I0824893

Art Fraud

Quarto

First published in 2025 by Ivy Press,
an imprint of The Quarto Group.
One Triptych Place, London, SE1 9SH,
United Kingdom
T (0)20 7700 9000
www.Quarto.com

EEA Representation, WTS Tax d.o.o., Žanova ulica 3, 4000 Kranj, Slovenia
www.wts-tax.si

A catalogue record for this book is available from the British Library.

ISBN 978-1-8360-0549-0
Ebook ISBN 978-1-8360-0550-6

10 9 8 7 6 5 4 3 2 1

Design by Ginny Zeal
Publisher: Richard Green
Editorial Director: Jennifer Barr
Editor: Katerina Menhennet
Editorial Assistant: Nayima Ali
Senior Designer: Renata Latipova
Production Controller: Rohana Yusof

Printed in Huizhou, Guangdong, China TT/Jun/2025

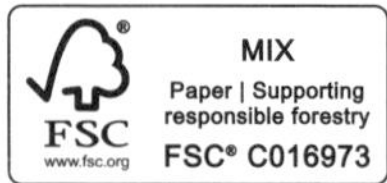

50 Fakes That Fooled The Art World

Susie Hodge

Contents

Introduction

Art fraud is rife. Many experts believe that as much as 50 per cent of all art on the market today is forgery. So what exactly is it? Who makes forgeries? Why? Who profits and who loses? What is the difference between a fake and a copy?

Forgery has always existed, but when produced in different places and at different times it can inspire divergent opinions. For example, in some countries throughout history, copying artworks exactingly has been admired, while in others it is seen as a crime. In much of the Western world, for instance, where art can be bought for extortionate prices, forgery is a crime – and yet copying in the

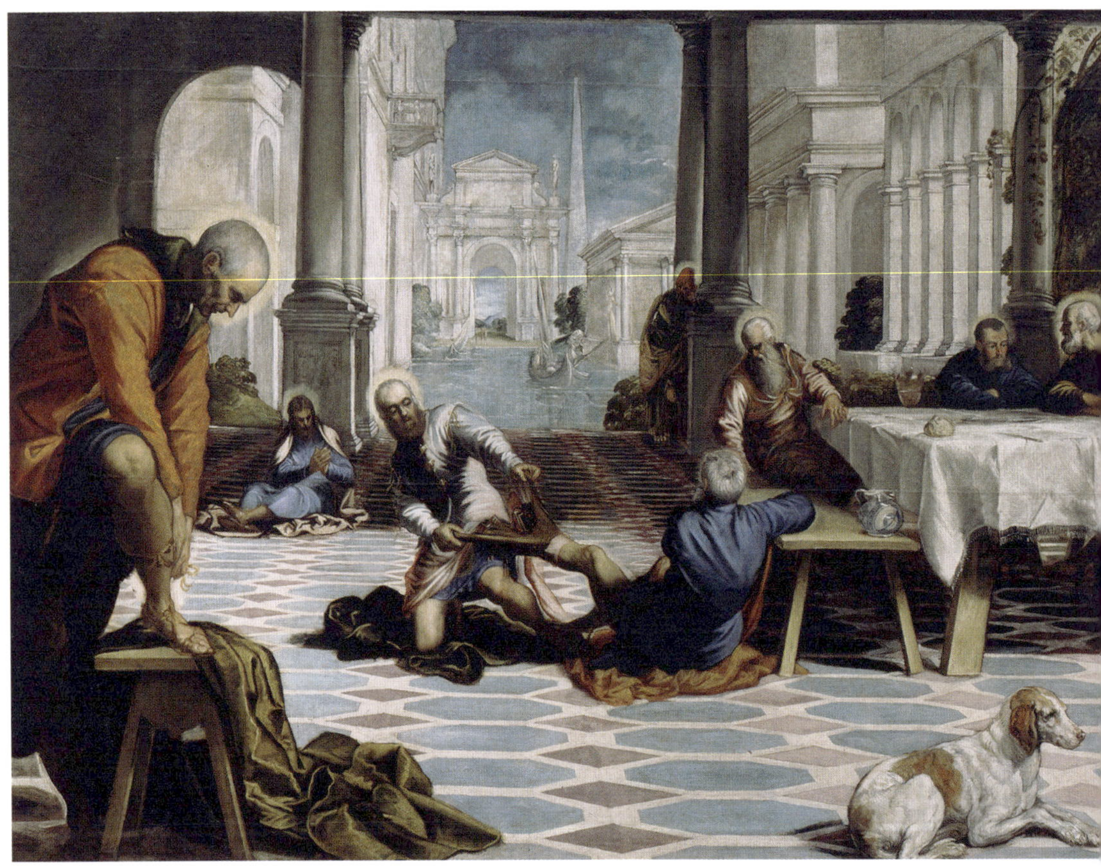

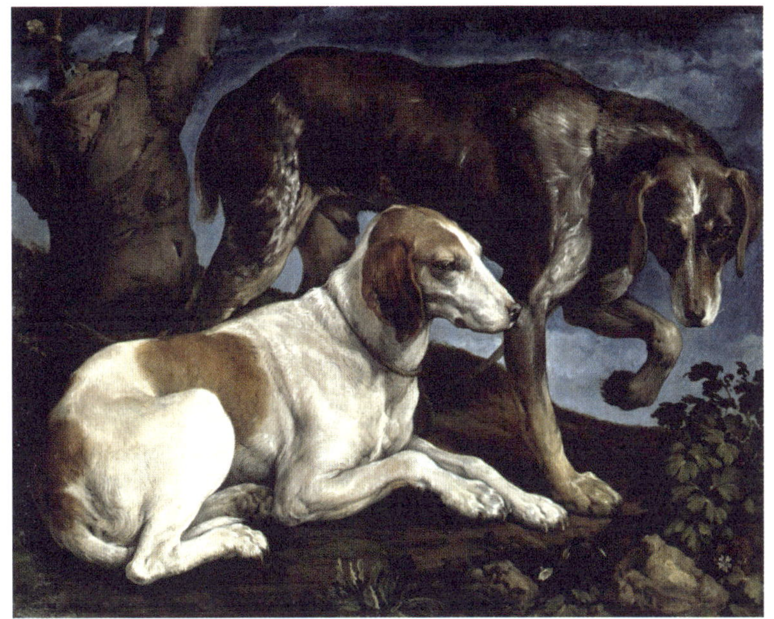

LEFT: *Two Hunting Dogs Tied to a Tree Stump*, Jacopo Bassano, c. 1548–9, oil on canvas, 61 x 80 cm (31⅓ x 24 in), the Louvre, Paris, France. Tintoretto and Bassano studied together in the 1530s, and mutually influenced each other and exchanged ideas. Tintoretto showed a particular interest in Bassano's natural style such as in this painting, and copied one of the dogs in his large-scale biblical work.

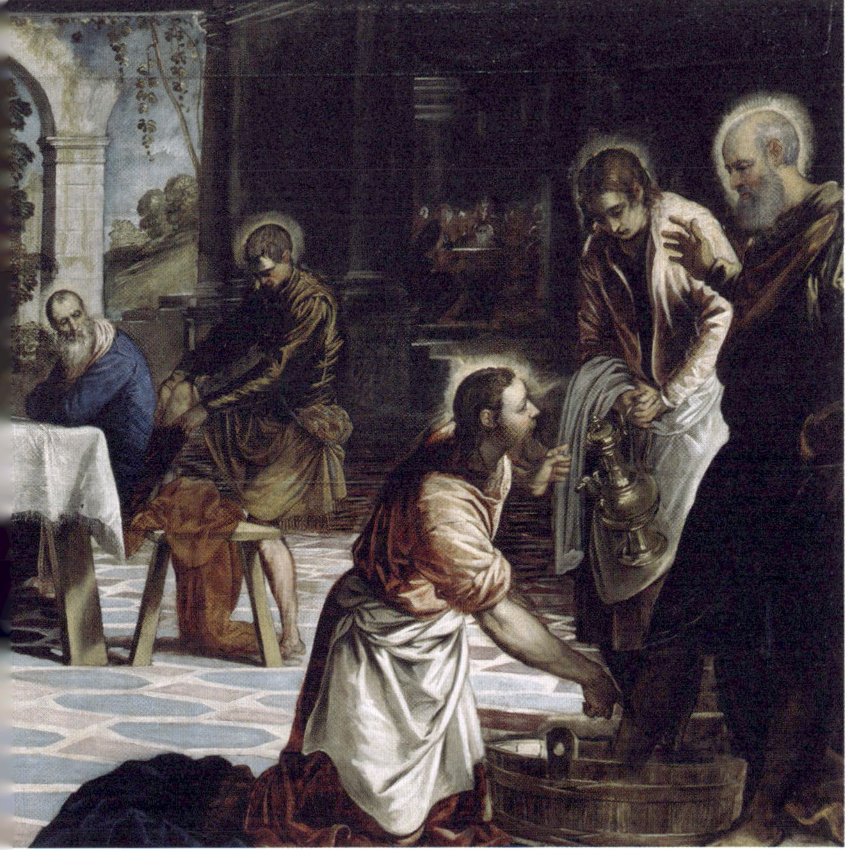

LEFT: *Christ Washing the Disciples' Feet*, Tintoretto, 1548–9, oil on canvas, 533.3 x 215.5 cm (210 x 84¾ in), Shipley Art Gallery, Gateshead, Tyne & Wear, UK. This painting represents a biblical scene of Jesus (on the far right), about to wash the feet of his disciple Peter. On the floor is a direct copy of one of the dogs from Bassano's painting.

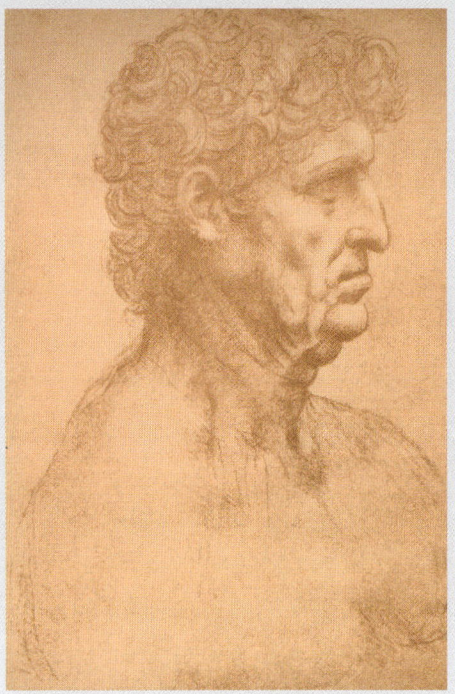

In August 2024, Spanish police arrested a man in Madrid for trying to sell a fake Leonardo da Vinci painting in Italy for €1.3 million. French customs officers had intercepted the suspect two years earlier when he was found travelling with the portrait in his vehicle. The man, in his forties, was suspected of being on his way to a buyer in Milan. Although initially everything looked in order, the customs officials found that the man's export permit, although verifying the legitimacy of the artwork, had expired, making the transportation of it illegal. They seized the portrait, supposedly of Italian aristocrat Gian Giacomo Trivulzio, and alerted the Spanish police, who went to the French border to recover the artwork. They sent it to the Museo Nacional del Prado in Madrid for expert analysis, which ultimately concluded that the work was a fake, so the man was arrested. The experts' report concluded that the work was a copy of a portrait by Leonardo when he was employed by Duke Ludovico Sforza in Milan between 1482 and 1499. The painting held by the man was probably painted with fraudulent intent at the beginning of the 20th century and its value was between €3,000 and €5,000.

Louvre, with the required permit, has been established since 1793. In 1548–50, Jacopo Bassano painted a double portrait of two dogs. Soon after, Tintoretto replicated one of the dogs in his huge painting *Christ Washing the Disciples' Feet* (1548–9). Both images have been admired ever since. Comparably, many contemporary street artists copy or use stencils to recreate famous artworks on pavements and walls. So what is the difference?

This book aims to clarify all these questions and more. The fact is there is nothing illegal in creating a copy of a famous painting. There is also nothing illegal about painting a work which can be described as 'school of' – in other words, in the style of a particular artist. Where the law is broken is when the artist of the copy asserts that it is an original. Creating a false provenance is against the law because this is deliberate deception and usually the intention is to make money from a fake through its association with the original artwork.

Why do it?

There are a few fundamental reasons why people engage in art forgery:

Financial gain: the primary motivation for many art forgers is the potential for significant profit. Authentic works by renowned artists can sell for millions, so creating convincing fakes allows forgers to cash in on the high market value.
Ego and recognition: some forgers are driven by a desire for recognition and a sense of accomplishment. By successfully passing off their work as that of a master artist, they can attain a level of prestige and acclaim they may not be able to achieve through their own artistic merits.
Satisfying artistic ambitions: in some cases, forgers may be skilled artists themselves but

lack the opportunity or acclaim to succeed in the legitimate art world. Forging allows them to vicariously fulfil their creative ambitions through the guise of another artist's identity.

Challenging the system: a small minority of forgers may be motivated by a desire to expose perceived weaknesses or flaws in the art authentication process. They see forgery as a way to challenge the exclusivity of the art establishment.

Ideology: rarely, forgers may have ideological reasons for faking art, such as a desire to make art more accessible to the masses by creating affordable alternatives to expensive originals.

Although these motivations vary, the common idea is the forger's belief that they can profit – either financially, psychologically or both – from deceiving collectors, museums and the public about the true origins of the artwork.

A long history

Art forgery dates back centuries. In ancient Rome, for example, sculpture and paintings were often copies of ancient Greek art, but in the main at that time buyers knew that they were copies and were happy to buy them.

BELOW: Two ancient Roman copies of ancient Greek works of sculpture: The Doryphoros ('Spear-Bearer') (left), a marble copy of the Greek sculptor Polykleitos, active in the 5th century BCE. It depicts a muscular standing warrior who originally held a spear on his left shoulder. The Discobolus ('Discus Thrower') (right), originally by Myron of Eleutherae, depicts an ancient Greek athlete throwing a discus.

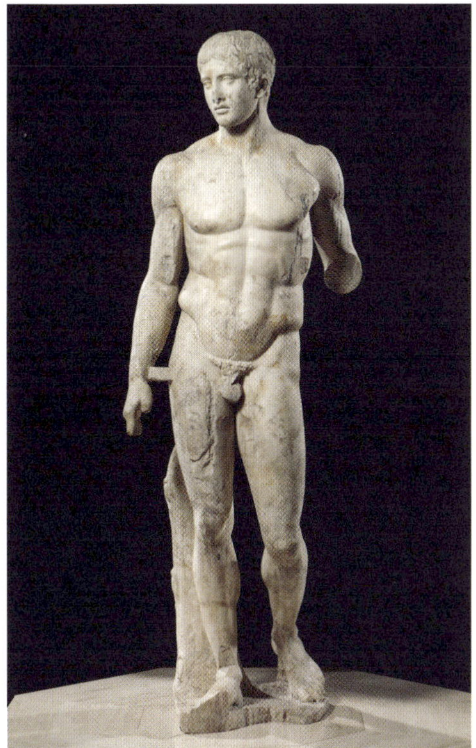

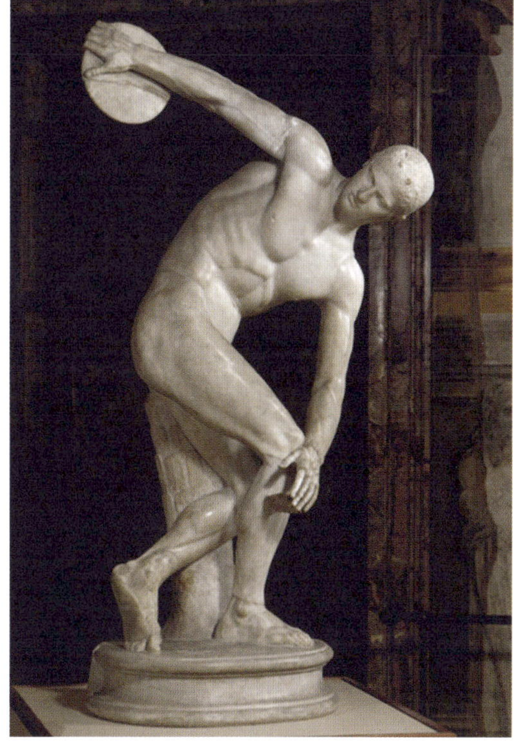

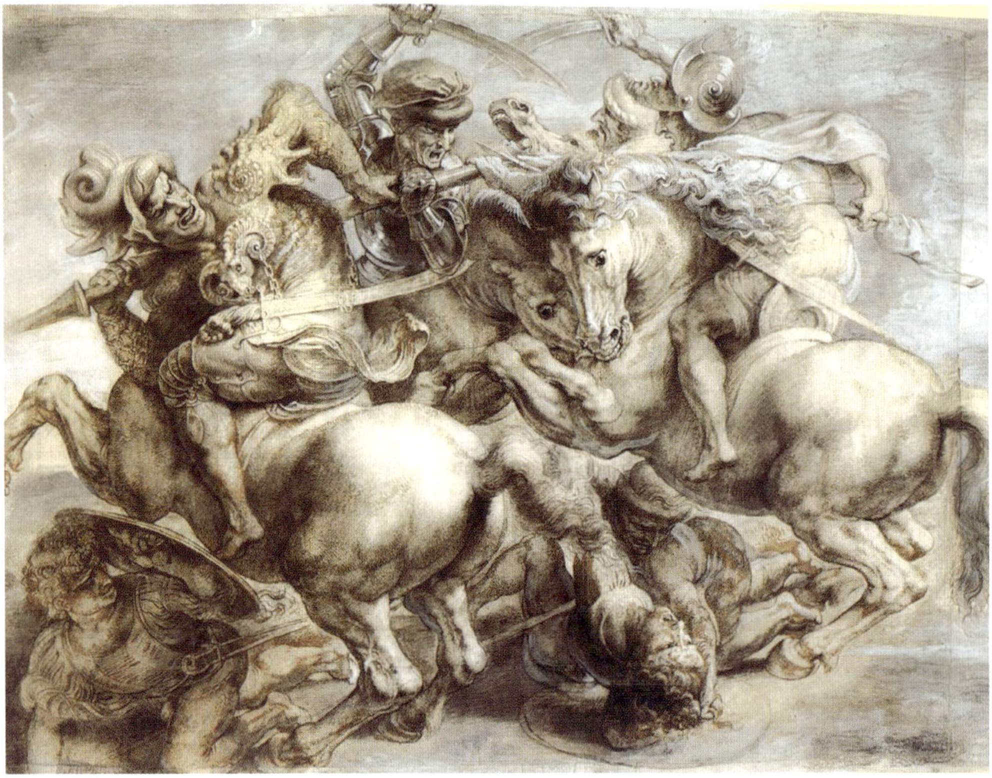

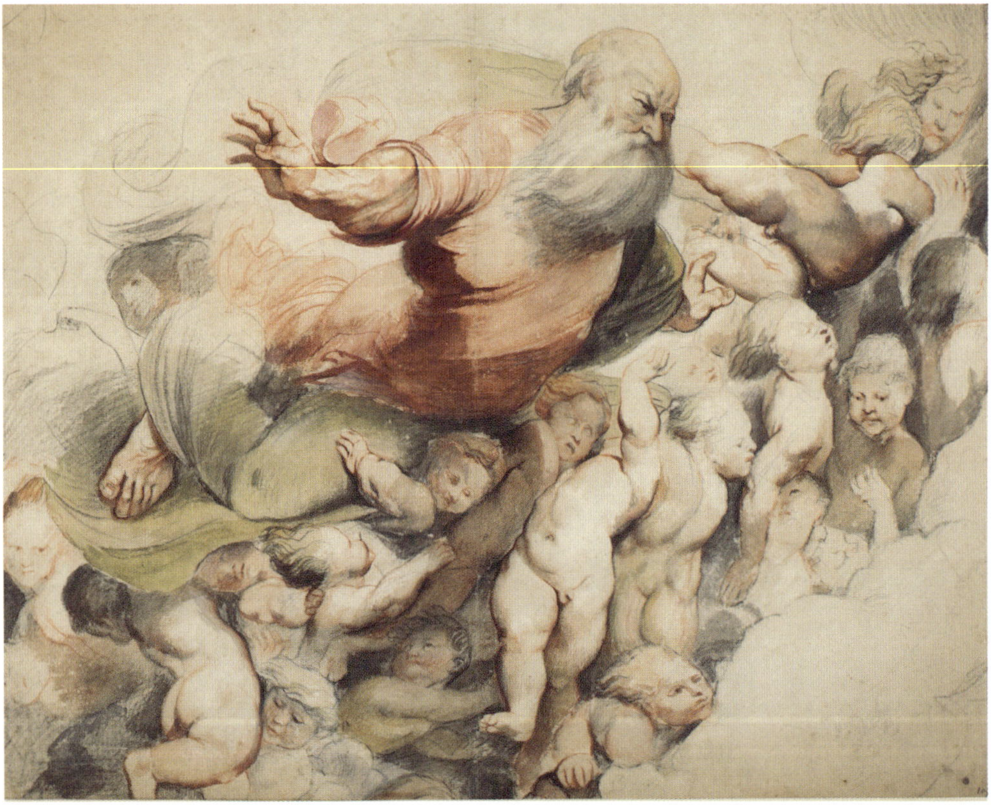

The Renaissance saw a surge in art forgery as the demand for classical and medieval artworks grew. In addition, skilled painters like Michelangelo (1475–1564) and Raphael (1483–1520) were sometimes commissioned to create copies of their own works or those of their contemporaries. In the 16th century, Italian painter Giorgione was particularly notorious for his forgeries, which he used to boost his own reputation. In 1496, Michelangelo sculpted a marble sleeping Cupid figure and treated it with acidic earth to make it appear old. He sold it to a dealer, Baldassare del Milanese, who then sold it to Cardinal Raffaele Riario. When Riario later discovered it was not genuine, he demanded his money back. However, Michelangelo was allowed to keep his share of the money for creating the work in the first place.

Traditionally, students learned by studying and copying great artists. In conventional apprenticeships and art schools, those students who could follow the professional artist most closely were deemed the best and the most likely to succeed in their future art careers. During the Middle Ages and the Renaissance, master artists often sold the copied works of art by their apprentices as part payment for their training.

However, even artists of the past did not want their work copied beyond apprenticeships or official art training, and galleries, dealers and collectors do not want fakes. Once apprenticeships and training are over, artists are meant to produce their own, original work, even if they 'borrow' elements, such as in Tintoretto's *Christ Washing the Disciples' Feet* discussed above.

OPPOSITE, ABOVE: Copy of *The Battle of Anghiari*, a fresco made by Leonardo da Vinci in 1504–05 and destroyed around 1560. Peter Paul Rubens made this in c. 1603 using black chalk, brown and grey ink applied with both a pen and a brush, and a grey wash, heightened in white and grey-blue.

OPPOSITE, BELOW: *God the Father Supported by Angels*, a copy of a work by Michelangelo, created by German-born Flemish painter Rubens in 1601-02. Rubens spent years studying classical and Renaissance art in Italy, and Michelangelo's art hugely influenced him. He made many drawings after Michelangelo's artwork that he used as references and for his apprentices and assistants to learn from.

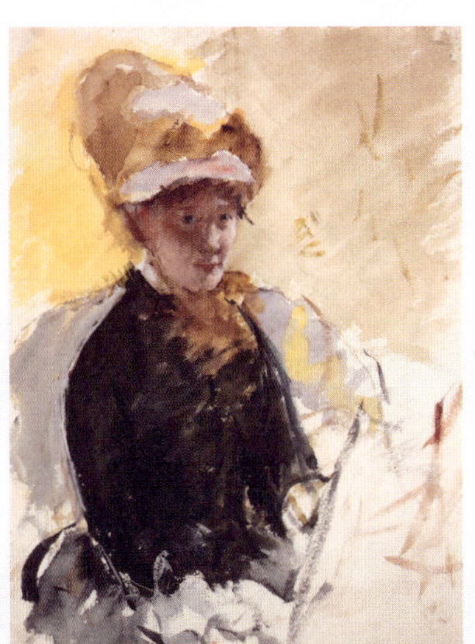

MARY CASSATT

In 1871, at the age of 27, Mary Cassatt, an American living in France, was considering giving up her ambitions of being a professional artist when her work attracted the attention of Roman Catholic Bishop Michael Domenec. The bishop commissioned her to paint two copies of paintings by Antonio Allegri da Correggio (1489–1534) in Parma, and advanced her enough money to cover her travel expenses and part of her stay while copying the paintings. Cassatt copied Correggio's *Il Giorno* and a copy of his *Virgin Crowned* made by Annibale Carracci (1560–1609). The copying exercise earned her money, revived her ambitions and helped to inspire her future, original style.

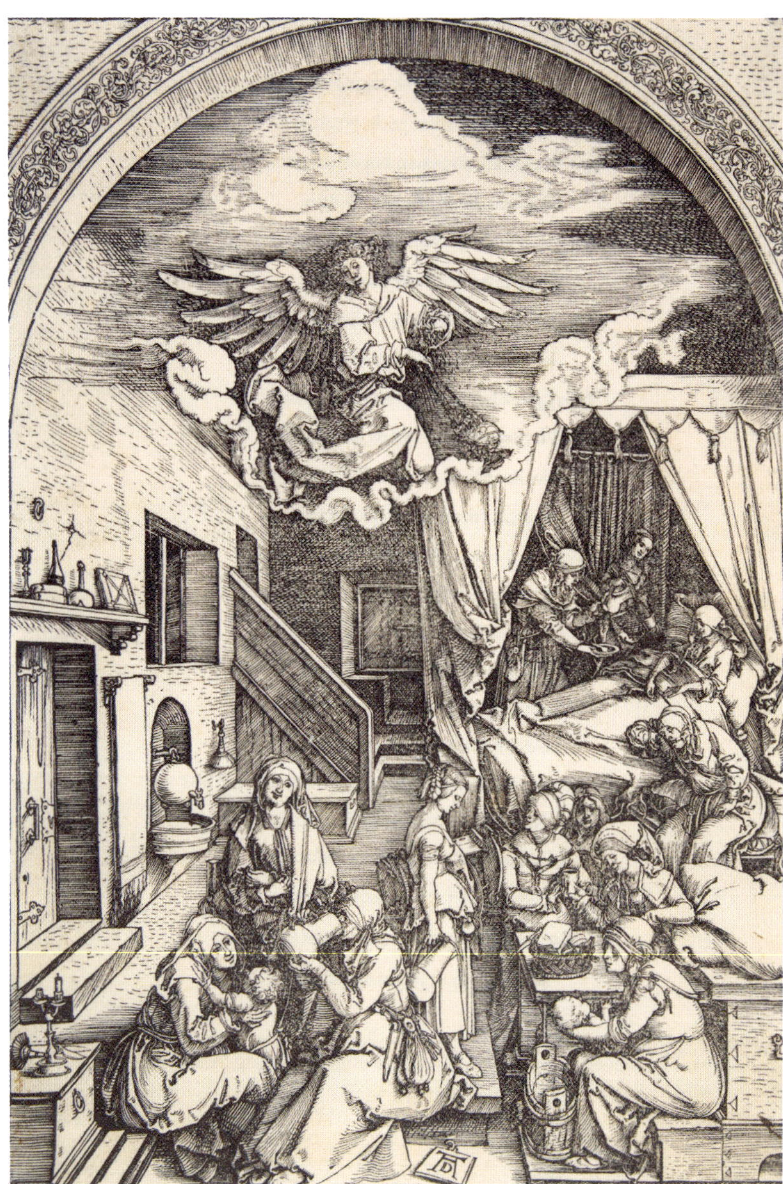

LEFT: *The Birth of the Virgin*, a woodcut from his series *Life of the Virgin* by Albrecht Dürer, created in c. 1503. Dürer made three woodcuts depicting the significant events in the Virgin Mary's youth. Raimondi copied this portrayal of a contemporary birthing scene, including midwives, friends and relatives.

In the early 16th century, the successful Northern Renaissance artist Albrecht Dürer wrote what is probably one of the first copyright notices. It read: 'Hold! You crafty ones, strangers to work, and pilferers of other men's brains! Think not rashly to lay your thievish hands upon my works. Beware! Know you not that I have a grant from the most glorious Emperor Maximilian that not one throughout the imperial dominion shall be allowed to print or sell fictitious imitations of these engravings? Listen! And bear in mind that if you do so, through spite or through covetousness, not only

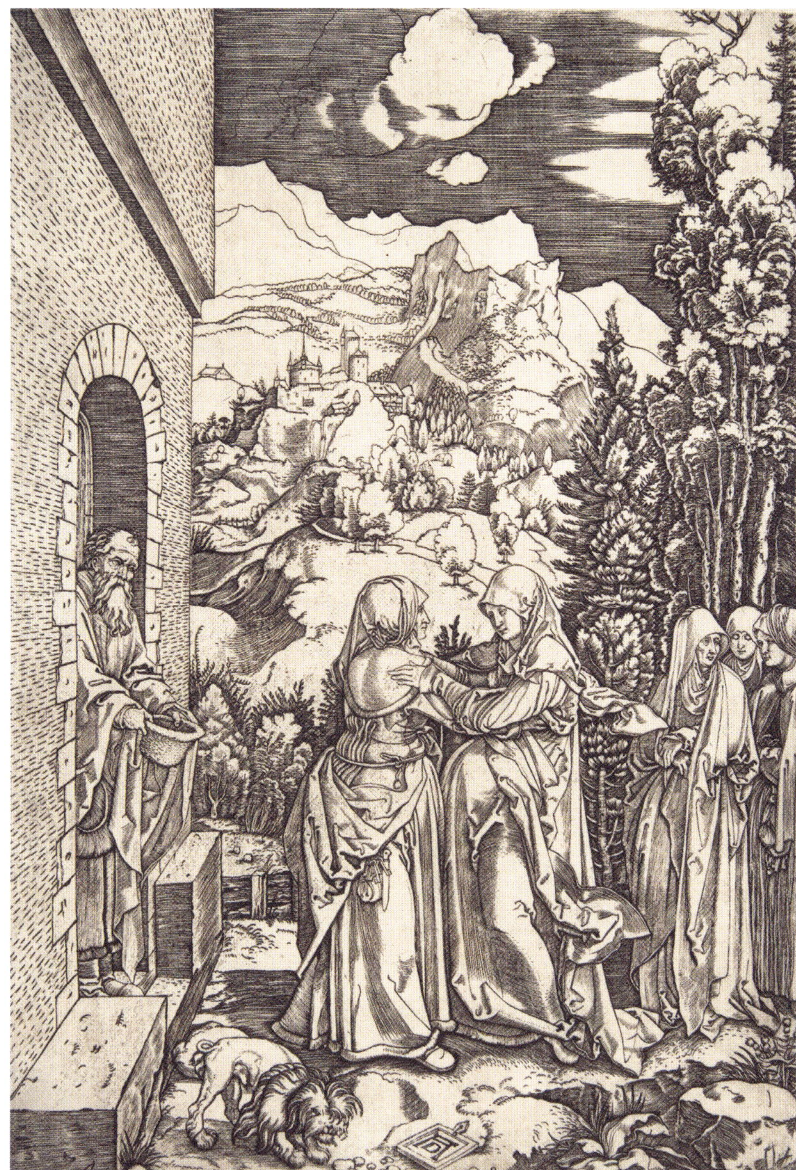

LEFT: Raimondo's copy of *Visitation*, another woodcut from Dürer's 1503 series. It depicts an episode in the Bible when Mary, heavily pregnant, travels to see her older cousin Elizabeth, who is also pregnant. The two women embrace, while Elizabeth's husband Zachariah stands at a doorway to the left.

will your goods be confiscated, but your bodies also placed in mortal danger.'

Dürer's prints – which were more affordable alternatives to paintings – were being bought across Europe, and he took great care to protect them from forgers. He even created a stylized 'AD' symbol to identify and ensure their authenticity. Yet in 1506, he discovered that some of these were being forged. A printmaker, Marcantonio Raimondi, had recreated every detail of Dürer's series *Life of the Virgin*, even including the 'AD' monogram. When Dürer took

Raimondi to court, Raimondi argued that he had changed three small aspects of the images and added his own monogram. In this way, he avoided a guilty verdict. It was the first known case of art-specific intellectual property being brought to trial. Raimondi was instructed to remove Dürer's monogram, and his prints of Dürer's work could only be sold as copies, not as originals.

After the Renaissance, demand for art grew and the monetary value of a work of art came to depend on the identity of the artist. The greatest artists began signing their works, and as the demand for certain artists' creations began to exceed the supply, fraudulent marks and signatures began appearing on the open market.

In 18th- and 19th-century Europe, the rise of the modern art market brought with it a new wave of forgeries, and art forgers reached new heights of sophistication in the 20th century. Henricus (Han) van Meegeren (1889–1947) was a Dutch painter who created

LEFT: *Self-Portrait*, painted by Rembrandt van Rijn in 1660. It is still unclear how many self-portraits Rembrandt produced himself or even how much of each image he produced, and how many were made by his students or with their assistance, not as forgeries but as part of their artistic training.

convincing fakes of paintings by Dutch masters including Johannes Vermeer (1632–1675) and Frans Hals (c. 1582–1666). Van Meegeren became a national hero after the Second World War when it was revealed that he had sold one of his forged paintings to Hitler's right-hand man, Hermann Göring, during the Nazi occupation of the Netherlands. Van Meegeren's forgeries went undetected for decades and earned him millions before he was eventually exposed.

Even though many forgers have been caught and sentenced, it is likely that fraudulent artworks remain in prestigious galleries and museums to this day. Advancing technology is helping experts to detect more fakes, but at the same time the forgers are using more sophisticated techniques to evade detection. Art fraud continues to be a persistent problem in the world. The lure of financial gain, coupled with the prestige associated with owning a masterpiece, continue to fuel the illicit trade.

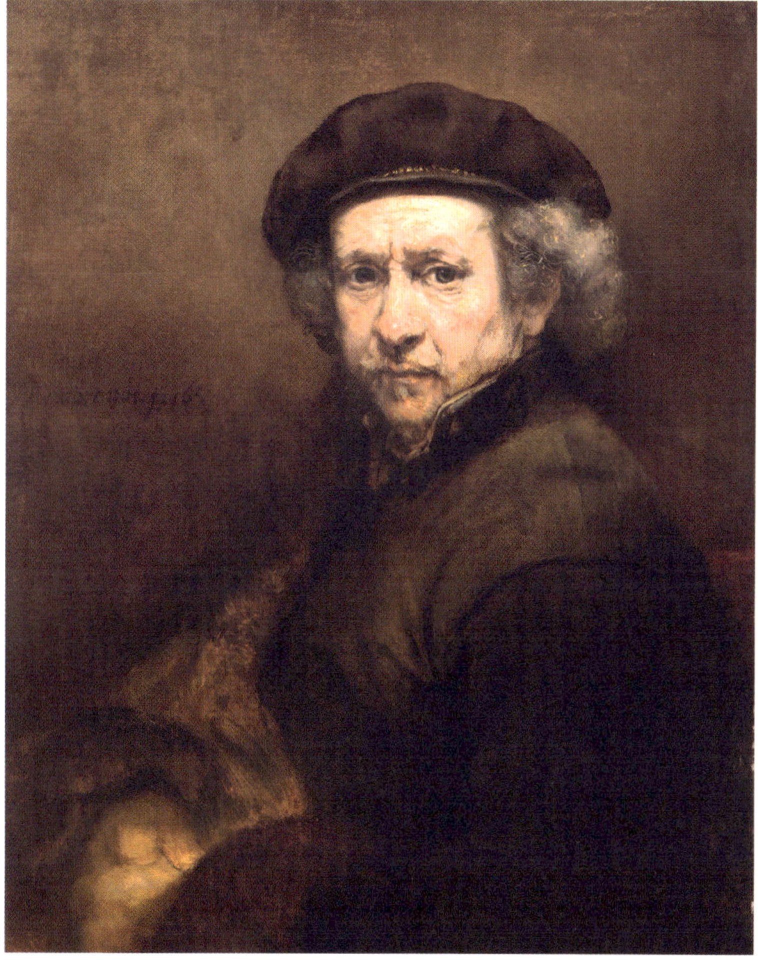

LEFT: *Self-Portrait,* painted by Rembrandt van Rijn in 1659. While recent scholarship has shown that some of the artworks previously thought to have been produced by Rembrandt were made by his students, he probably produced 40–50 self-portraits, 7 drawings and 32 etchings.

Why is art forgery illegal?

Art has been copied and misattributed probably for as long as it has been made. Fundamentally, a forgery is an object that is a complete imitation of another artist's work without that artist's knowledge or agreement, and often with a copy of the artist's signature or mark.

However, as we have seen, during the 14th to 18th centuries many successful artists had large studios filled with apprentices and assistants, and commissions were regularly fulfilled by the workshop, with the master designing and supervising, perhaps completing particularly complex details. In many cases, the master barely touched a work of art. For instance, it is not clear how many of the self-portraits that Rembrandt van Rijn (1609–1669) produced were painted by him and how many were made by his students. When authenticated, artworks made by an artist's studio are described as 'studio of'. When artworks are in the style of a particular artist or created by one of his or her students or assistants, the artworks are described as 'school of.'

Of course, these are not forgeries. Art forgery is the creation and sale of works of art that are credited to other – usually more famous – artists: a deliberate deception. In exploiting the art trade, forgery involves skill, treachery, deception and both science and mystique. Most art forgery is illegal for several key reasons:

Misrepresentation and deception: when a forged artwork is passed off as an original, it involves intentional misrepresentation and deception. This undermines the integrity and transparency of the art market, eroding trust between artists, collectors and the public.
Economic damage: forged artworks can diminish the value of genuine works by the same artist, harming the livelihoods of legitimate artists and dealers. The sale of fakes also deprives the rightful owners and creators of economic benefits from selling their real work.
Cultural heritage preservation: many valuable artworks are part of a culture's shared heritage. Forging such works undermines our ability to preserve and study genuine art history, threatening the integrity of our cultural legacy.
Legal ownership rights: forged artworks are often sold without the consent of the rightful owners, which is a violation of their property rights. This can lead to lengthy legal battles and the seizure of illegally obtained works.

The protection of artistic integrity and heritage is crucial in maintaining a transparent and trustworthy art market, while the dishonesty of imitating a famous artist, and deliberately seeking financial gain through this dishonesty, is what makes forgery so condemned in most societies. Art forgery does irreparable damage to our shared cultural history, but most forgers are mercenary without a real understanding of how the art world affects us all.

Sometimes, when they are caught, fraudsters attempt to pretend that the fakes are jokes, but they cause damage by eroding the reliability of the artistic record of our most important cultural objects – art. Art forgery is rarely linked to organized crime as, for example, art heists are. Forgers are frequently characters with complex psychological problems. They are also overwhelmingly men. There have been no known female art forgers.

LEGAL COPYING

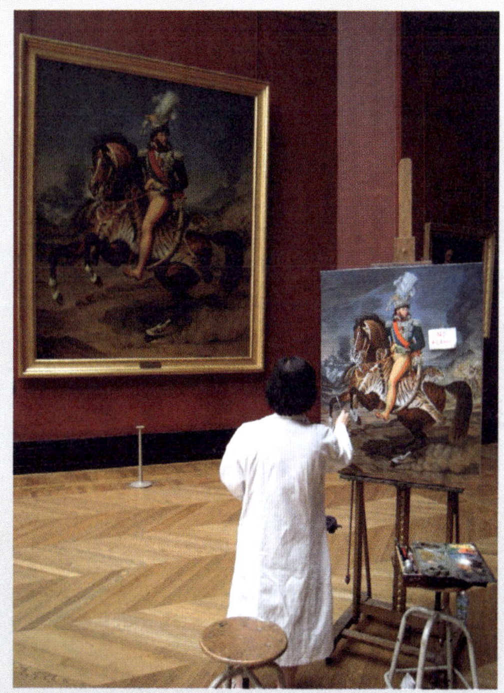

Obtaining an official permit to copy in the Louvre has always been necessary to keep the copying under control. In the 19th century, copyists there were often low-paid women who were banned from official art schools or they were student artists (see Mary Cassatt, page 11). So both men and women regularly filled the museum to paint copies, to learn from the original artists who made them, as well as to sell their paintings later. In 1863, Paul Cézanne first registered to copy a work in the Louvre by Nicolas Poussin (1594–1665), reflecting: 'The Louvre is the book from which we learn to read.' Édouard Manet first met young Berthe Morisot when she was in the Louvre in the late 1850s copying a canvas by the Venetian Paolo Veronese (1528–1588). Manet also met Edgar Degas at the Louvre in around 1860 while 27-year-old Degas was copying a work by Diego Velázquez (1599–1660) on to a copper plate with no prior drawing, which was both bold and unusual. Manet, two years older than Degas, was fascinated. It became the beginning of a brief but intense relationship, in which the two artists both admired and competed with each other.

Even today, Louvre copyists are allowed to work for up to three months, having access to the galleries for certain times, during certain months and on certain days. Once their artworks are finished, they are inspected closely by Louvre officials, who make sure that they meet the rigorous requirements. These requirements include that the canvases must be 20 per cent smaller or larger than the original, and the original artist's signature is not to be reproduced anywhere. Once these precautions against forgeries are met, the copy is stamped and signed by the head of the Louvre's copy office. Similar measures are in place in many galleries and museums around the world.

CHAPTER 1

Did He or Didn't He?

Born in Cremona, Alceo Dossena (1878–1937) was one of the 20th century's most prolific and successful art forgers. But whether his deceit was deliberate or engineered by others remains a mystery.

Simone Martini

In 1923, the respected and wealthy American art collector Helen Clay Frick, daughter of steel magnate Henry Clay Frick, founder of the Frick Collection in New York, saw a marble sculptural group in the collection of Italian antiquarian Elia Volpi. Representing the Annunciation, the work comprised the two figures of the Angel Gabriel and the Virgin Mary, and it was attributed to one of the greatest 14th-century Sienese artists: sculptor Simone Martini. This attribution was substantiated by the quality and style of the work, as well as the initials 'S.M.' inscribed on the base of the angel and the date '1316' on the base of the Madonna. After also viewing the work, the respected collector, critic and art historian Frederick Mason Perkins told Frick that he believed the attribution to be correct.

The two marble figures closely resembled the style of Martini's 1333 painting of the Annunciation in the Uffizi Gallery in Florence, but although Perkins and Volpi (who was one of the most prominent antiquarians in the world at the time) assured Frick that they believed the work was genuine, there was no documentation and no known provenance. So two further scholars, Charles Loeser and Giacomo de Nicola, were asked for their opinions, and they too evaluated the artwork as a genuine Simone Martini. After this, Frick decided to complete her negotiations. The Pre-Renaissance work would be a marvellous asset to the collection. She paid Volpi the agreed sum of $150,000 and in March 1924, the sculpture arrived safely at the museum in New York. Soon after it was put on display, however, it began to crack, and various independent scholars, art historians and collectors expressed their doubts about its authenticity. So Frick called for another assessment. German art historian and museum curator Wilhelm von Bode came and studied it. After much deliberation, he noted that with an absence of information about any such sculpture being produced by Martini, it was problematic, but he also wrote in a letter to Volpi that 'the anatomy, the folds, the expression, everything is Simone's art'.

Yet Frick still felt concerned, and so she had the statues examined by a commission of further experts. After deliberating for several months, they gave their verdict. Their collective belief was that the artwork was a forgery. Their reasoning, they explained, was due to several factors, including the way the initials and date had been inscribed, the positions of the heads of the figures, and the 'general effect elicited by the two statues' that made it seem unlikely to them to have been created by Martini. By November 1928, four

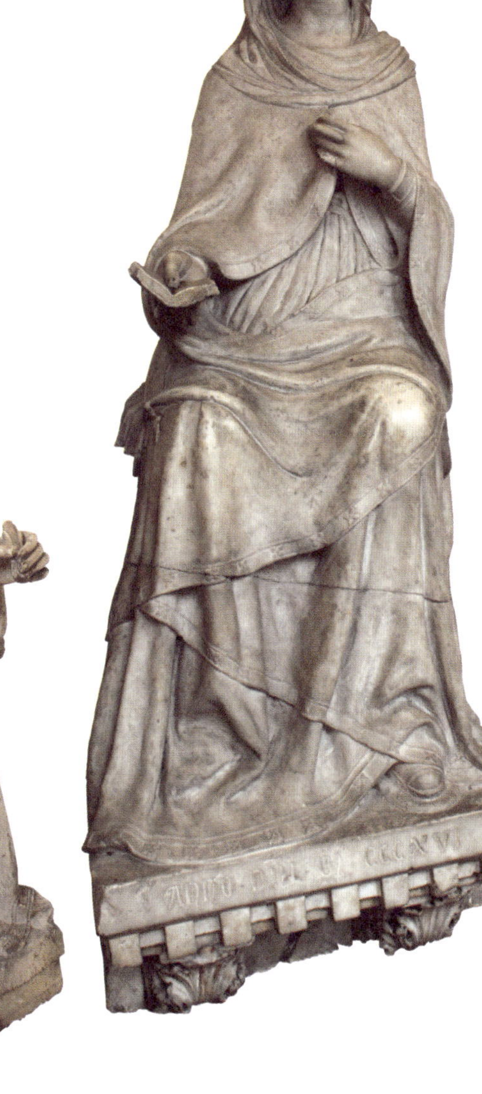

RIGHT: The two marble figures made by Dossena, representing the Angel Gabriel (left) and the Virgin Mary (right) at the Annunciation, were initially attributed to Simone Martini. Their poses resemble the painted figures in the image on page 20. Due to the quality and style of the sculptures, many experts believed that the Early Renaissance master created them.

and a half years after it had arrived in America, the sculpture was attributed not to Martini, but to a living Italian artist named Alceo Dossena. Frick asked Volpi for the return of her payment, but professing to be in financial difficulty, he offered her a drawing by Leonardo da Vinci instead. In February 1933, the sculpture was given to the University of Pittsburgh.

Giovanni Pisano

'Skilled above all men in the art of pure sculpture, who carved, in fitting fashion, glorious works in stone and gilded wood' is a 1310 description of Italian artist Giovanni Pisano (c. 1250–1314). An important contributor to Gothic sculpture and an influential precursor of Italian Renaissance sculpture, Pisano's work evolved markedly from the stiff, elongated style of the Romanesque style into a more naturalistic approach, emulating ancient Greek and Roman sculpture's treatment of drapery, facial expressions and postures.

BELOW: *Annunciation with St Maxima and St Ansanus*, Simone Martini, tempera on wood, gold background, 1333, from the collection of the Uffizi Gallery in Florence, Italy. This was made for the altar of St Ansanus in Siena Cathedral, dedicated to the Assumption of the Virgin Mary.

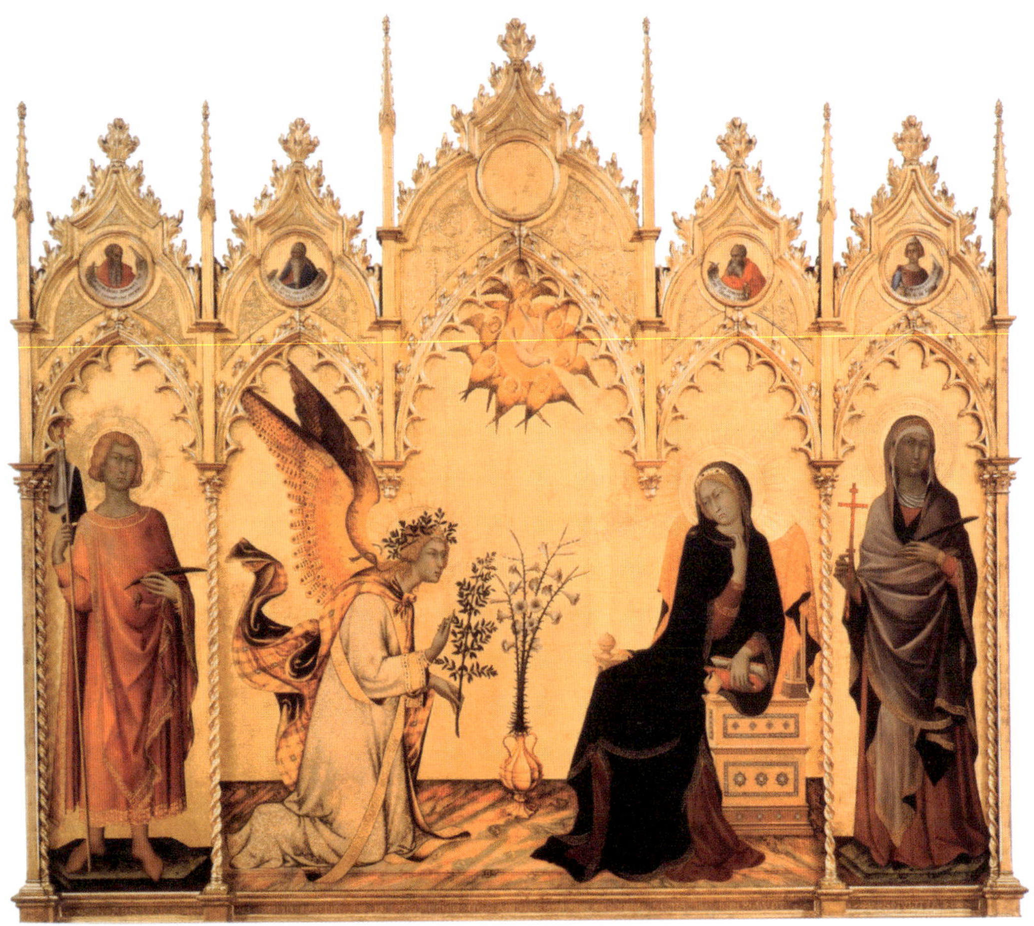

In 1924, a life-sized wooden statue of the Madonna and Child, believed to be a previously unknown work by Pisano, was discovered in a secluded convent chapel in the town of Montefiascone in central Italy. Soon after, at a dinner party in Ohio, Harold Parsons, who worked for the Cleveland Museum of Art, heard about the sculpture and arranged to view it in secret. As soon as he saw the statue, he was convinced, and he bought it for $18,000 for the Cleveland Museum. By March 1925, the statue was in Ohio. Delighted with the acquisition, the Cleveland's curator, William Milliken, wrote in the museum's *Bulletin* that although 'No exact attribution can be made . . . it is no school piece, and at this moment there is no known artist to whom it could be logically ascribed if not to Giovanni.'

BELOW: *Madonna and Child*, an ivory statuette by Giovanni Pisano, was made in c. 1300 and is from the Treasury of Pisa Cathedral, Italy.

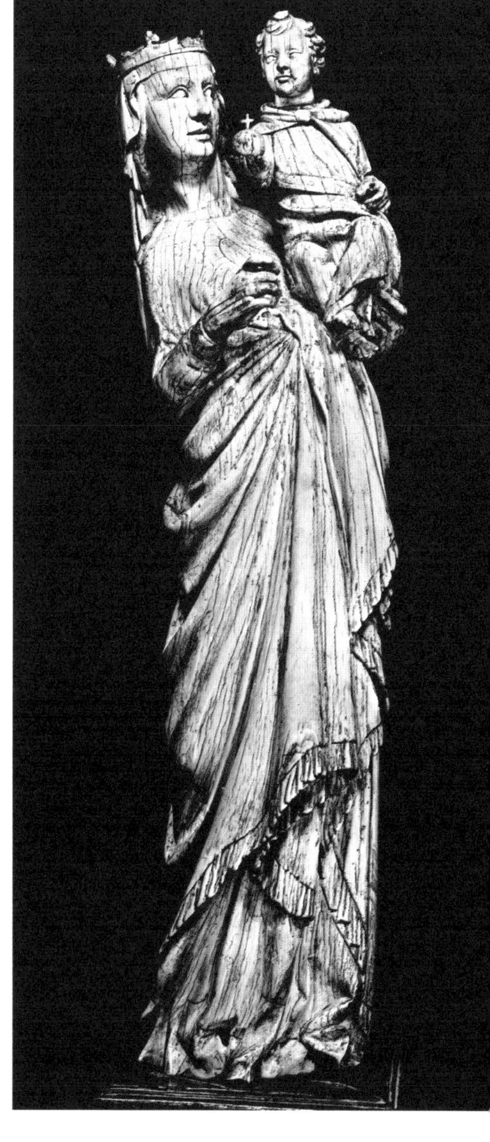

Yet just two years later, in June 1927, motivated by the doubts of several independent scholars, a series of X-rays were taken of the statue. They revealed that parts of it were held together with 20th-century nails. The work was returned quietly to Europe. Frustration, anger and embarrassment were assuaged, however, by a new purchase of the Cleveland Museum. A life-sized marble statue of Athena had been discovered dating from the 5th century BCE. The museum paid $120,000 for it. The following year, the Athena's maker was traced to a studio in the Lungotevere district of Rome. His name was Alceo Dossena.

Innocent or guilty?

From a young age, Dossena found that he had a gift for art. He attended the Istituto Ala Ponzone where he learned basic painting and sculpture, copying classical models, and then worked for art restorers in Cremona and Milan, repairing numerous marble and wooden fittings in churches throughout northern Italy. Through this, he refined his skills and acquired a thorough knowledge of how to artificially age materials and an understanding of the work of famed medieval and Renaissance sculptors, including Martini, Pisano, Donatello, Michelangelo and Giambologna.

In the early 1900s, he sold a series of sculptures he attributed to Michelangelo to a wealthy Italian collector. These were so convincing that they were later acquired by the Louvre in Paris, where they remained on display for years before the deception was uncovered.

In 1916, during the First World War, Dossena was serving in the Italian army. On leave for Christmas, he was in Rome and in need of money. He made a small bas-relief in terracotta of the Madonna and Child, and – patinated in urine to falsely age it – he offered to sell it to the owner of a bar. Not knowing about art and not wanting it for himself, the barman called for Alfredo Fasoli, the owner of a small antique store nearby, to give his opinion and see if he wanted to buy it. Fasoli was astonished by the work and believed that it may have been made by the great Renaissance sculptor Donatello and that Dossena had probably stolen it from a church. He paid Dossena 100 lire (a very small amount), believing that Dossena did not know what a masterpiece he was letting go. Dossena was delighted to have some money for Christmas and Fasoli thought he had a priceless work of art. However, when he arrived home, Fasoli studied the artwork and realized that it was not what it had seemed. Rather than feel disappointment, however, he was delighted, and after the war ended, he and his well-connected colleague, Romano Palesi, arranged for Dossena to work for them in a studio in Rome near the River Tiber. They planned to buy as many fake works of art that Dossena could make.

For ten years, from 1918 until 1928, Fasoli constantly commissioned Dossena. He and Palesi discussed what would be the most marketable works, and they benefited from the harsh economic conditions after the war, which fostered a black market in genuine masterpieces illicitly sold by impoverished European institutions to wealthy patrons of aspiring American museums.

Even now, it is not certain whether Dossena was innocent or as guilty as Fasoli and Palesi. Ten years later, he claimed that he had no idea what the dealers were doing and that he was innocent of their crimes; that he was simply making old-looking art but not claiming that it was by anyone but himself. This is still unclear, although he probably had no idea how much they earned from his talents. They pocketed an estimated $2 million over the decade, but they paid him a fraction of that. For example, his terracotta 'Donatello' was sold for a four- or five-figure sum, and for the $120,000 Athena, it is likely that Dossena was paid about $7,500.

Reincarnated master or plain cheat?

Dossena created hundreds of forged sculptures, paintings and drawings that were marketed as the work of celebrated Renaissance and Baroque artists. He developed a knack for simulating the styles, materials and even the physical imperfections of genuine masterpieces, making his forgeries virtually indistinguishable from the originals. Many highly respected art experts were fooled, probably because he appealed to the art world's hunger for respect and rarity.

Soon after the Athena scandal made worldwide headlines in 1928, amidst revelations of several dozen more forged attributions, the German documentary filmmaker and art historian Hans Cürlis filmed Dossena at work. As he sculpted clay and chiselled marble, he hummed popular tunes. Curlis observed: 'The figures were first thoroughly shaped in the nude from the living model, a pair of large wooden dividers being frequently used to measure the lengths of limbs, head and dimensions on his models then transfer them to the clay figure. Then he draped his model and reproduced the robing in clay.' This was the same process followed during the Renaissance and ancient Greece. 'The abnormality of his work became so natural that it only later occurred to us that we had witnessed the reincarnation of a Renaissance master and an Attic sculptor,' Cürlis reflected. Dossena explained: 'Even as a boy in the industrial art school at Cremona, I grew to be perfectly familiar with the various styles of the past. I could not assimilate them in any other way.'

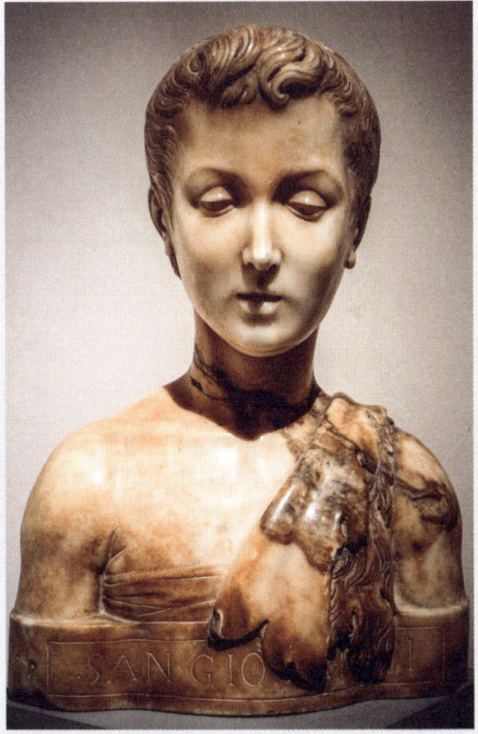

AGEING TECHNIQUES

For his 'ancient Greek' artworks, after completing the carving, Dossena would smash it with a hammer, and then sandblast the fractures to emulate erosion. Next, fragments were lowered by winch into an acid bath sunk into his studio floor and soaked up to 40 times, in between which the stone was blazed with a torch to crackle the surface. Other chemicals were applied to produce chalky deposits. Another early method of ageing a sculpture was to place it in urine. This technique became more sophisticated over the years, but Dossena never revealed his exact methods. It is believed that for his marble sculptures, he worked them almost to completion, then applied a liquid patina made of permanganate, rust water and oak earth (a type of dark brown soil or substrate rich in organic matter and nutrients, often associated with oak trees and their surroundings) that had been dried in the heat of a gas flame. This masked the entire surface of the sculpture with a blackish coating, and then, using flat chisels, he scraped the surface. Next, he covered it with lead and oxalic acid, causing polymerization (a chemical process where small molecules combine to form larger molecules which, for Dossena, created an aged-looking surface).

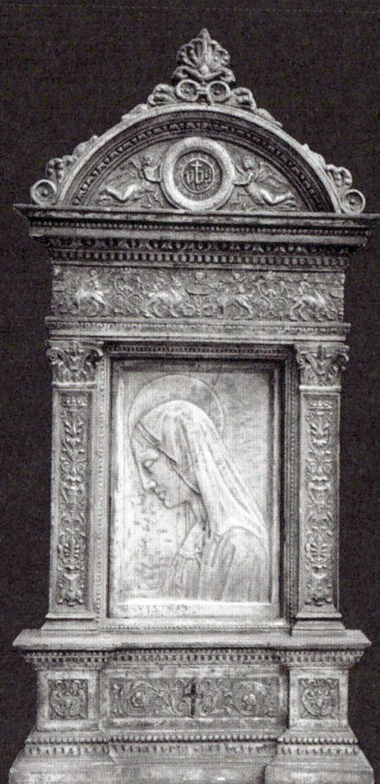

Head of the Virgin, probably made by Dossena, now in The Metropolitan Museum of Art, New York, USA.

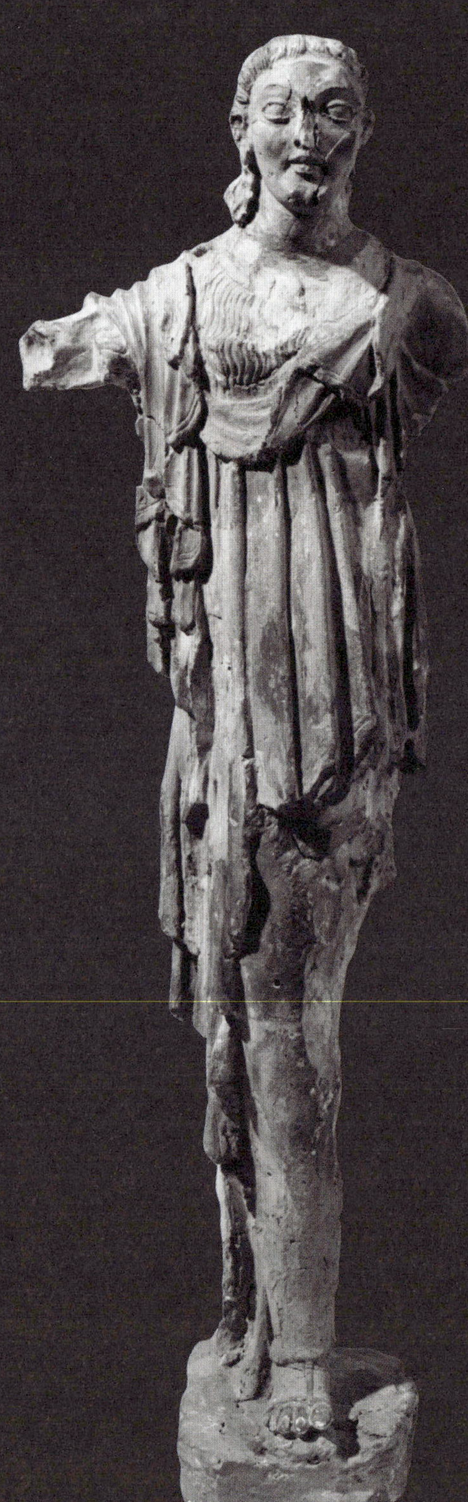

Imitation of an Etruscan kore, by Dossena, made in terracotta, 1920–30.

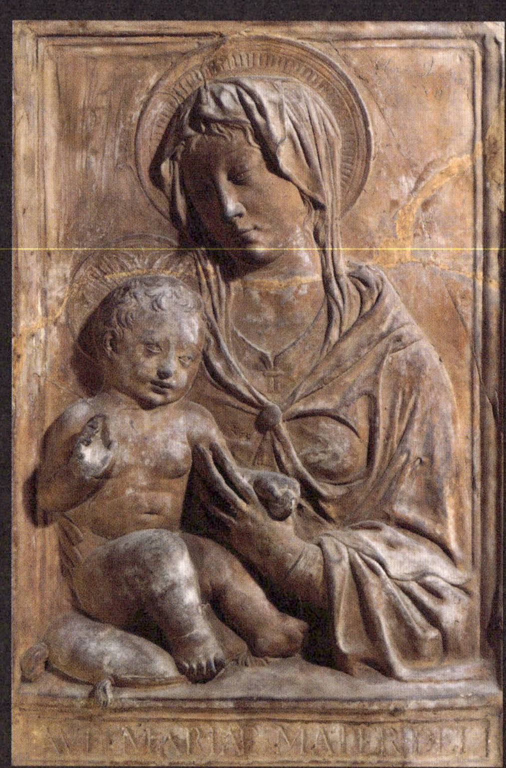

Madonna and Child, a terracotta relief made by Dossena in 1929.

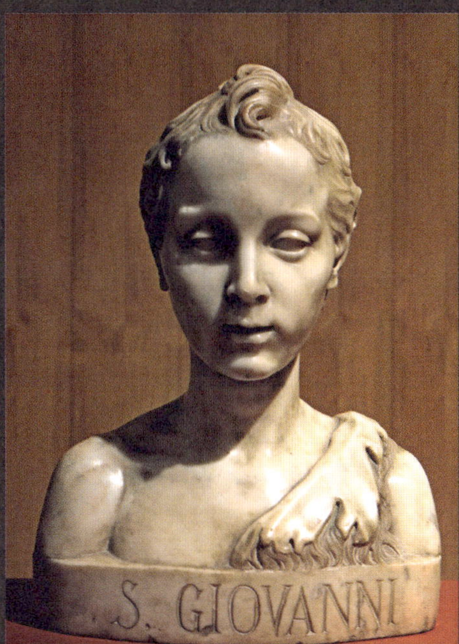

A sensitively carved bust of a young *Saint John the Baptist*, carved by Dossena in 1936.

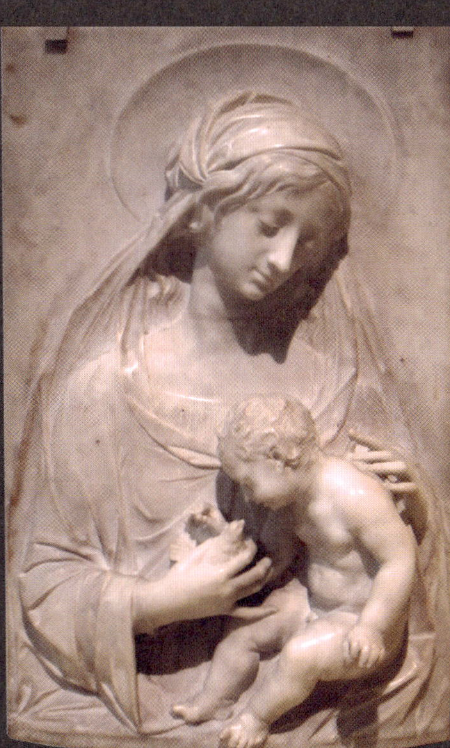

Madonna and Child, marble, Alceo Dossena, 1930, now in the San Diego Museum of Art.

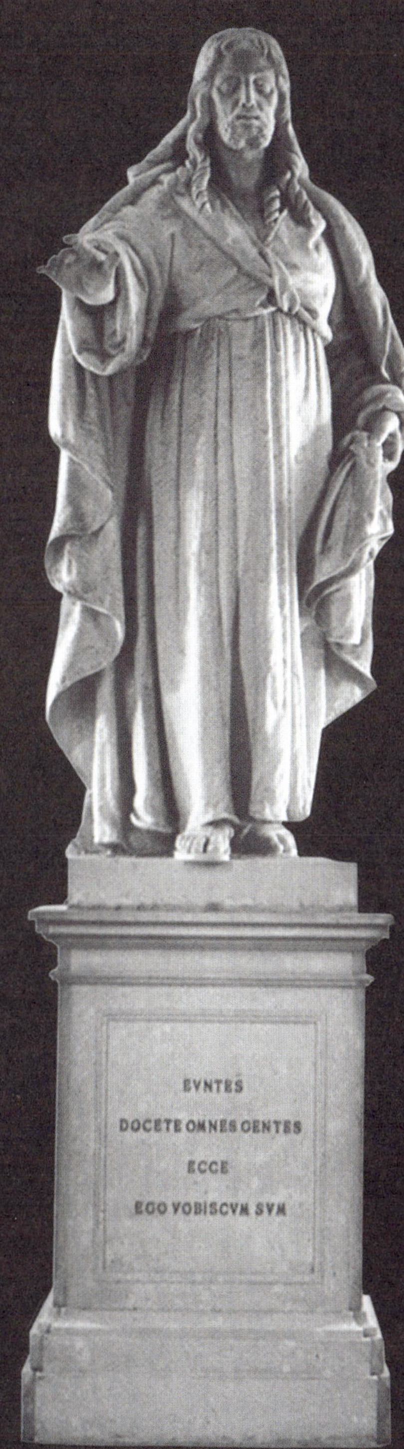

Jesus Christ, created by Dossena, at the Pontifical Gregorian University of Rome.

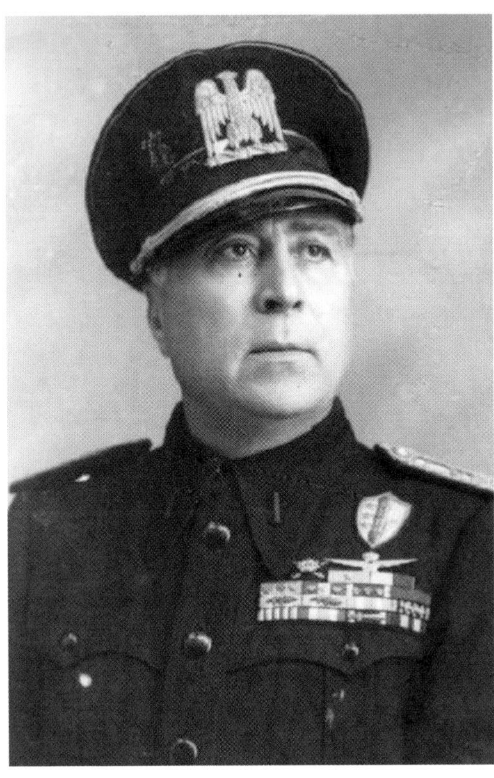

LEFT: Roberto Farinacci (1892–1945) was a leading Italian Fascist politician and a significant member of the National Fascist Party before and during the Second World War. Dossena hired him in his counter-claim against Fasoli, which ultimately led to Dossena not being charged with a crime.

This idea – that Dossena was a modern, almost reincarnated master – was taken up by some of the institutions who had been duped, perhaps because it made their mistakes seem less foolish, and because Dossena's work was extremely skilful. A 1928 article in *The New York Times* quoted the Cleveland Art Museum curators calling Dossena 'among the greatest sculptors of the day'. In a 1931 interview in *The Times*, Frick trustee J. Horace Harding said, 'Dossena deserves to be recognised as one of the greatest sculptors the world has known. In my opinion, his sculptures, which have found their way into American collections, are treasures that are cheap at any price.'

The problem, of course, is that the works were accredited to past masters. When Fasoli commissioned a sculpture, he provided photographs for Dossena. For the Simone Martini, for example, Dossena referred to pictures of the Annunciation by Martini in the Uffizi Gallery in Florence and copied the work closely, then 'aged' it.

The trial

In May 1927, Dossena asked Fasoli for several thousand dollars he was owed for a statue. By that time, Fasoli was probably aware that the deception was wearing thin, that too many of the forgeries were being questioned, and that Dossena was likely to be discovered soon, so he refused to pay him. However, Dossena needed the money urgently. His girlfriend had just died after months of illness, and he had a huge bill for her medical treatment and funeral. So when Fasoli refused to pay him, Dossena sought the advice of a lawyer, who, on hearing the story, quickly calculated the amount of money that Fasoli and Palesi were probably making out of Dossena. Infuriated, Dossena decided to prosecute.

Sueing Fasoli for fraud, embezzlement and slander, Dossena claimed that he was being underpaid from the profits made by his own work from his business partners. He had discovered more about their financial deceit. They had sold his most recent artwork, for instance, for nearly 4 million lire, but had paid him just 20,000 lire for it. In response, Fasoli reported Dossena to the police as an enemy of the Fascist regime, accusing him of verbally slandering Mussolini. In the late 1920s, this was a dangerous accusation. To add credibility to this, Fasoli hired the secretary of the Roman Fascist Federation, Aldo Vecchini, as his lawyer. In a counter move, Dossena then hired Roberto Farinacci, secretary of the National Fascist Party, who was second in command to Mussolini.

In court, Dossena claimed that he had no idea what the two dealers had been doing with his works, to whom they had been sold or for how much, and that he was not involved in selling the art. The case was challenged by art collectors and connoisseurs, mainly because they did not want to admit that the art they had bought were fakes and that they had been duped in their own area of expertise. Dossena needed to prove that the artworks were both by him and that they were sold as being by famous artists without his knowledge or consent by Fasoli and Palesi. According to Dossena's statements, Fasoli allegedly told him that a Renaissance-style church was being built in the United States and it needed to be appropriately decorated with sculptures similar to those made in the 15th century. He argued that he had done nothing illegal, as he had only created art in the styles of the masters and had not created replications of any specific works. It was Fasoli, he said, who was the dealer who had sold them under false pretences.

Dossena was not charged with a crime. He was acquitted for lack of evidence. As it could not be proved that the art was created with the intention to deceive, the court cleared him of any wrongdoing. Most accounts suggest that he was awarded damages, but that he never actually received any money from Fasoli. Fasoli was also acquitted for lack of evidence. In the press and in public opinion, however, Dossena was believed to have been a victim of the crooked dealings of Fasoli and Palesi. It is possible that he had been duped by Fasoli, but the truth will never be known.

Braggart

During the trial, as many experts either did not believe Dossena or did not want to, numerous art experts visited him in his studio, including a curator from The Metropolitan Museum of Art in New York, Gisela Richter. Among other works, Dossena showed her his plaster model for the kore (a free-standing ancient Greek figure statue) that was bought by The Metropolitan, studio photos of the Athena sold to the Cleveland Art Museum, and numerous works in progress including a marble relief of a Madonna and Child in the style of Mino da Fiesole (c. 1429–1484), a Gothic baptismal font and a French 17th-century helmeted head. As he showed Richter and others around, he declared, 'All my own work. None are copies, none are imitations, I created them all – paintings, sculpture, architecture, wood carvings.' He was equally forthcoming with other visitors and told the newspapers that his sculptures 'really deserve to be prized as highly as those of Donatello, Verrocchio, Vecchietta or da Fiesole'.

He said he never pretended that his work was by anyone else but that he believed himself to be the old masters' equal. When he was interviewed by *Art News* in 1929, he protested about 'the mistaken supposition that I meant to make false representations. The truth is that I have never made any but original things, modelling them from nature in an antique character and style.'

After the trial, between 1929 and 1931, he had exhibitions in some of the most important museums in Paris, Berlin and Vienna, and in March 1933 a public auction of his work was held in the ballroom of New York's Plaza Hotel. The catalogue contained an essay by the editor-in-chief of *Art News*, Alfred Frankfurter, who wrote of the 'quality of sincerity in Dossena, the almost incredible ability of the man to have worked without affectation and without malevolence in the spirit of the dead past and its masters'. Nevertheless, buyers were restrained. The 39 works of sculpture at the Plaza Hotel sold in total for just $9,125. The highest price paid for one item was $675 for the relief of the Madonna and Child in the style of da Fiesole.

In 1937, Alceo Dossena died a poor man in Rome.

OPPOSITE: Alceo Dossena, whose artworks deceived many experts, came from humble origins, but he had a passion for art throughout his life.

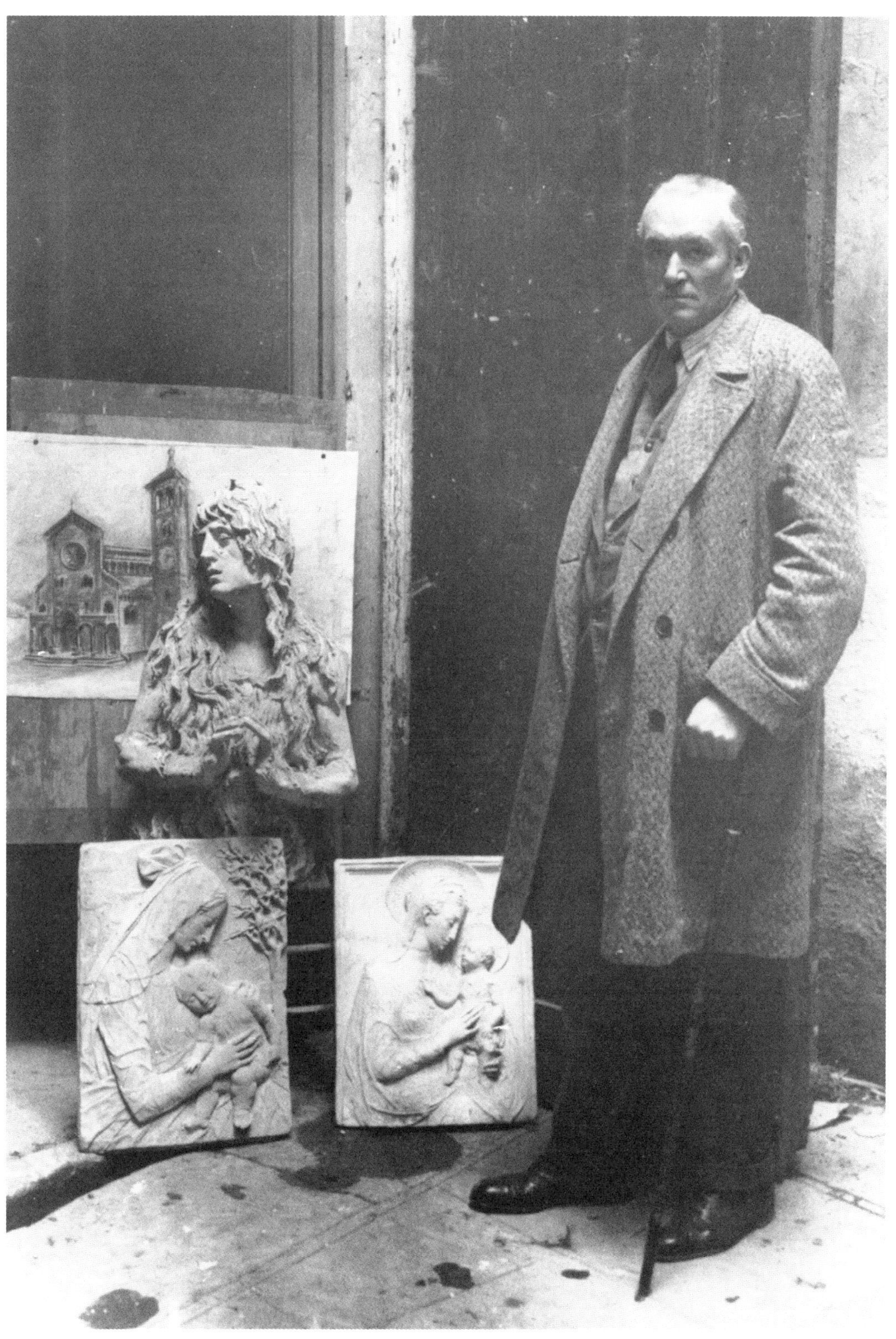

CHAPTER 2

The 'Vermeer' That Fooled the Nazis

Dutch painter and portraitist Henricus 'Han' van Meegeren (1889–1947) is infamous as one of the cleverest art forgers of the 20th century.

Honest beginnings

Initially, van Meegeren attempted to make an honest career as an artist, but critics dismissed his work as being mediocre. Hurt and also incensed, he decided to prove everyone wrong by forging paintings from the Dutch Golden Age (c. 1588–1672). He spent years deceiving many leading art experts of the time that his paintings were genuine 17th-century works. His victims even included the Netherlandish government.

Born in Deventer in the Netherlands, Han van Meegeren showed great promise as an artist from a young age. At the Higher Burger School, his teacher, painter Bartus Korteling, became his mentor. Korteling was a huge admirer of Johannes Vermeer, and he taught van Meegeren some of Vermeer's techniques. However, van Meegeren's father had other ideas and made the boy enrol to study architecture at the Delft University of Technology. At first, van Meegeren applied himself. He passed his preliminary architectural exams with ease, and was awarded a prestigious Gold Medal for a drawing of the interior of the Church of St Lawrence in Rotterdam, but at the end of the course he simply refused to take his finals because he had no intention of becoming an architect.

In 1913, at the age of 24, he walked away from the University of Technology and instead enrolled at the Royal Academy of Art in The Hague, where he studied drawing and painting. After a year, he had completed the diploma examination, which enabled him to teach, and he became employed as the assistant to the Professor of Drawing and Art History at the Royal Academy. Married by now and with a daughter, to supplement his income he designed posters and painted pictures for Christmas cards, as well as still lifes, landscapes and portraits for the commercial art trade.

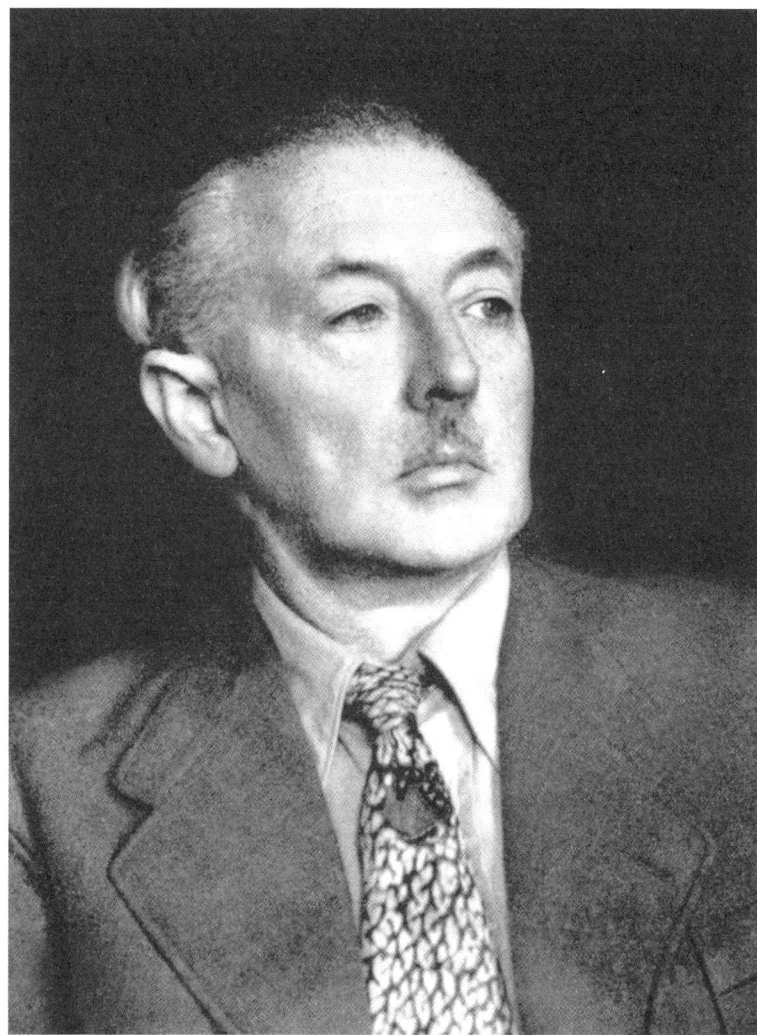

LEFT: Han van Meegeren worked undetected as a forger, until an Allied art commission after the Second World War tried to identify and restore works of art that the Nazis had stolen to their rightful owners. Van Meegeren was arrested and charged with collaboration with the Nazis, until he confessed to having forged several of the paintings.

Although he also held exhibitions of his artwork, reviewers wrote that he had limited talent. His distinctive painting style resembled Vermeer's, but he struggled to achieve originality, and the fame and recognition he believed he deserved eluded him. Frustrated and annoyed, he determined to prove those critics wrong, and he devised a cunning plan. He would create his own 'lost' masterpieces by Vermeer and pass them off as authentic.

Success

Van Meegeren's first major success was the sale of *The Supper at Emmaus* in 1937. The painting was both in the style of Vermeer and treated with his ageing process, and it was well received. As soon as he saw it, the highly esteemed art collector, historian and curator

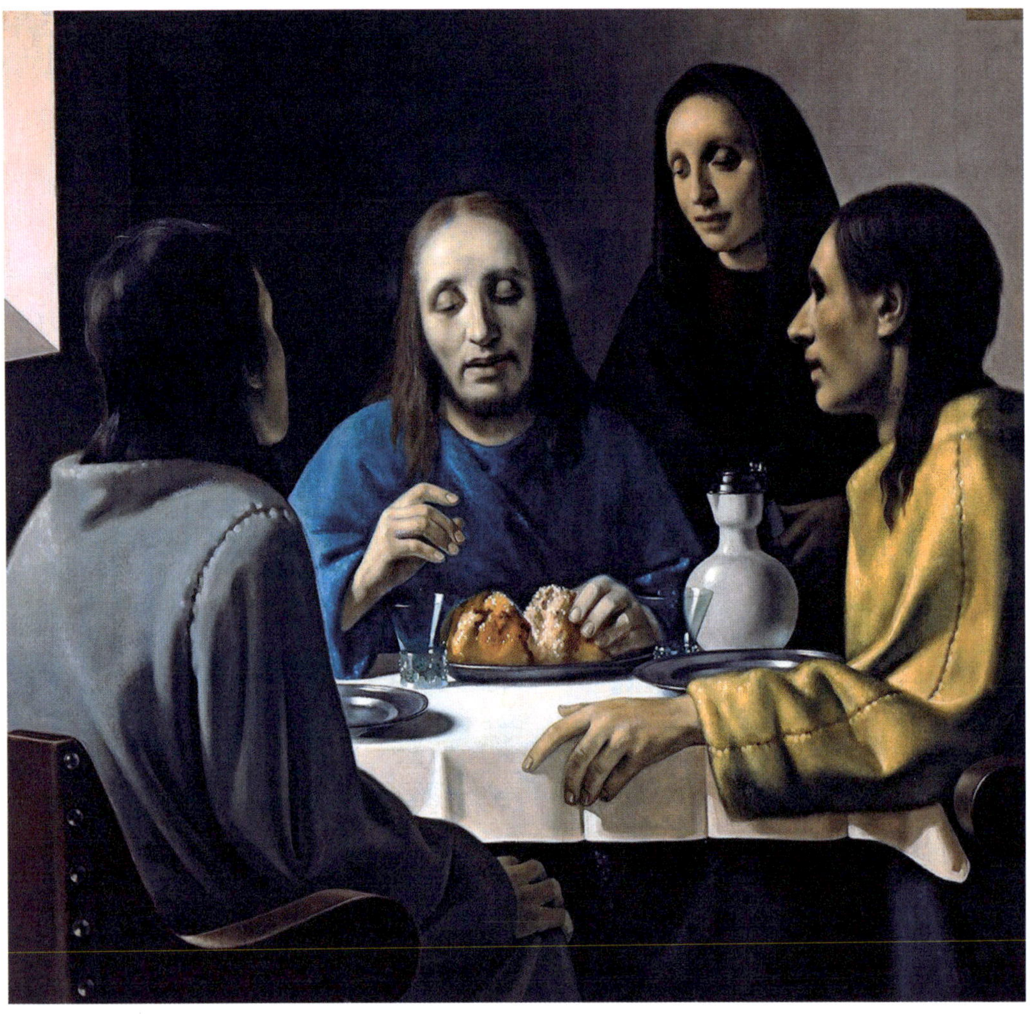

Abraham Bredius described the painting as a rediscovered lost work by Vermeer, writing in a respected English art journal, the *Burlington Magazine*: 'It is a wonderful moment in the life of a lover of art when he finds himself suddenly confronted with a hitherto unknown painting by a great master, untouched, on the original canvas, and without any restoration – just as it left the painter's studio. And what a picture! Neither the beautiful signature . . . nor the pointillés on the bread which Christ is blessing, are necessary to convince us that we have here – I am inclined to say – the masterpiece of Johannes Vermeer of Delft . . . quite different from all his other paintings and yet every inch a Vermeer. In no other picture by the great master of Delft do we find such sentiment, such a profound understanding of the Bible story – a sentiment so nobly human expressed through the medium of highest art.' Within just a few months, the Museum

ABOVE: In 1937, van Meegeren painted *The Supper at Emmaus*. Experts believed that Vermeer had studied in Italy, so van Meegeren used Caravaggio's *Supper at Emmaus* in Milan as a model. Respected art historians thought that sthe painting was an authentic Vermeer.

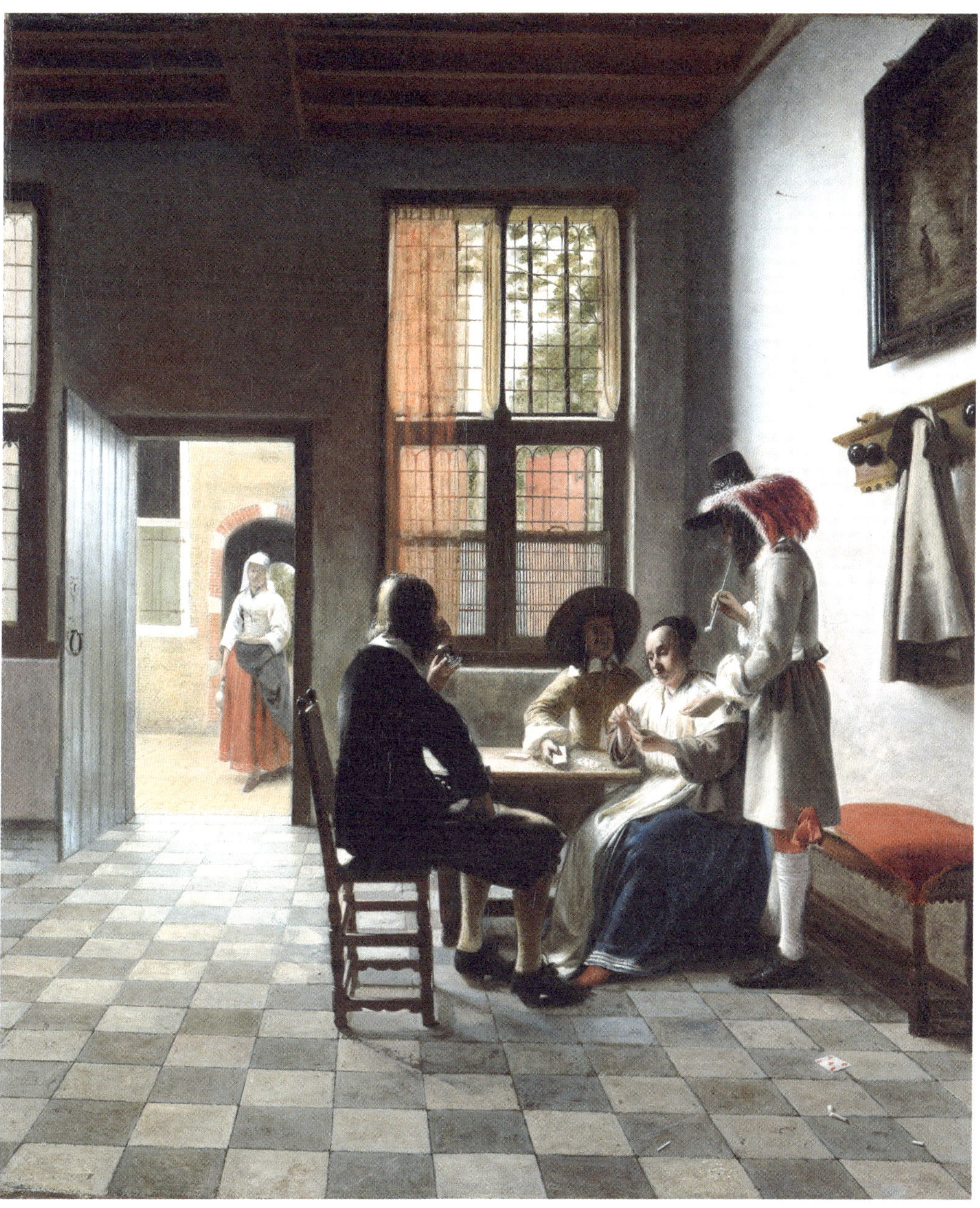

ABOVE: The Dutch painter Pieter de Hooch painted *Card Players in a Sunlit Room* in 1658. He explored many similar subjects, featuring softly lit interiors, a sense of stillness and figures occupied with their daily lives. The paintings usually involve a moral message, and his was one of the styles that van Meegeren often copied.

Boijmans van Beuningen in Rotterdam bought the painting for 520,000 Dutch guilders.

In 1938, with the proceeds from the sale of the painting, van Meegeren bought a 12-bedroom home at Les Arènes de Cimiez in Nice. He decorated the walls with several genuine old masters, and there he produced more forgeries, including *Interior with Card Players* and *Interior with Drinkers*, both 'signed by' Pieter de Hooch (1629–after 1684), and *Last Supper* 'by' Vermeer. He returned to the Netherlands in September 1939 just before the Second World War broke out. As he was 50 in 1939, he was not conscripted, and during the war he created several forgeries in Vermeer's style. The money he was earning went on more properties, jewellery, works of art and a lavish lifestyle. Over the years, he forged many more paintings 'by' Vermeer and other Dutch masters. His command of 17th-century painting styles and his ability to artificially age the canvases made his forgeries nearly indistinguishable from genuine paintings of the time, and in total it is estimated that they earned him the equivalent of around $60 million.

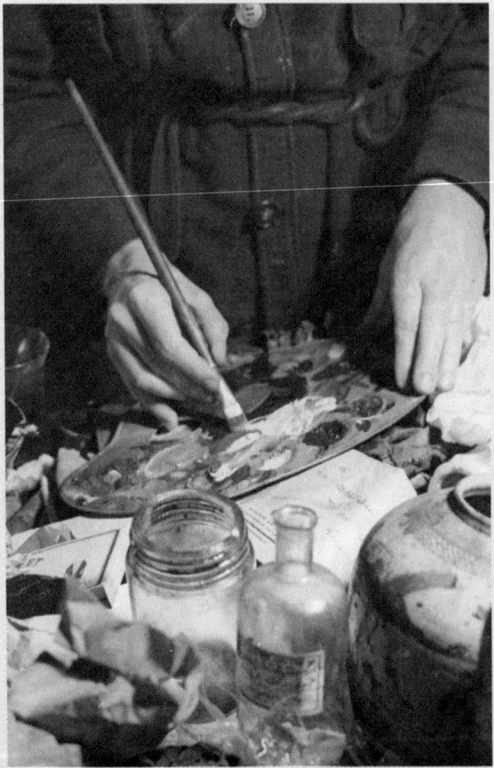

CHEMICAL AND TECHNICAL PROCEDURES

In 1932, van Meegeren set out to define the chemical and technical procedures that would be necessary to create his forgeries. He bought authentic 17th-century canvases and mixed his own paints from raw materials (such as lapis lazuli, white lead, indigo and cinnabar) using old formulas to ensure that they could pass as authentic. He also created his own badger-hair paintbrushes that emulated Vermeer's. He invented a scheme of using phenol formaldehyde (Bakelite) to harden his paints after application, making the paintings seem about 300 years old. He first mixed his paints with lilac oil to stop the colours from fading or yellowing in heat. After completing a painting, he baked it to harden the paint again, and then rolled it over a cylinder to multiply the cracks. Later, he doused the painting in black India ink to fill in cracks with what would look like years of grime.

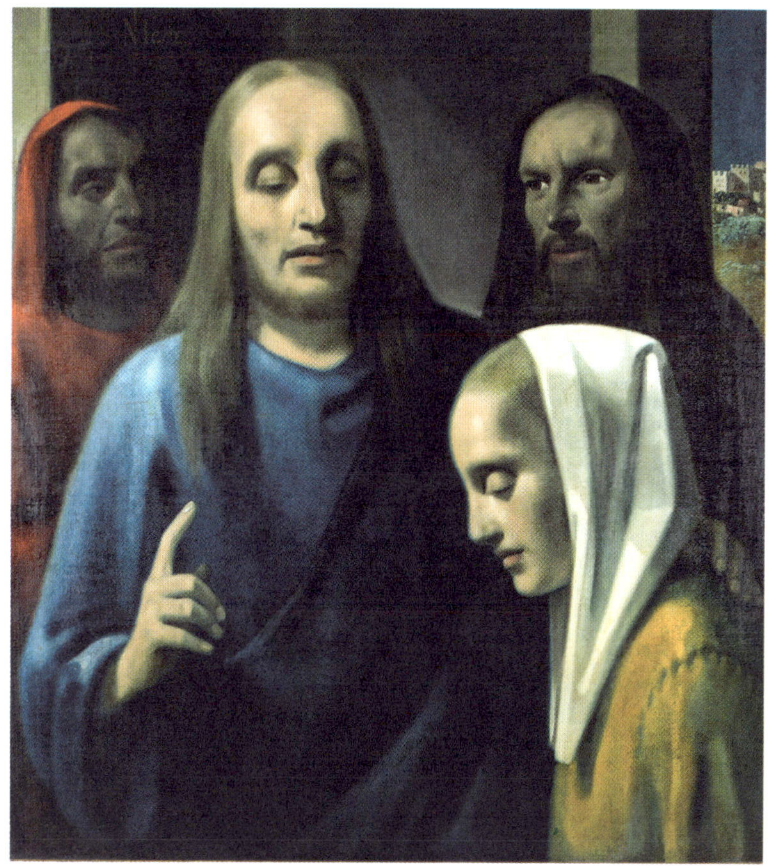

LEFT: This painting, *Christ with the Adulteress*, was stolen by Hermann Göring during the Second World War, believing that Vermeer created it. However, it was painted in 1942 by van Meegeren and its discovery after the war forced him to confess to his forgeries.

Caught!

Van Meegeren's deception might have continued undetected if not for the Nazi occupation of the Netherlands during the war. In 1942, one of van Meegeren's agents sold his painting *Christ with the Adulteress* that purported to be a Vermeer to a Nazi banker and art dealer. Reichsmarschall Göring saw it and wanted it, and in order to obtain it, he gave the banker 137 looted paintings. A year later, Göring hid *Christ with the Adulteress* along with 6,750 other artworks stolen by the Nazis in an Austrian salt mine. However, in May 1945, a group of Allied forces (now known as 'the Monuments Men') were commissioned to try to recover the art that had been plundered by the Nazis and they located the salt mine. Among all the other works of art, they discovered van Meegeren's 'Vermeer', and they traced it back to the banker and eventually to van Meegeren. At the end of May 1945, van Meegeren was arrested and charged with being a Nazi collaborator and plunderer of Dutch cultural property, threatened by the authorities with the death penalty. To save his life, in court he admitted his forgeries, which carried a far more lenient sentence.

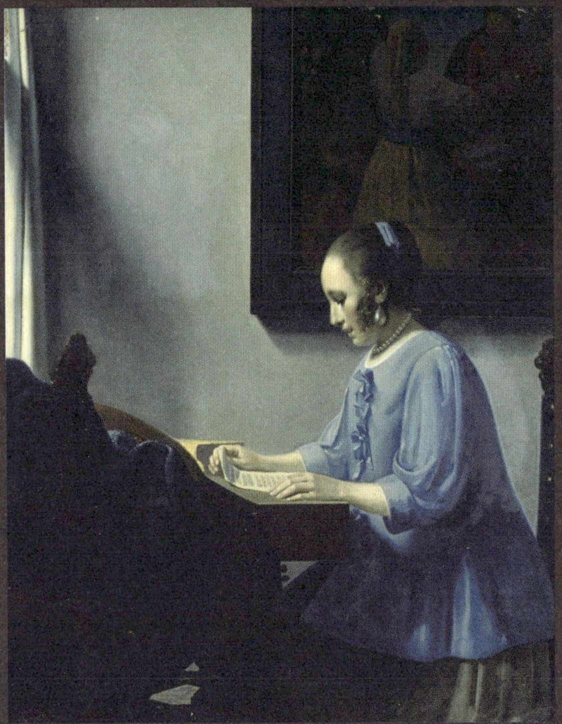

Woman Reading Music, a painting in the style of Vermeer by van Meegeren, 1935–40.

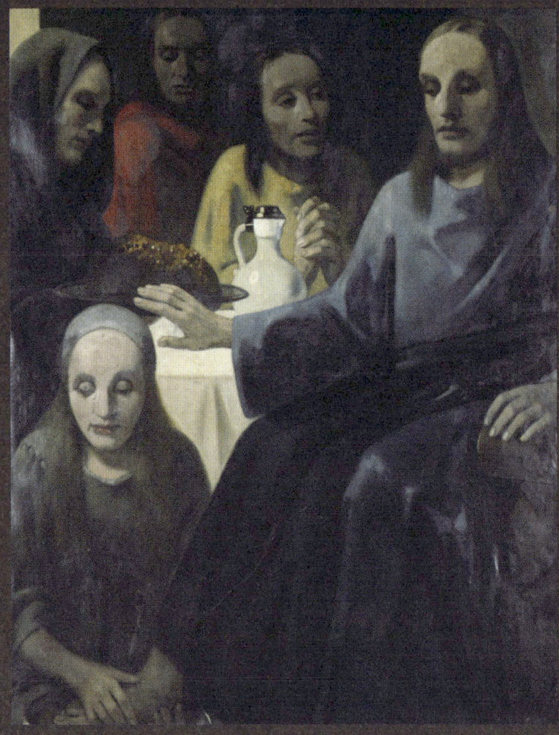

The Foot Washing, Mary anoints Christ's feet, painted by van Meegeren in the style of Vermeer, 1935–43.

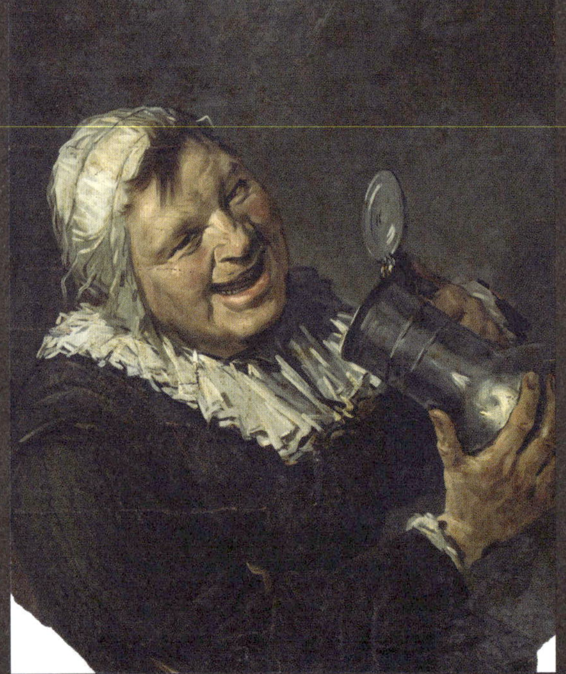

Malle Babbe, a copy of a work by Frans Hals, painted by van Meegeren, 1930–40.

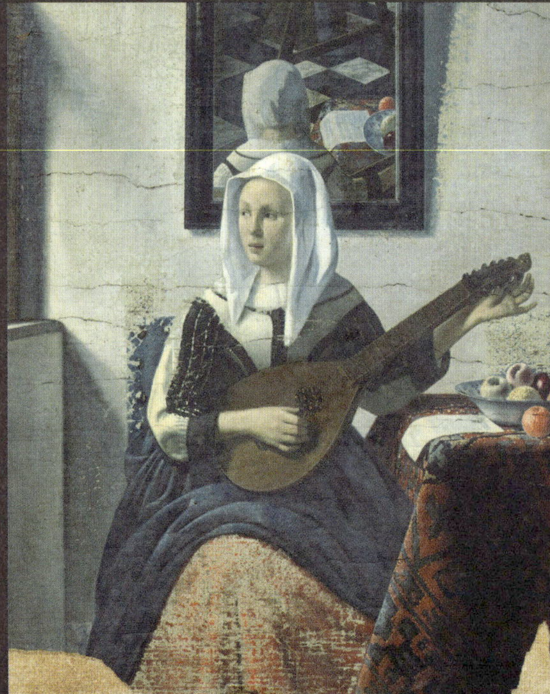

Woman Playing a Cittern, in the style of Vermeer, painted by van Meegeren, 1930-40.

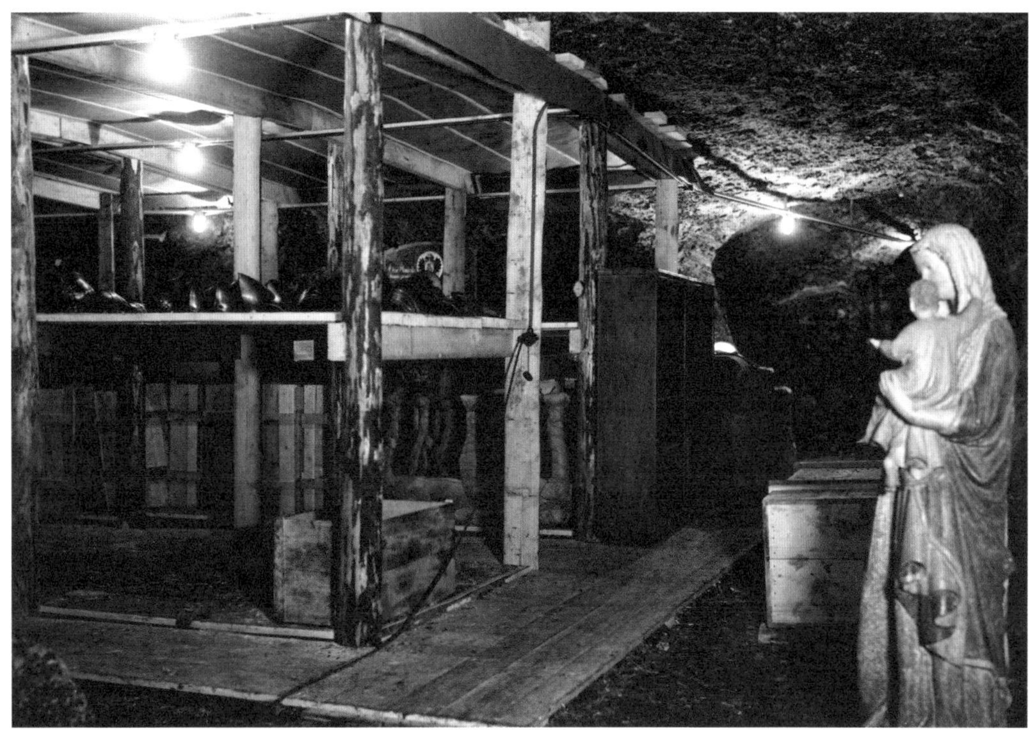

ABOVE: During the Second World War, the German Nazi Party stored paintings, sculptures, furniture, gold and other objects that they had plundered at various storage sites, including salt mines at Altaussee and Merkers and a copper mine at Siegen.

His revelation stunned everyone in court, and at first no one believed him. So, to prove his claims, he painted another 'Vermeer' with witnesses. Under police guard and documented by reporters, he painted *Jesus among the Doctors* in the style of Vermeer, painstakingly demonstrating both his painting and his ageing techniques. Ultimately, in November 1947, he was cleared of being a Nazi collaborator but found guilty of fraud and forgery, and sentenced to one year in prison. The trial was widely covered in the media, and van Meegeren's audacious deception captured the public imagination, especially having duped Göring. However, one month after he was sentenced, following years of drug and alcohol abuse, at the age of 58, van Meegeren died of a heart attack. Two years later, his belongings were auctioned. Although he had spent much of his earnings on his extravagant lifestyle, the money raised was used to pay back some of those who had bought his fraudulent paintings.

Continuing story

Since that time, several more fake works of art have been proved to be by van Meegeren. For example, in July 2011, the BBC TV series *Fake or Fortune* investigated *The Procuress*. This painting, in the collection of the Courtauld Institute of Art in London, was believed to be a 17th-century anonymous copy of a 1620s brothel scene by Dutch

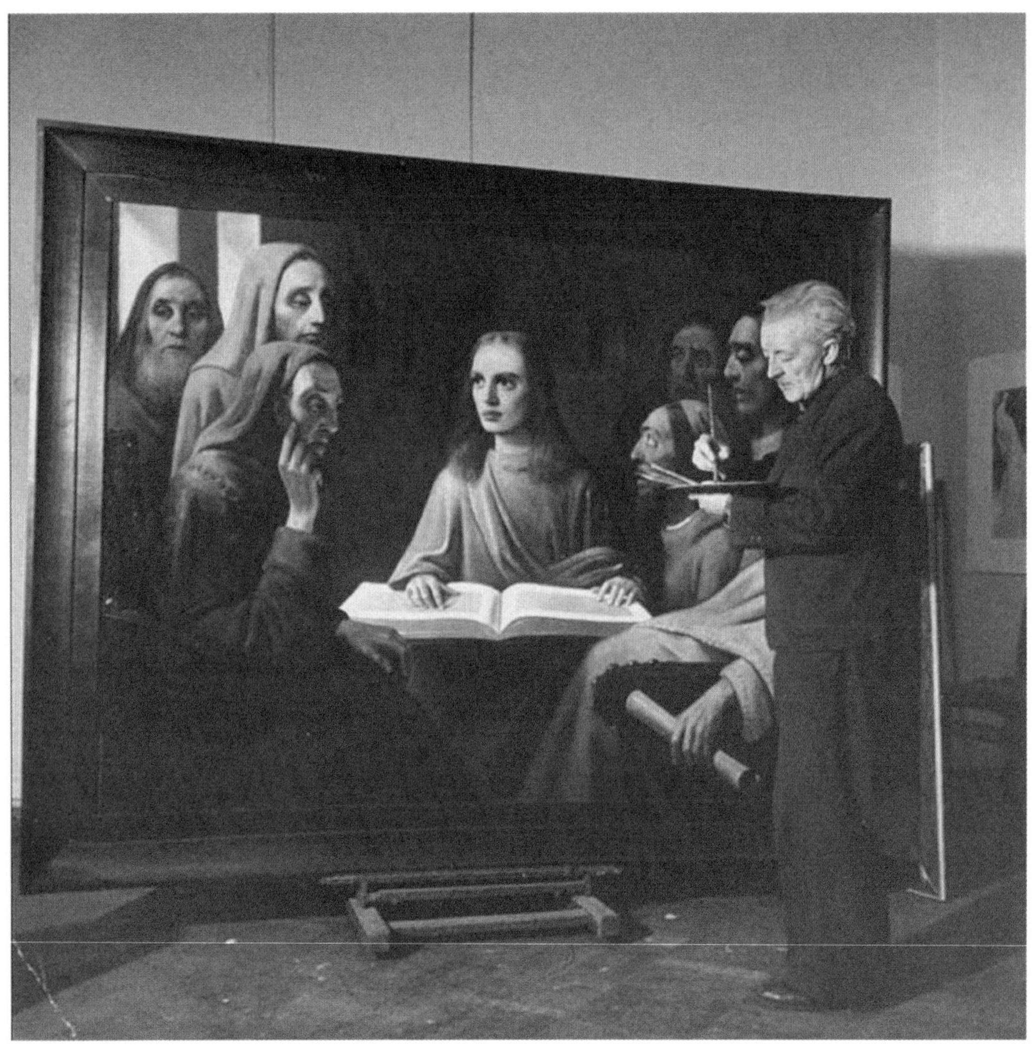

master Dirck van Baburen. Scientific tests that were commissioned for the series detected a synthetic resin – probably Bakelite, the 20th-century material used extensively by van Meegeren to mimic age. It is highly likely that more paintings exist in collections today that are believed to have been made by 17th-century masters, but were, in fact, executed by van Meegeren.

Van Meegeren swindled his buyers out of millions, but the money lost is not the only problem. His dishonesty has affected art collectors, museums and art historians everywhere. Much art has had to be re-evaluated – or will have to be. The art world has become less trusting, more wary and less confident. As there is no knowing exactly which works he painted, the uncertainty continues.

ABOVE: *Jesus Among the Doctors*, painted by van Meegeren in 1945 to prove his innocence and sold to a reputable gallery. Jesus is in the centre of the composition, looking young, with a book on his lap.

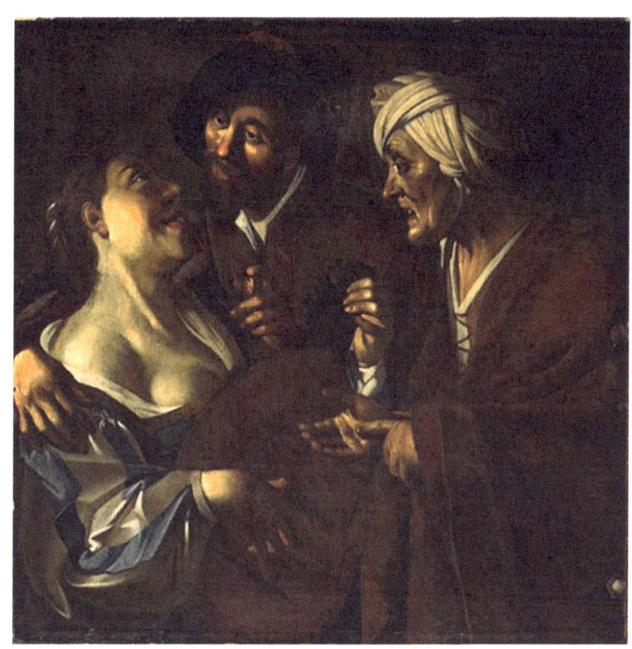

LEFT AND BELOW: Van Meegeren's forgery in the style of Dirk van Baburen's painting *The Procuress*, painted c. 1930 (left). Below, the painting is being examined by an expert at the Courtauld Gallery, London, where the artwork is now held.

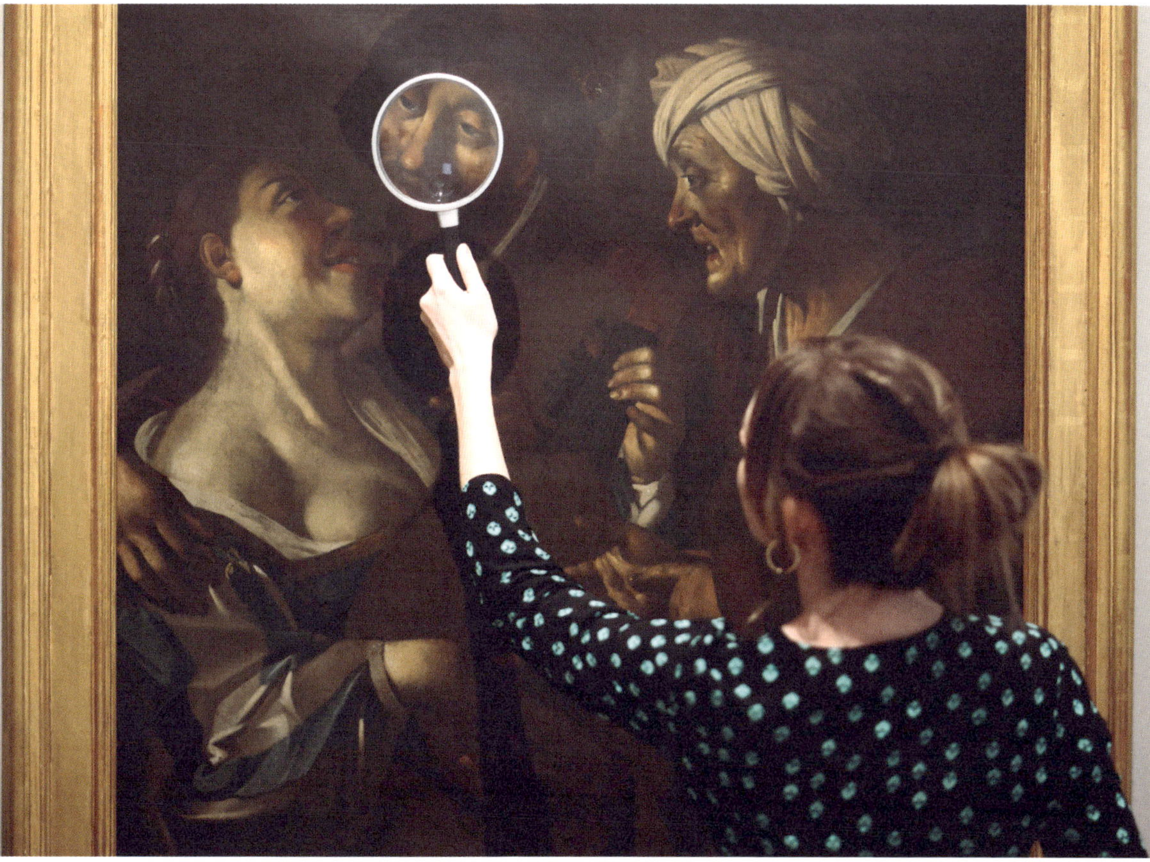

CHAPTER 3

Genuine Fakes

In 1985, having failed to make a living as a painter, farmer's son John Myatt (b. 1945) placed an advertisement in *Private Eye* magazine which read: 'Genuine Fakes. Nineteenth and twentieth century paintings from £150.'

Myatt was born in Staffordshire in the UK. He won a scholarship to boarding school, where he discovered a talent for copying artists' styles, and he often amused his friends with his paintings. He eventually became an art teacher at a local secondary school. During the 1960s and 1970s, in his spare time he continued to paint, experimenting with different styles and techniques, but he made little money from them. Then, in 1985, his first wife left him, and in order to spend more time with his two young children he gave up teaching and decided to place the fateful ad in *Private Eye*.

Myatt executed copies of any painting ordered, signing his own name on the copy. However, although he sold several of these, he was barely making ends meet. Then he met John Drewe. Born John Cockett in 1948 in Sussex, Drewe had a fairly unremarkable background. In 1965, he had dropped out of school, changed his surname, and lied about his qualifications. In 1986, Drewe contacted Myatt to say that he had bought several of his 'Genuine Fakes', and one – a copy of a painting by Cubist artist Albert Gleizes (1881–1953) – had just sold at Christie's auction house in London for £25,000. Drewe had paid Myatt £150 for the painting, but Christie's had accepted it as a genuine work by Gleizes. Drewe offered Myatt a cheque for £12,500 and a business plan. Until that point, Myatt had been struggling financially, but suddenly he felt hopeful and he accepted Drewe's offer.

From 1986, he began to paint forgeries, signing them with the artists' names and delivering them to Drewe in London. His paintings emulated the styles of a wide range of 19th- and 20th-century artists, including Claude Monet, Vincent van Gogh, Roger Bissière, Marc Chagall, John Everett Millais, Le Corbusier, Jean Dubuffet, Alberto Giacometti, Henri Matisse, Ben Nicholson, Nicolas

OPPOSITE: John Myatt in his studio, painting one of his colourful works. Myatt initially left his day job to produce art so that he could spend more time with his children. He always maintained that his modern materials proved he never attempted to fool anyone.

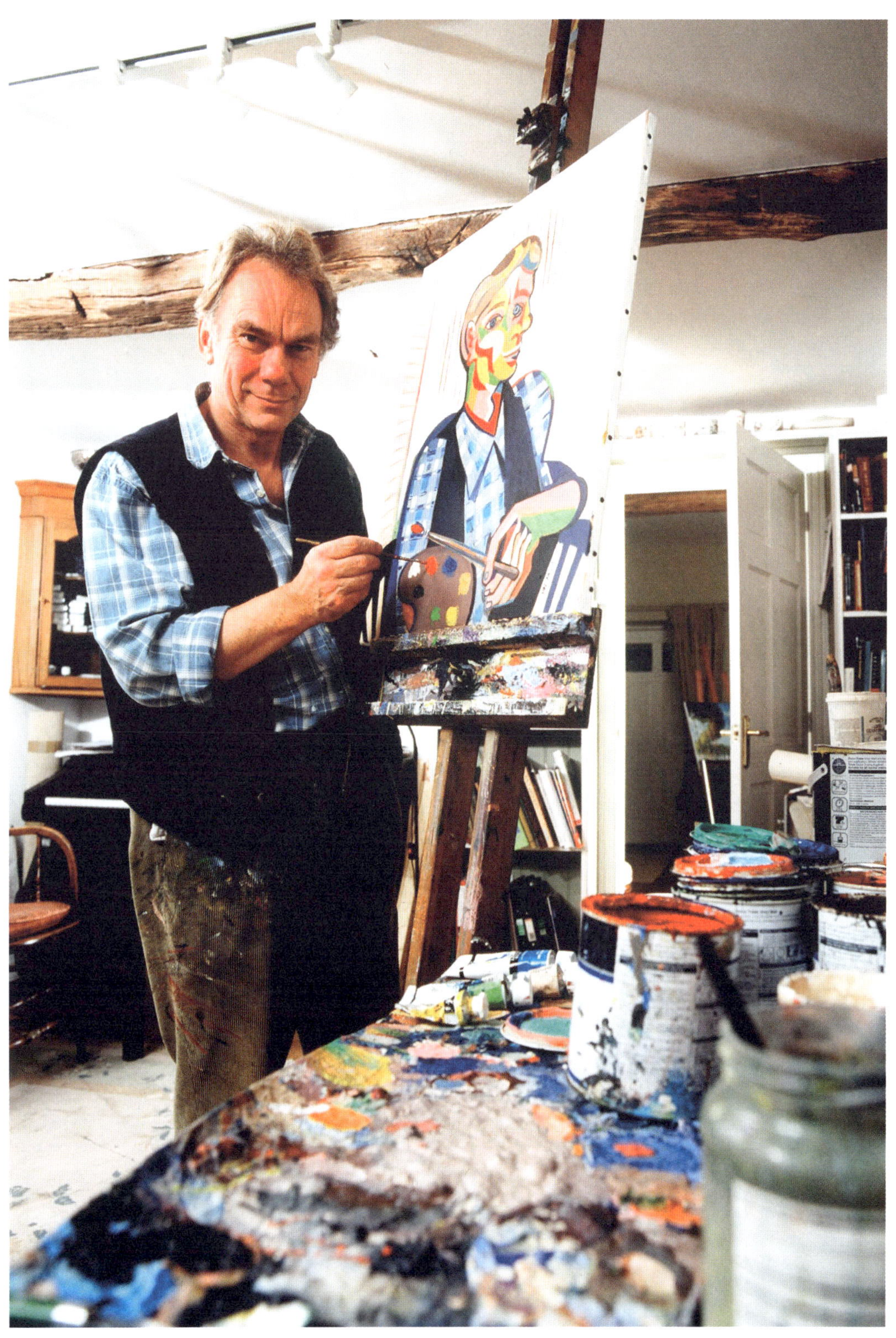

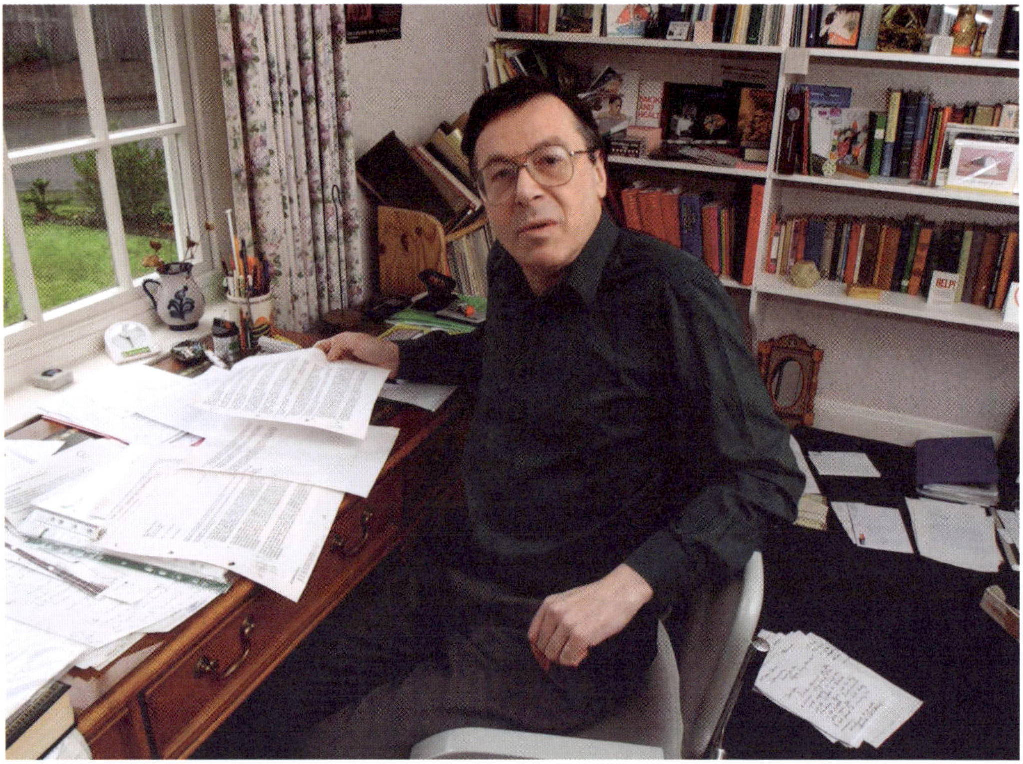

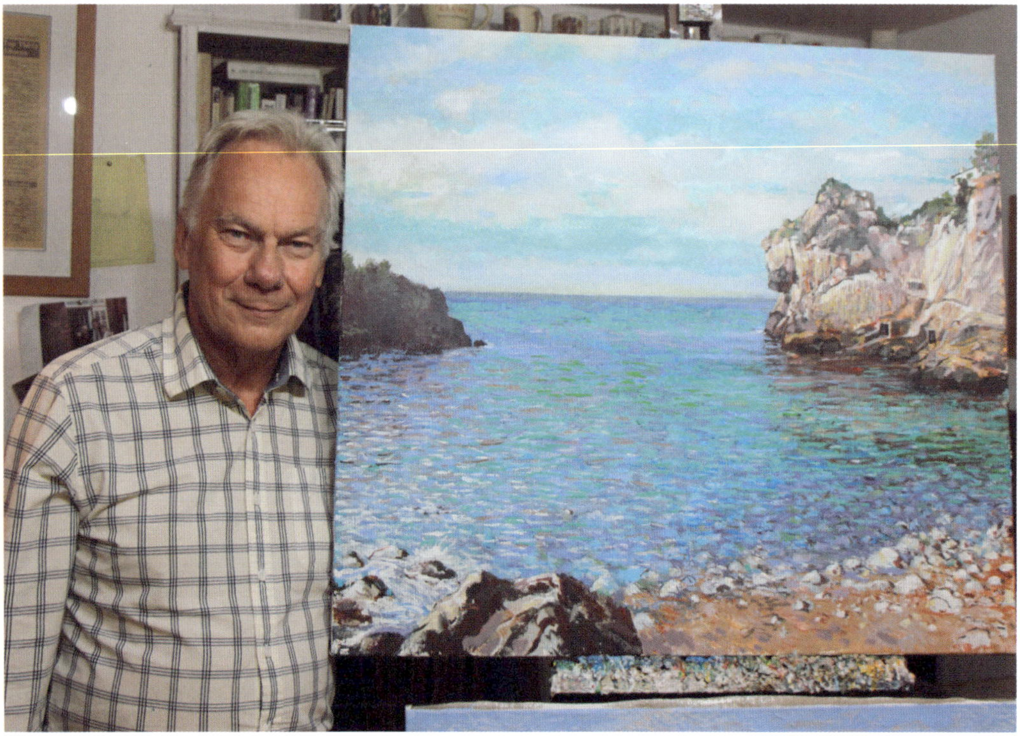

de Staël and Graham Sutherland. Everything that Myatt produced was different from any actual works but in the style of the artists. Even though he used emulsion paint and K-Y jelly to imitate the texture of oil paintings rather than genuine oils, reputable dealers in London, Paris, New York and Japan were fooled by his artworks.

Historical records

If they had been scientifically analysed, Myatt's paintings would have been discovered immediately, but it seems that the experts believed what they saw, augmented by Drewe's elaborate back stories. For along with each of Myatt's paintings, Drewe had forged invented provenances, including fake historical and archival documents: letters, receipts and inventory notices that alleged to be from obscure but defunct galleries and museums or deceased individuals, making the paintings impossible to authenticate.

When an auction house is offered a work of art, it usually checks the historical records to see if it is genuine. This includes archives, provenance and the catalogue raisonné, which is a complete annotated listing of all the known artworks by that artist. Just like buying a car, these checks validate the artwork and can be used to reassure potential buyers of its authenticity. Although Drewe could not change the published catalogue raisonnés, he managed to insert fake documents into relevant archives by pretending to be researching particular artists. In 1989, he gained access to the archives of the Institute of Contemporary Arts (ICA) in London by claiming to be an interested collector. He donated two of Myatt's forgeries for a fundraising auction, and later he used the ICA's stationery in his fake documents. He donated two paintings by Roger Bissière to the Tate, but Bissière's son did not accept them, so Drewe withdrew the paintings and instead donated £20,000 to the gallery. As a result, the Tate opened its archives to him. He provided a false reference to become accepted by the Victoria and Albert Museum. Once he had access to these archives, he put false records into them, and even replaced old pages and inserted other new pages into old art catalogues – all about Myatt's forgeries. To this day, it is not known how many archives Drewe tampered with or where he placed his fake information. Although those institutions and others have conducted extensive examinations of their archival systems, fake historical evidence is difficult to find when it has been inserted into genuine documents.

Drewe also forged documents about previous 'owners' of the paintings, sometimes using records of dead people, including some of his own old acquaintances. By offering them money or convincing them that they would be helping someone in need, he convinced

OPPOSITE, ABOVE: Born John Cockett in Sussex, England, John Drewe spent much of his life fabricating stories about his experiences and achievements. After he met John Myatt, Drewe became a regular client and convinced Myatt to create forgeries through which he could earn large amounts of money.

OPPOSITE, BELOW: Myatt at his studio holding one of his paintings that closely resembles Claude Monet's work, which Myatt now sells legitimately, calling them 'Genuine Fakes'. Arguing that this is no different to a 'copy band' of a famous musical group, Myatt's works are proving popular.

some of his living friends to sign documents as though they were previous owners of the paintings. Some of his friends were struggling for money; one old childhood friend believed Drewe's story about an alcoholic wife and deprived children and was convinced to pretend to be the owner of another painting by Myatt. Several other real people were bribed, while some were simply fictitious people; others were even the descendants of deceased artists whom Drewe persuaded into believing that some of Myatt's paintings had been, in fact, painted by their relations and they authenticated them.

'The biggest art fraud of the 20th century'

In 1995, Drewe made a mistake. He left his girlfriend to marry another woman. Drewe's scorned girlfriend wasted no time in telling the police and the Tate about Drewe and Myatt's activities. The police began tracking Myatt, and in September 1995 they arrested him.

BELOW: Myatt at his home in Staffordshire in September 2015 with his version of a self-portrait of Vincent van Gogh. Myatt insists that greed in the art world has distorted our appreciation of art. 'The fact is that when you're looking at a real van Gogh, what you're actually looking at is the money. You're considering its worth, those millions of pounds. The art gets lost.'

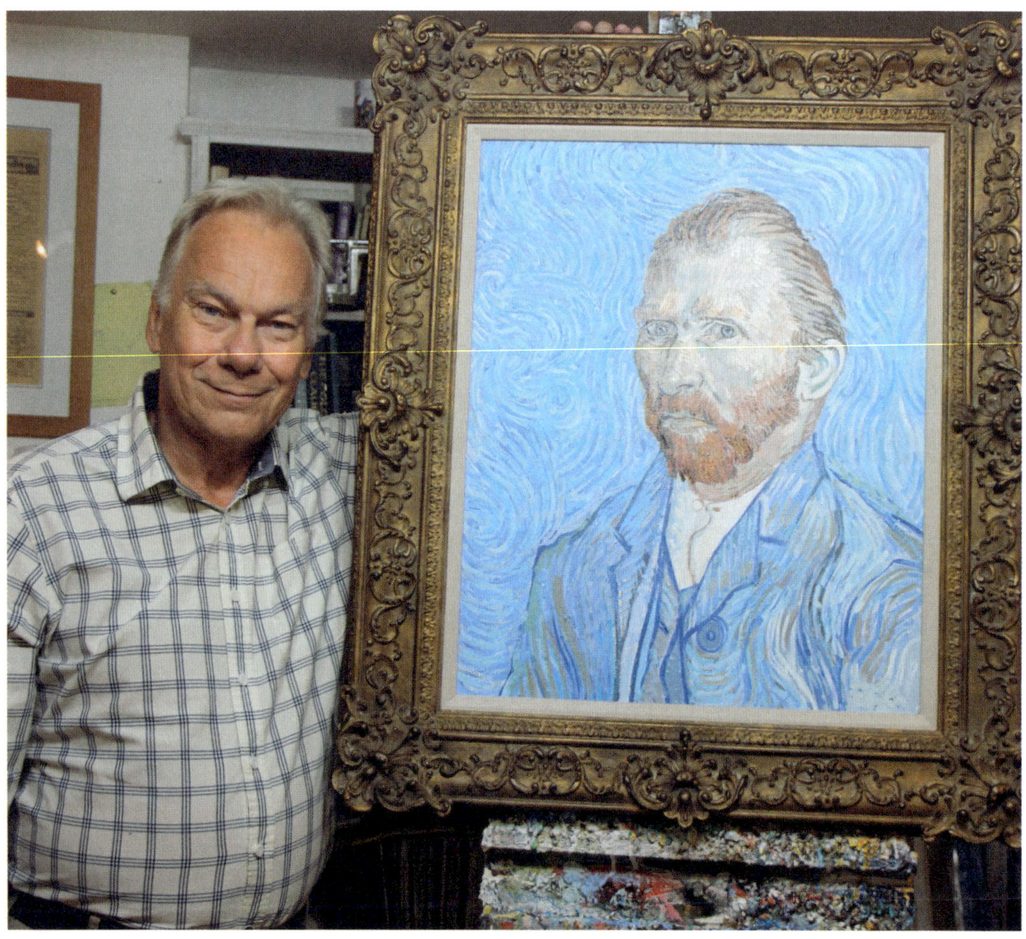

Myatt instantly confessed. For various reasons, he had grown to dislike Drewe, and he helped the police track him down. Myatt explained how he forged his paintings, showing that he did not even use the same media as the artists, so experts should have been able to tell the difference. He also offered to help Scotland Yard investigate other forgers.

The police believe that Myatt made approximately £275,000 from Drewe, while Drewe made millions. In April 1996, they arrested Drewe at his home, where they found the materials and some of the documents he was using to falsely validate the paintings. The police

BELOW: John Myatt surrounded by just a few of his paintings, showing his skill at emulating various artists' different styles and approaches.

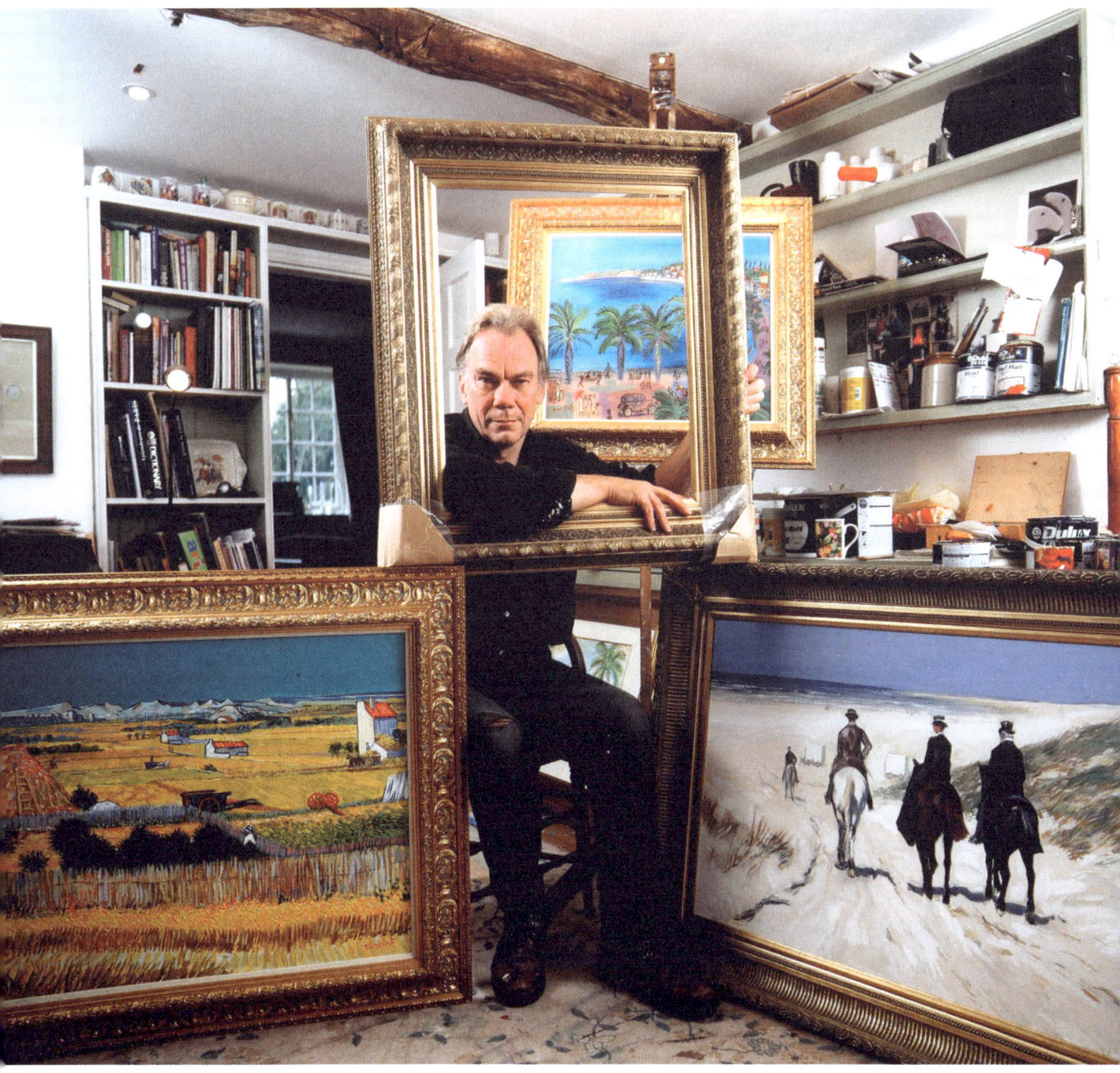

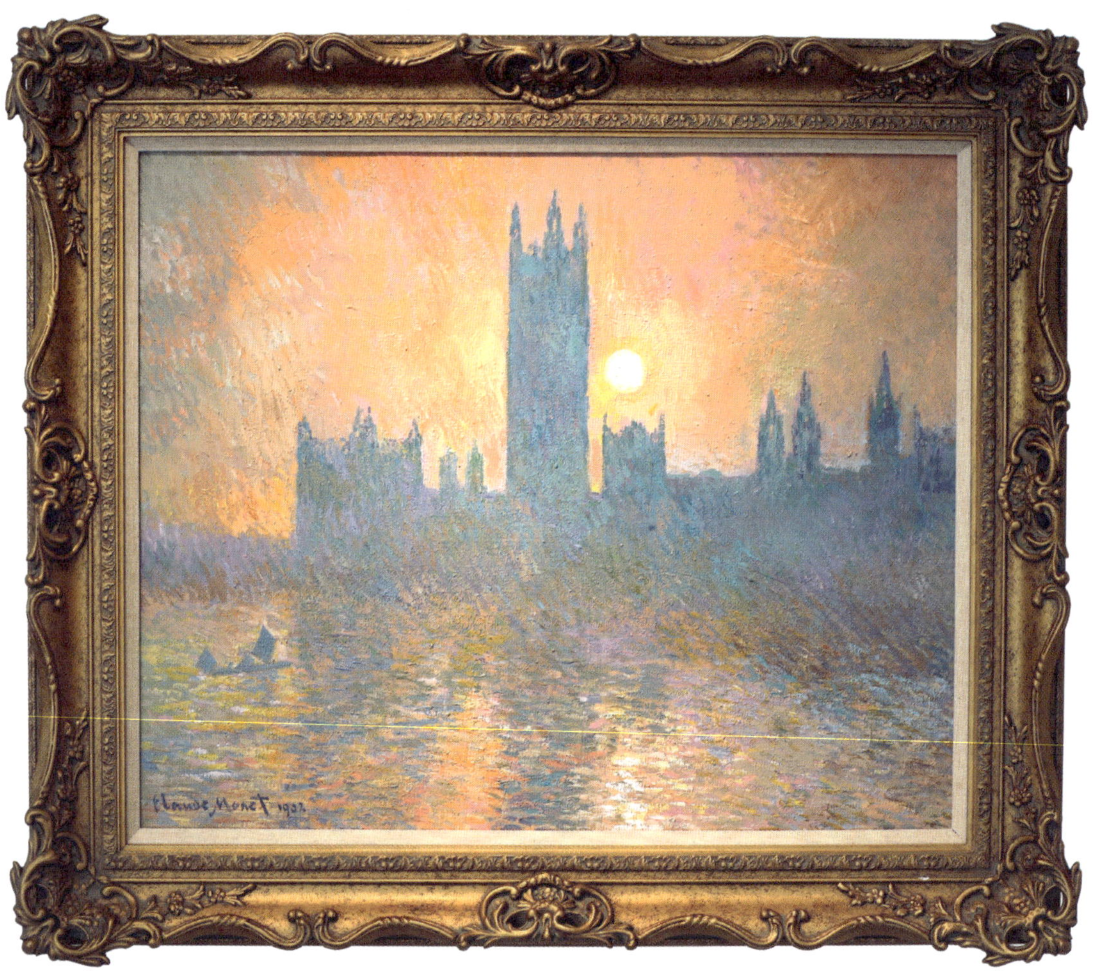

ABOVE: Another of Myatt's paintings closely following a series of images of London by Monet between 1899 and 1901. Monet painted the River Thames and the Houses of Parliament from St Thomas's Hospital. This work by Myatt features the sun in a different place from Monet's original works.

described the affair as 'the biggest art fraud of the 20th century'. In February 1999, Myatt was sentenced to one year in Brixton Prison. He was released in June after serving four months of his sentence. Drewe was sentenced to six years for conspiracy and served two. According to the police, Myatt painted about 200 forgeries, but only 80 have so far been recovered.

In prison, Myatt was nicknamed 'Picasso'. He reflected: 'Prison was horrible. But I suppose I was lucky because I was old. I made some lovely friends and just kept my head down . . . I had a business on the side drawing pencil portraits in exchange for phone cards.' While there, the police officer who had arrested him commissioned him to paint a family portrait and paid £5,000 for it. Myatt said that the policeman sent art materials into Brixton for him, and the barristers who ran the case against him wanted a memento too. He was suddenly making money legitimately as an artist. He said: 'I left prison in June and by October I had £10,000 in the bank that I'd earned legally through painting.'

After his release, Myatt continued to paint commissioned portraits and what he still calls 'Genuine Fakes'. He now exhibits his own work and is recognized for his skill as an artist, rather than for his involvement in the forgeries. He has appeared on TV, in

BELOW: Myatt in his studio. On his easel is a painting that resembles a work by Monet, and on the floor just behind him is a copy of the famous Portrait of Pope Innocent X, a portrait by the Spanish painter Diego Velázquez.

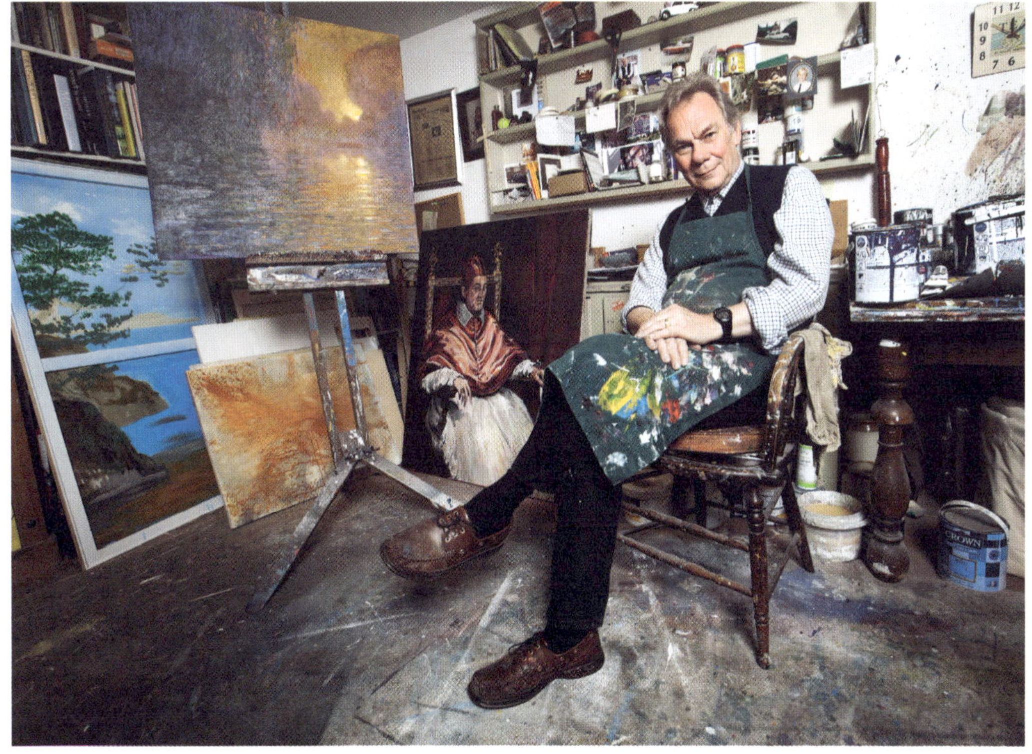

documentaries and educational programmes, and works alongside law enforcement officers helping to expose other fraudsters. He had a television show where he painted celebrities in styles that emulate the old masters, including Johannes Vermeer and Diego Velázquez.

He said of his forgeries, 'When I paint in the style of one of the greats . . . Monet, Picasso, van Gogh . . . I am not simply creating a copy or pale imitation of the original. Just as an actor immerses himself into a character, I climb into the minds and lives of each artist. I adopt their techniques and search for the inspiration behind each great artist's view of the world. Then, and only then, do I start to paint a "Legitimate Fake".'

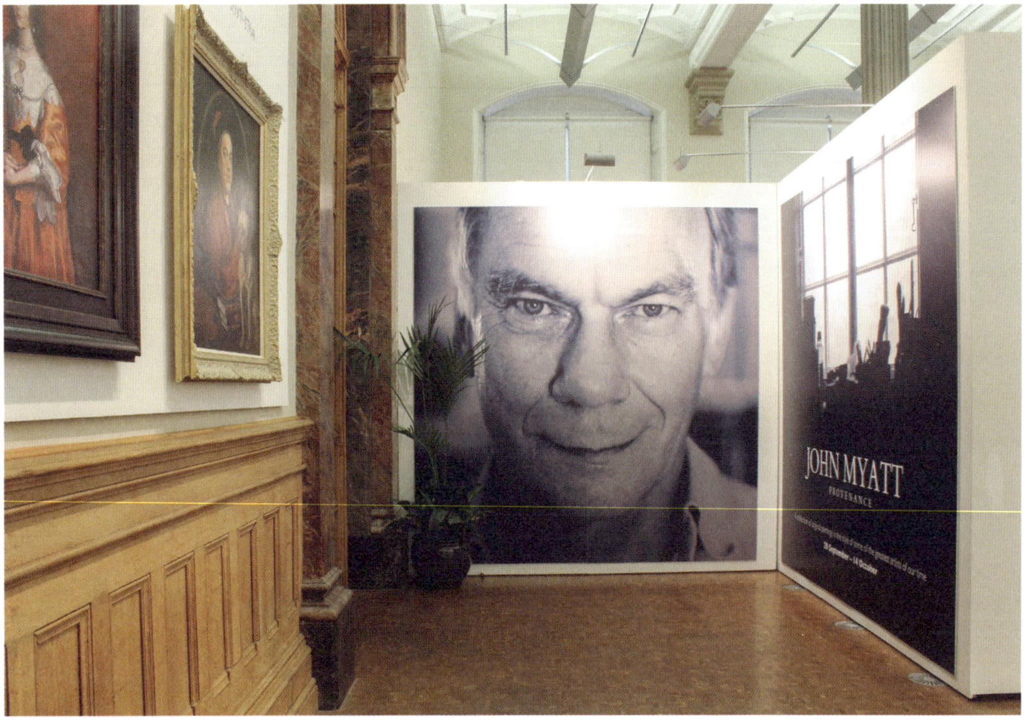

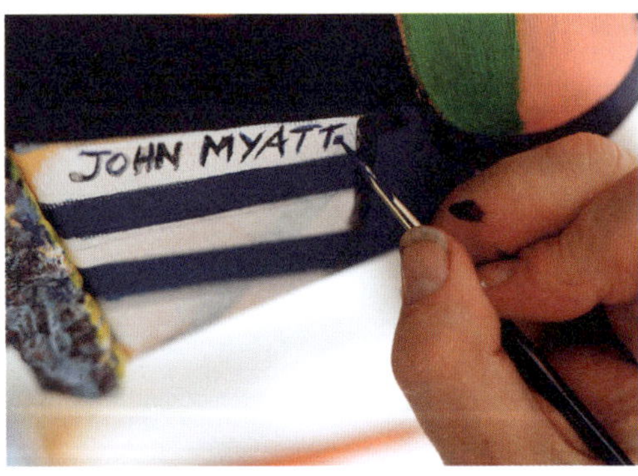

LEFT: Myatt now signs all his paintings with his own signature.

OPPOSITE, ABOVE AND THIS PAGE, BELOW: In the summer and autumn of 2024, two exhibitions of John Myatt's work were held. Called 'Genuine Fakes', the exhibition was promoted as 'a way to understand the spirit and methods of history's greatest artists'.

Descriptions continued: 'From Monet to Matisse and Van Gogh to Vermeer, Myatt's past portfolio of "genuine fakes" traverses most styles and subjects of any note from the annals of art history.' The exhibition significantly boosted Myatt's popularity.

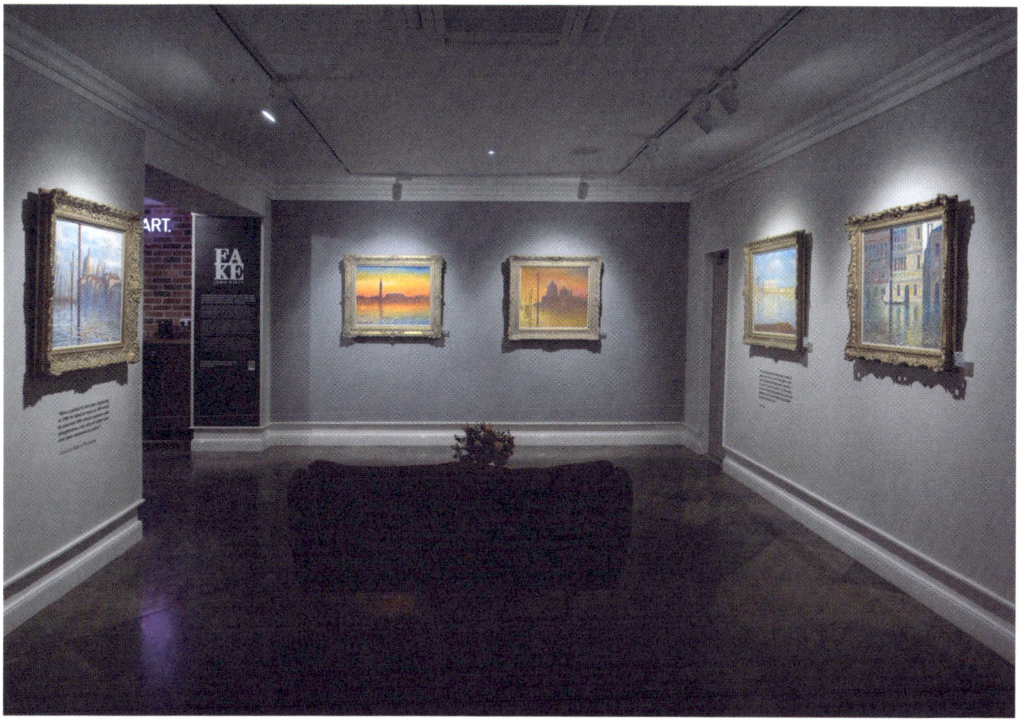

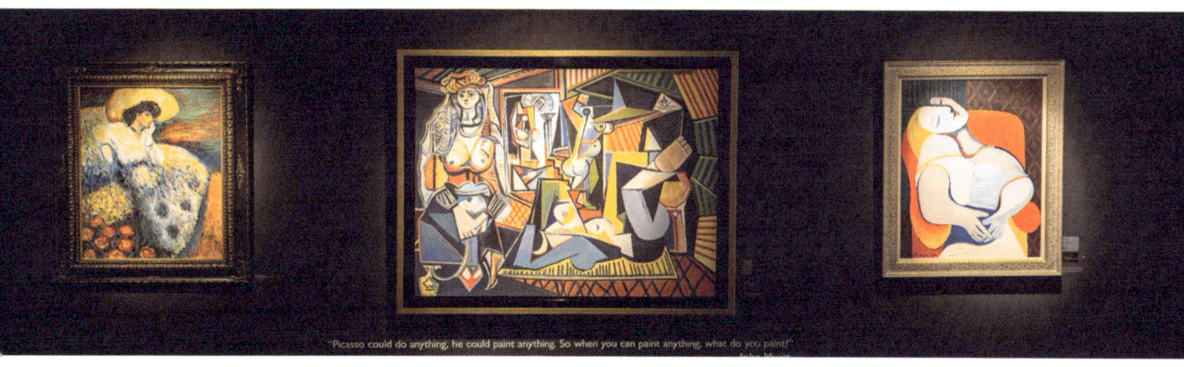

CHAPTER 4

Crusade Against the Art World

Hailed as the most versatile and prolific forger of the 20th century, Tom Keating (1917–1984) was an English artist, art restorer and art counterfeiter who claimed to have faked more than 2,000 paintings by over 160 different artists.

Growing up in a poor area of London with a father who worked as a house painter, Keating helped with the family finances by collecting and selling horse manure, running errands for neighbours, and taking and collecting parcels to and from the local pawnshop. At the age of 11, he ran away from home to his grandmother 7 miles away in Kent and stayed with her for three years. While living there, he attended Eltham College Primary School, where the headmistress was also an art teacher. She encouraged his early love of painting and drawing. However, three years later, his grandmother died, and he returned to his parents in Forest Hill. At 14, he passed a difficult entrance exam for St Dunstan's College, but then discovered the fees would be far too high for his parents to pay, so he left school and took various jobs, including selling parts for early wirelesses, working as a barber's assistant and house painting with his father. Like the famous Cubist Georges Braque (1882–1963), he developed specialist decorating techniques, including graining and marbling wood, and sign writing.

In the early months of the Second World War, Keating joined the Royal Navy. He was deployed to various locations, then spent a short time at home on leave after his ship was torpedoed. During that time, he married. In 1943 he was invalided out, severely injured both physically and mentally. He spent two weeks in an induced coma and was then discharged with a basic disability pension, plus a grant to study art for two years at Goldsmiths, University of London. While his wife worked in munitions, Keating continued working at odd jobs, including as a door-to-door salesman selling furniture polish.

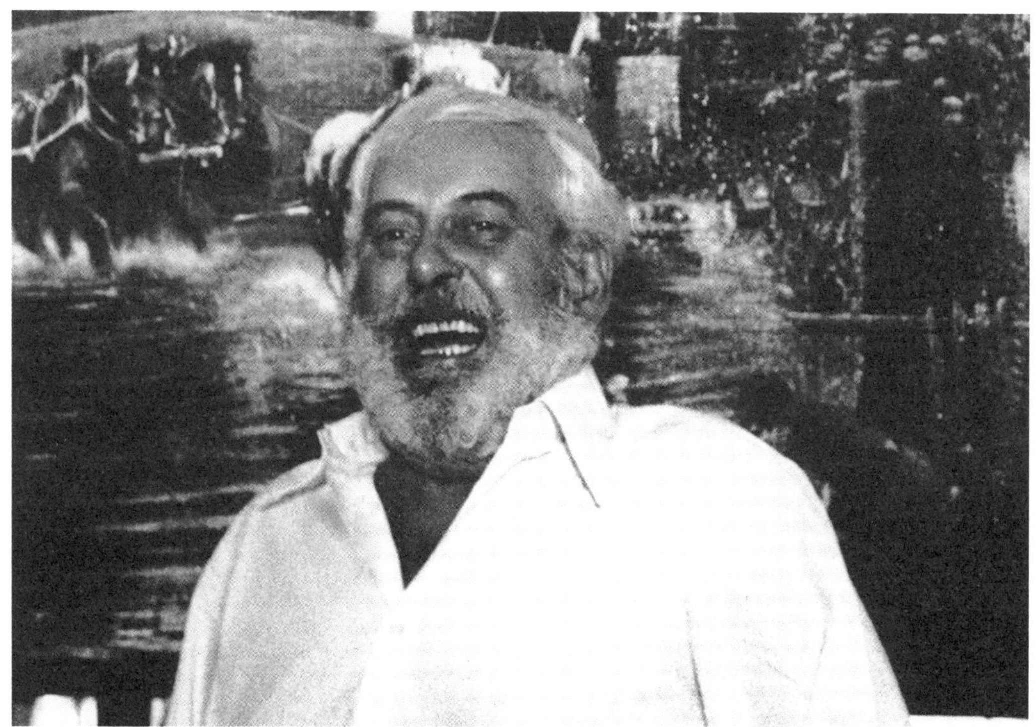

ABOVE: Keating claimed to have faked paintings by more than 160 different artists, including Holbein, Titian, Tintoretto, Klee, Kandinsky and Matisse.

The couple had two children, but in 1952 they separated. Meanwhile, at Goldsmiths he dreamed of becoming an art teacher, but discovered that he did not have the required entrance qualifications, so he abandoned the idea. By then, he was already working part-time in London as an art restorer at the well-respected Hahn Brothers in Mayfair, and he decided to focus on that. Soon, he was expertly repairing the work of various artists, carefully imitating their individual methods.

Exclusive club

Keating secured a full-time job in a small art restoration shop owned by a man he knew as 'Fred Roberts'. Roberts asked him to repair a 19th-century painting by Thomas Sidney Cooper that had been damaged by shrapnel during the war. The resulting hole had obliterated part of the painting depicting a herd of grazing cattle, and at Roberts's suggestion Keating replaced this with a maypole. When Roberts saw the finished painting, he was so impressed that he gave Keating more paintings to repair or copy. Without Keating's knowledge, however, Roberts began framing these paintings, adding forged signatures, and displaying them in a nearby showroom for sale for hundreds or thousands of pounds, while still paying Keating around £5–10 a week. One day, Keating saw some paintings for sale in an upmarket West End gallery, priced between £1,500 and £3,000, by British artist Frank Moss Bennett (1874–1952). But the paintings were not by Bennett; they were the same artworks that Keating had almost completely repainted for Roberts. Fuming, he rushed back to Roberts's shop, told him exactly what he thought of him, hurled a paint palette across the room and quit the job.

In common with many forgers, Keating yearned to become a recognized artist in his own right, but he could not make a living through it. He saw the art world as an exclusive club – you needed a certain background to enter, and experimental art attracted more attention than art that displayed dexterity. Angry at the dealers, critics and gallery owners, he determined to crusade against them all, especially the dealers, believing they were only interested in fine art as a commodity for which shock value or particular connections always eclipsed skill. In his autobiography *The Fake's Progress* (1978) he wrote of artists: 'It seemed disgraceful to me how many of them had died in poverty. All their lives they had been exploited by unscrupulous dealers and then, as if to dishonour their memory, these same dealers continued to exploit them in death.' He believed that the commercial art establishment needed to learn a lesson, and that he was the man for the job. He continued: 'I was determined to do what I could to avenge my brothers and it was to this end that I decided to turn my hand to Sexton Blaking' (see page 53).

Creating the fakes

In the early 1950s, Keating began scouring antique shops around south London for cheap old canvases and frames. Then, once these were acquired, using descriptions he found in old sale catalogues and with scrupulous background research, he began creating copies of many different paintings.

Keating always claimed that he learned his most important skills as an artist through independent study and experimentation. His early sources of inspiration included the Venetian Renaissance artist Titian, Dutch master Rembrandt, British landscape painters Thomas Gainsborough, J.M.W. Turner and John Constable, and Spanish artist Francisco Goya. Keating spent hours studying and copying their work in Britain's greatest museums, especially the National Gallery, the Royal Academy and the Tate.

He began flooding the London art market with hundreds of fakes, often giving them to friends and acquaintances, guessing that many would soon end up in respected auction houses or galleries. Among the 2,000 paintings that he claimed to have faked was a huge range of styles. These included Renaissance works by artists such as Hans Holbein the Younger, Titian and Tintoretto; Modernist,

Expressionist and Fauvist paintings by Wassily Kandinsky, Paul Klee and Henri Matisse, plus paintings that mimicked English landscape artists, Romanticists and French Impressionists. He escalated his crusade in the late 1960s and early 1970s by directing his business partner and lover, Jane Kelly, to sell several fakes of the then little known Romanticist Samuel Palmer (1805–1881). To create his many Palmer fakes he mixed sepia with glutinous tree gum and applied thick coats of this as varnish, then heated them to develop craquelure, to make the paintings appear old. For his Rembrandt drawings he used 18th-century paper and made walnut ink by boiling nuts for 10 hours, then filtering the result through silk stockings.

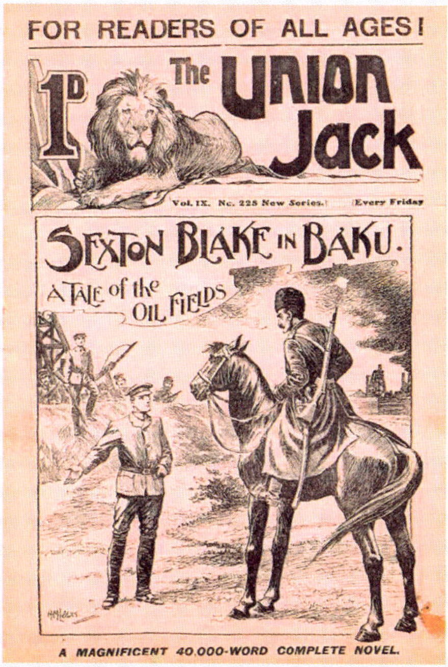

Time bombs

Keating never became wealthy through his fakes, as he usually gave them away as gifts, bartered them for food, alcohol or rent, or sold them for a pittance to people he knew. Because his resentment was against the corrupt, greedy art world, especially dealers, he was aiming to destabilize the system rather than make a fortune. At one point in the 1950s, so many previously unknown paintings by the 19th-century Dutch-born Canadian-American Cornelius Krieghoff came on the market that prices for his work dropped drastically over fears that many were fake. This achieved two of Keating's goals: to reduce the profits of greedy art dealers and to make paintings by one of his favourite artists more affordable for all. For years, paintings that looked like Krieghoff's work were labelled as 'attributed to' Krieghoff rather than 'by' Krieghoff in case any of them were forgeries.

Keating considered himself to be a socialist and used his political views to justify his actions. He claimed that his goal was never to make a fortune but to expose the art world and the many frauds within it. He wanted his work to be discovered. So within his paintings he inserted what he called 'time bombs'. For example, he

SEXTON BLAKE

Sexton Blake was a fictional detective, created by Harry Blyth, popular in British comic strips, novels and dramatic productions from 1893. The name also became popularly used in Cockney rhyming slang for cake, but Keating used it as rhyming slang for fake, so he often talked about 'Sexton Blaking' or described one of his paintings as a 'Sexton Blake'.

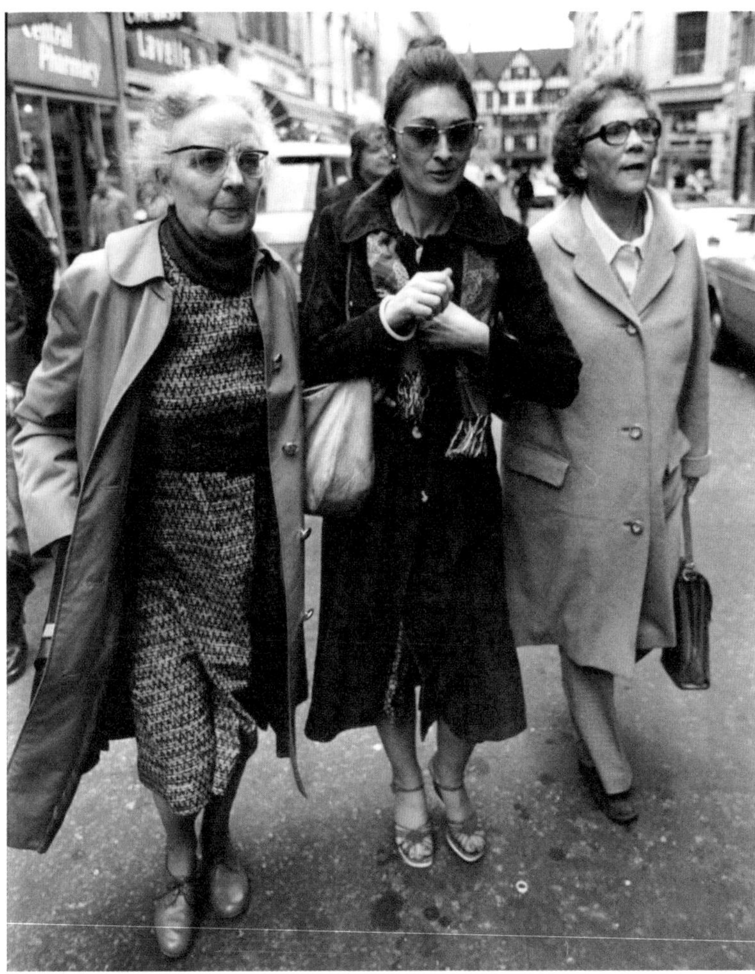

LEFT: Jane Kelly. This photograph was published in newspapers in 1978 after the court case, with the heading: 'Jane Maurice, Tom Keating's former girlfriend, leaving court with her aunt Margaret Beeston and mother Mary Kelly.'

OPPOSITE: Tom Keating's studio with a self-portrait on an easel. Keating always claimed his aim was not material gain but a crusade against art dealers, who he believed were only interested in fine art as a commodity.

would write on a canvas before he painted it so that this would be seen if it was X-rayed. Sometimes he would paint an incongruous object in a composition. For other works he put a layer of glycerine under the oil paint so that when the painting was cleaned, the glycerine dissolved and the paint layer disintegrated. He also used modern acrylics and varnishes for paintings that were supposedly created centuries before, so that when tested it would quickly be realized that they were not old masters after all.

Jane Kelly

In the summer of 1963, 46-year-old Keating met 16-year-old Jane Kelly in the Railway Café at Kew Gardens Station opposite his flat. When Jane walked into the café, Keating was entertaining a group of young people with stories about the Second World War and treachery in the art world. Having recently moved from Llangyndeyrn in

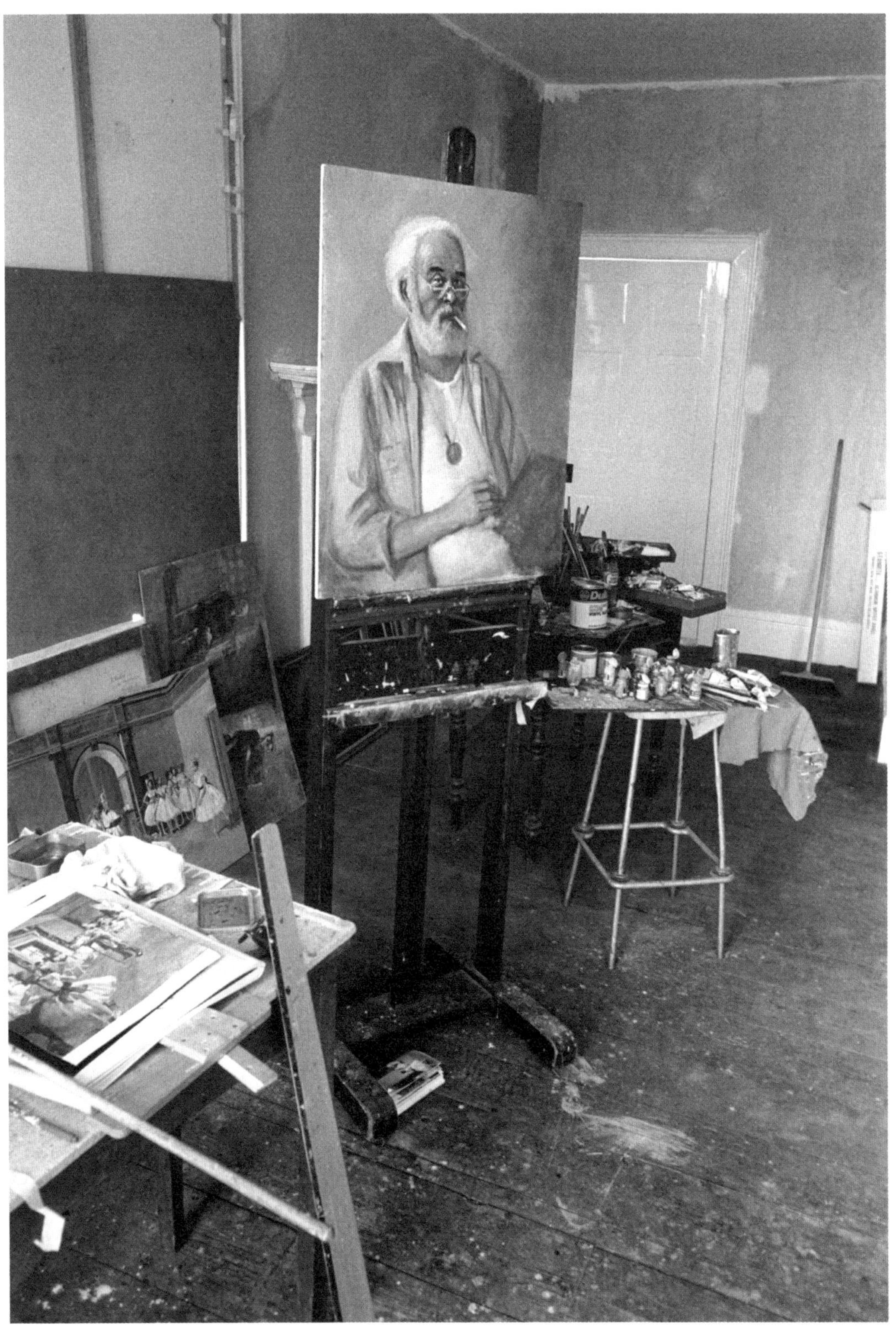

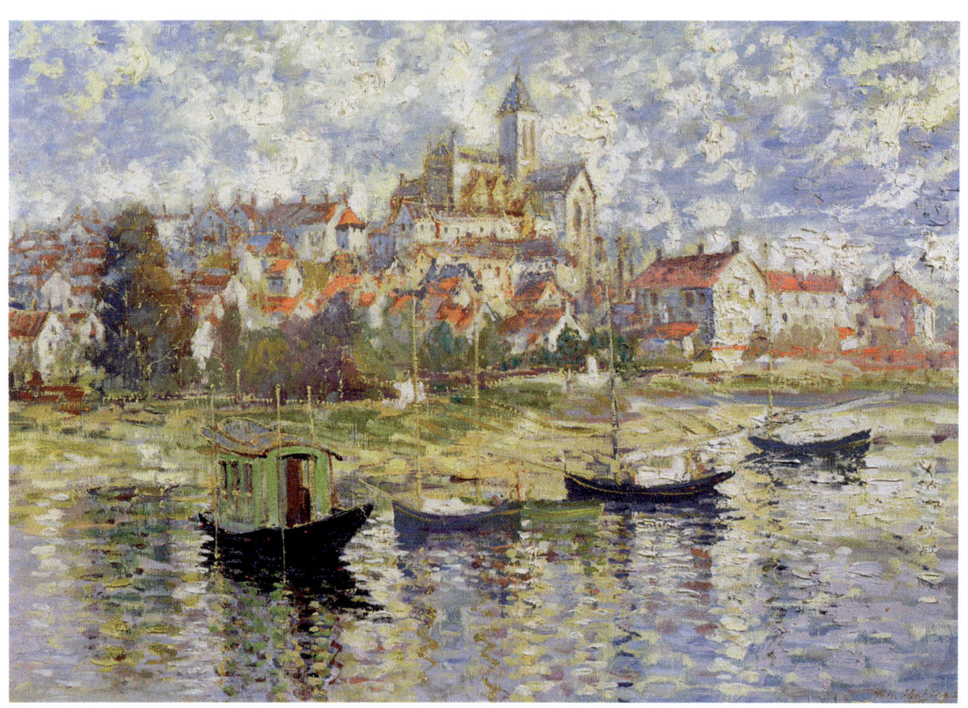

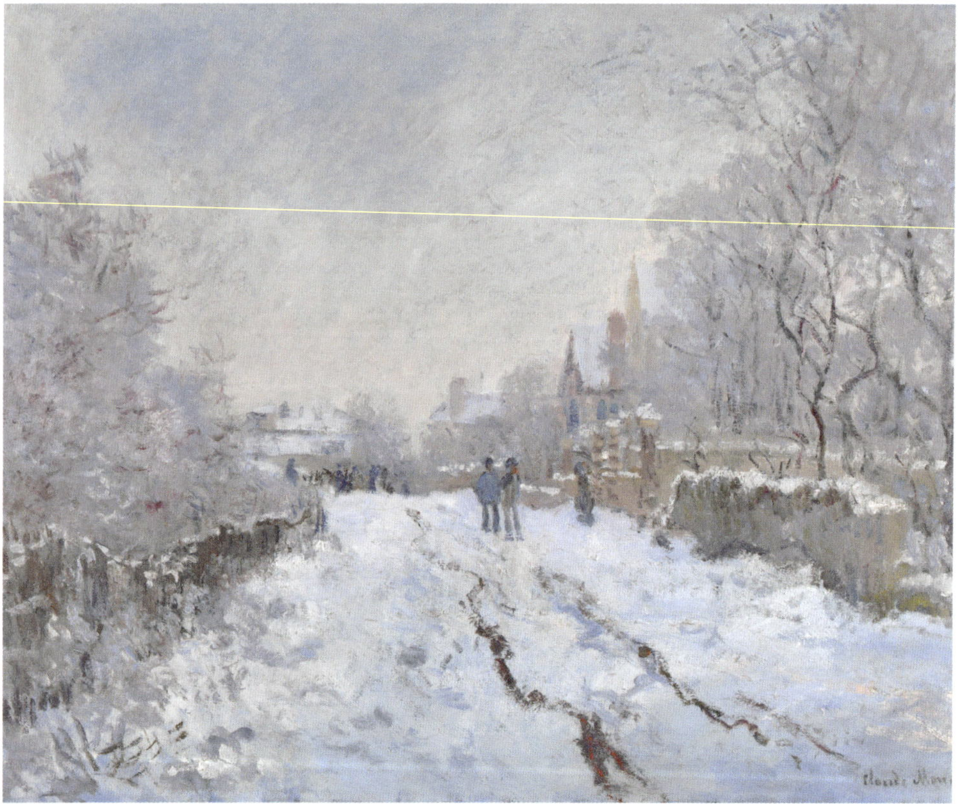

Wales, Kelly joined the group and discovered that the amusing man also gave informal painting lessons. She and Keating began chatting more about art, and he was taken by her enthusiasm and intelligence. As a young child, Kelly had studied several sketchbooks that had been made by her great-grandfather, Thomas Farr, in British Ceylon (now Sri Lanka) in the 1890s. Farr had been a pioneering tea planter, artist and early conservationist, and he had filled numerous sketchbooks with detailed drawings and watercolours, which inspired Kelly to become an artist. Within a short time, she was Keating's full-time student and apprentice. Keating taught her all he knew as an artist and restorer, and they spent practically every day together. Four years later, the two moved to Suffolk and started an art restoration business.

DIFFERENTIATING IMITATIONS

Keating always maintained that he was not a forger, that he never exactly copied any images, but instead painted pictures that resembled those painted by well-known artists. In a 1977 BBC documentary, he described the various types of imitation:

- 'A ***copy*** is an exact duplicate.
- A ***repainting*** is the result of careless restoration.
- A ***pastiche*** is a variant of an existing painting, or a new work of art that simulates another artist's style.
- A ***fake*** is a pastiche that has been modified to look like an original.
- A ***forgery*** is a fake with another artist's signature added and a false provenance provided.'

Discovered

In February 1970, Geraldine Norman, the Sale Room Correspondent for *The Times* newspaper, wrote an article about a previously unknown painting by Samuel Palmer that had been bought by a major Bond Street gallery for £9,400. The painting, *Sepham Barn*, was dated c. 1831 and depicted a dreamlike image of the landscape around Shoreham in Kent. A month later, *The Times* published a letter from art expert David Gould, who claimed that the painting was a fake. Norman continued to receive news of further new paintings by Palmer appearing in the market, along with assertions from David Gould that all of these were fakes. Six years after her article on *Sepham Barn*, in March 1976, Norman began specifically investigating forgeries. She studied 13 newly discovered paintings that were alleged to have been executed by Palmer and asked experts from prestigious museums across the UK – the British Museum, Ashmolean, Tate and Fitzwilliam – as well as author Geoffrey Grigson, who was an authority on Palmer's work, to study them and tell her what they thought.

That July, Norman wrote the first of a series of articles on the paintings by Palmer – exposing them as fakes. Five of the 13 works were traced back to Jane Kelly. Norman delved further and finally discovered that Tom Keating was probably the forger. She drove to Suffolk and found him at his studio in Dedham, and she was

OPPOSITE, ABOVE: *Houseboat on the Seine,* Tom Keating in the manner of Claude Monet, oil on canvas.

OPPOSITE, BELOW: *Snow Scene at Argenteuil,* Claude Monet, 1875. Painted in Argenteuil, where Monet was living during a heavy snowfall in the winter of 1874–5, this is the boulevard Saint-Denis. The River Seine and local railway were behind Monet as he worked. Keating emulated Monet's loose, short, directional brush marks.

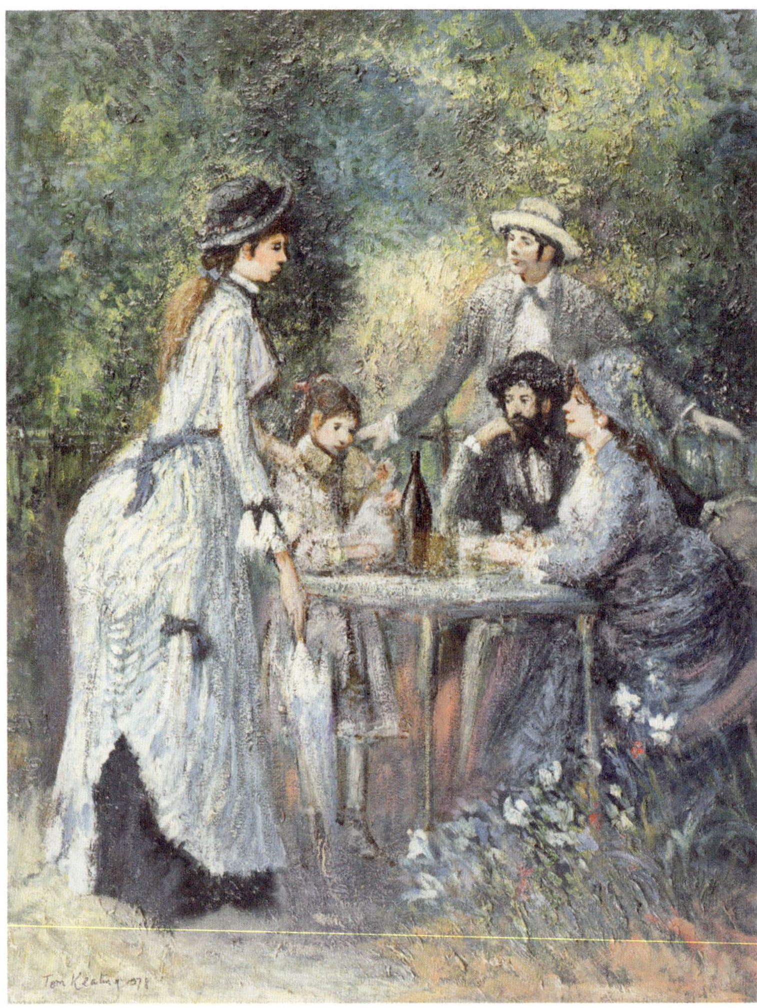

LEFT: *Garden Scene,* painted by Tom Keating, 1982, emulating the work of Renoir – as seen opposite. Keating has used a similar palette and loose, sketchy brush marks. However, when viewed knowing that it is fake, the work seems quite unlike a genuine Renoir.

surprised when he welcomed her in, told her all about his life as a restorer and artist, and then ranted about his opinion of the art establishment. Approximately a week later, Norman had another article published in *The Times* that described Keating and the many accusations of forgery against him. Keating responded with a letter to the newspaper: 'I do not deny these allegations. In fact, I openly confess to having done them.' He explained that money was not his motivation, and that he always left obvious traces of fakery, such as his use of paper that was the wrong age for the artist. He continued, 'Quite frankly, and with, I trust, due modesty, I cannot imagine how anyone could begin to believe that the crude daubs being marketed as Samuel Palmers were authentic. Anyone with a true love of this kindly, generous and devout artist (who was unable to afford a pinch of snuff in his declining years) will know that he could not possibly

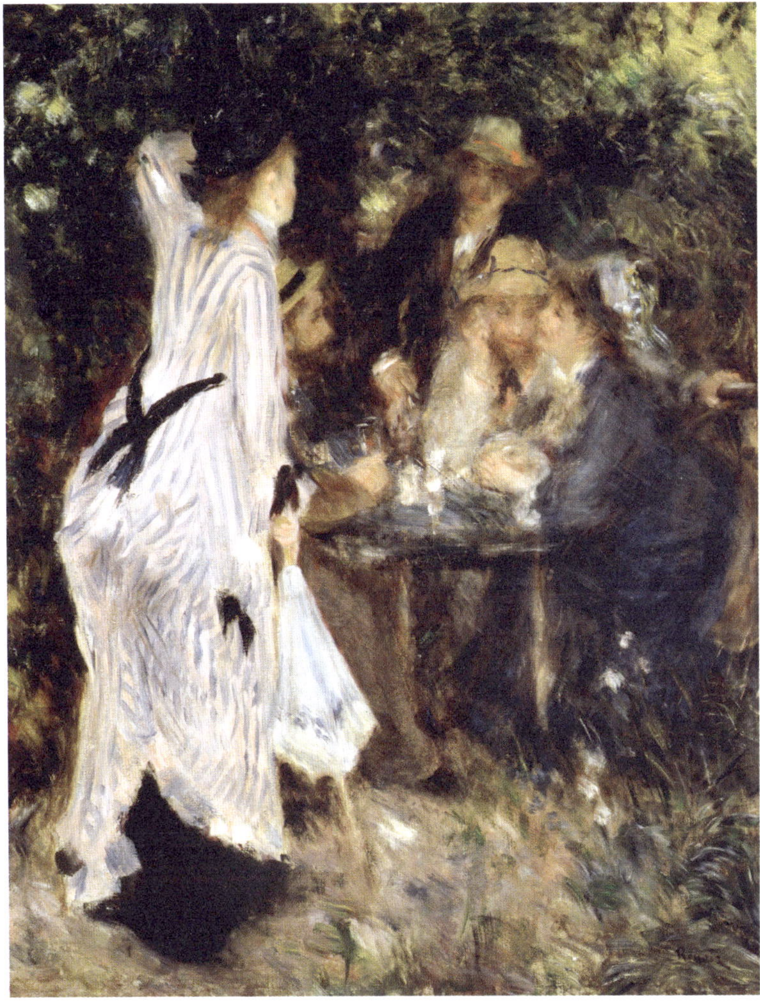

LEFT: *In the Garden (Under the Arbour, Moulin de la Galette)*, Auguste Renoir, 1876. This is a genuine painting by Renoir, made in his Paris studio on rue Cortot in Montmartre. He had a secluded garden that became an extension of his indoor studio.

have done this work, even on an off day.' Keating wrote that he felt no resentment towards Norman for her exposition. He said that she was sympathetic, respectful and appreciative of his art. Ultimately, she wrote a series of nine articles about Keating, and in 1976 was awarded the British Press Awards News Reporter of the Year for all her work on the subject.

Court case and notoriety

In 1977, Keating and Kelly were arrested, both accused of conspiracy to defraud and obtaining payments through deception amounting to £21,416. The decision to try their case at the top criminal court in Britain was extraordinary. No art fraud case had ever been heard at Court No. 1 of the Old Bailey. Proceedings began in January 1979 and for six weeks the story featured hugely in the British press.

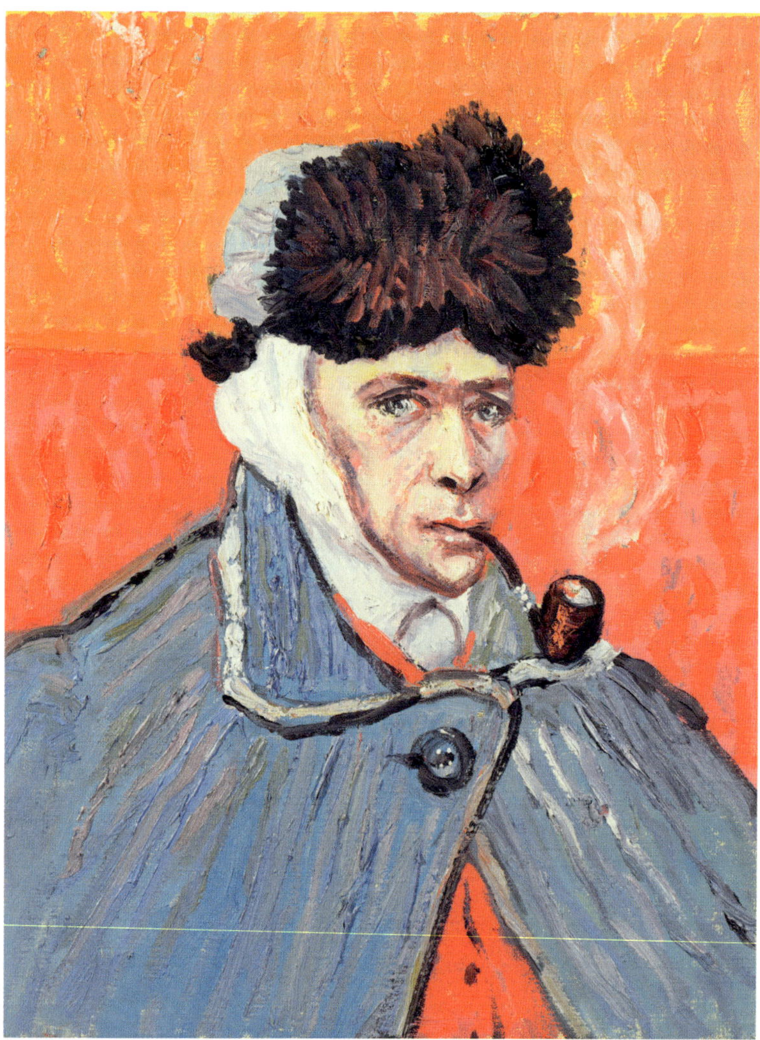

LEFT: Painted after Keating's trial, when he became a TV celebrity, this is his version of one of van Gogh's self-portraits. It lacks van Gogh's passion, ingenuity and individualism, but Keating helped the general public understand the techniques of some of the greatest artists in history.

The *Observer* described the courtroom scene as 'the best show in town, where they have been packing them in for weeks'. The *Daily Express* put words in Keating's mouth with, 'I FAKED THE LOT!' The *Daily Mirror* declared: 'Fake artist draws in the crowds.' Umpteen letters were sent to various papers, some from art dealers expressing their anger towards Keating, but most from readers who described their amusement at Keating's activities and roguish charm. In America, an article in *TIME* magazine was headed: 'Art: Palming off the Palmers'. *The New York Times* professed: 'London painter and restorer admits flooding art market with forgeries', with the headline 'Watercolorgate – Whimsey, Fakery, and Esthetic Truth'.

Kelly was convicted of obtaining money by deception, and given an 18-month sentence that was suspended for two years. In the dock,

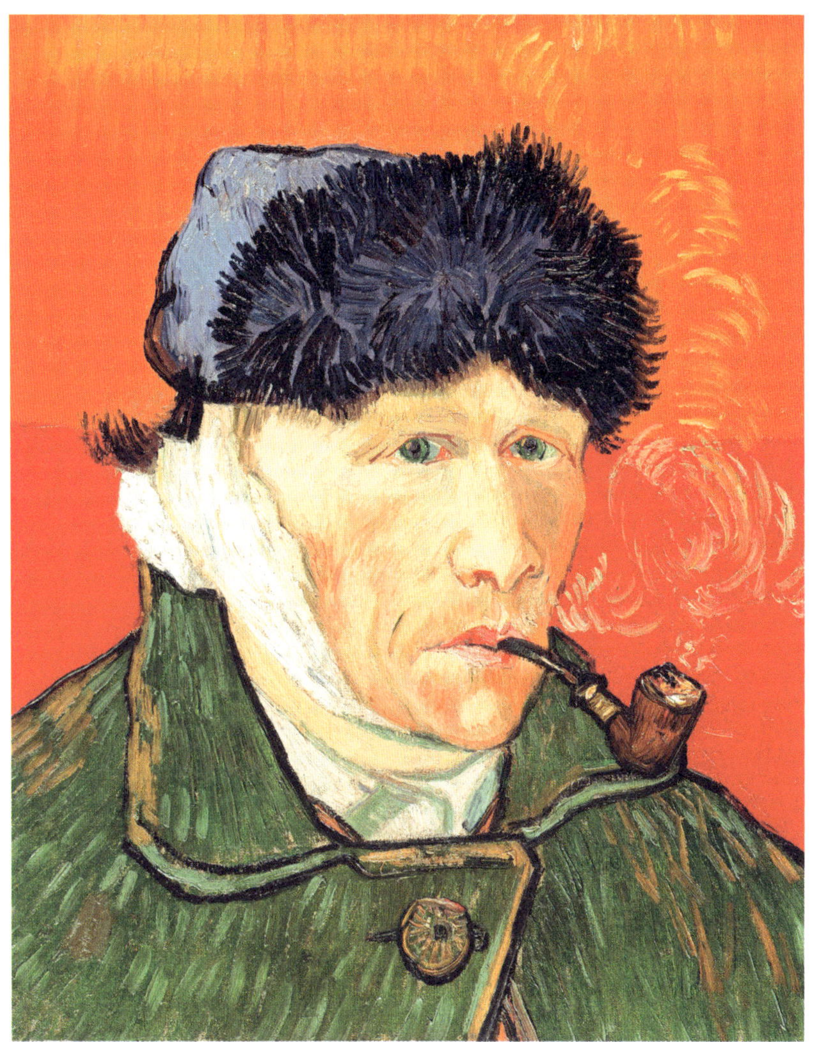

LEFT: This is an authentic self-portrait by Vincent van Gogh, *Self-Portrait with Bandaged Ear and Pipe*, 1889. Two days before Christmas in 1888, van Gogh cut off his ear after a row with his friend Paul Gauguin. Afterwards, he often painted his portrait from the same angle, applying swirling strokes of impasto paint in intense colours.

Keating gave evidence for two days, pleading innocence, claiming that he had never intentionally defrauded anyone and had left clues that ought to have revealed his deceptions to any expert who examined them. His defence barrister, Jeremy Hutchinson QC, described 'greedy dealers' as being 'aware that the works might not be genuine, but that the possibility of making a substantial profit overcame their scruples'. On the night of the second day in court, Keating had a motorbike accident. He returned to the Old Bailey the next day, but collapsed in the witness box and was taken to hospital. He had contracted bronchitis, aggravated by pulmonary disease and a heart condition. Doctors did not expect him to live. His prosecutor dropped the case, declaring 'nolle prosequi', which is a legal term meaning 'to be unwilling to pursue'. He was released without charge.

Final years

In 1977, the year that Keating was arrested, he published his autobiography with Geraldine and Frank Norman. He had become friends with the married couple since she had visited him at his studio, and together they collaborated to tell his tale. *The Fake's Progress* was quite a success. By the end of the 1970s, however, Keating was in ill health. He had chain-smoked for years and the effects of breathing in the chemical fumes that he used in art restoring, such as ammonia, turpentine and methyl alcohol, together with the stress induced by the court case, had all affected him adversely.

Despite his fragile health, in 1982 he starred in an award-winning Channel 4 television series called *Tom Keating on Painters*, showing viewers how to paint like the old masters. His direct language demystified art. Two years later, a further series was aired that focused on him demonstrating Impressionist techniques. He maintained to audiences that he was not a particularly good artist, but by then art collectors and celebrities were starting to collect his work. In December 1983, hoping to raise sufficient funds to buy a new cottage, Keating sent 137 of his pictures to be auctioned at Christie's in London. These were signed by him but painted in the style of other artists, and Christie's accepted them. Exceeding all expectations, the auction raised £72,000, but Keating died before receiving the proceeds. Five more auctions of his works were held in 1984, and overall, they raised £274,000. He had always longed to earn a living from his own work, but the money came too late.

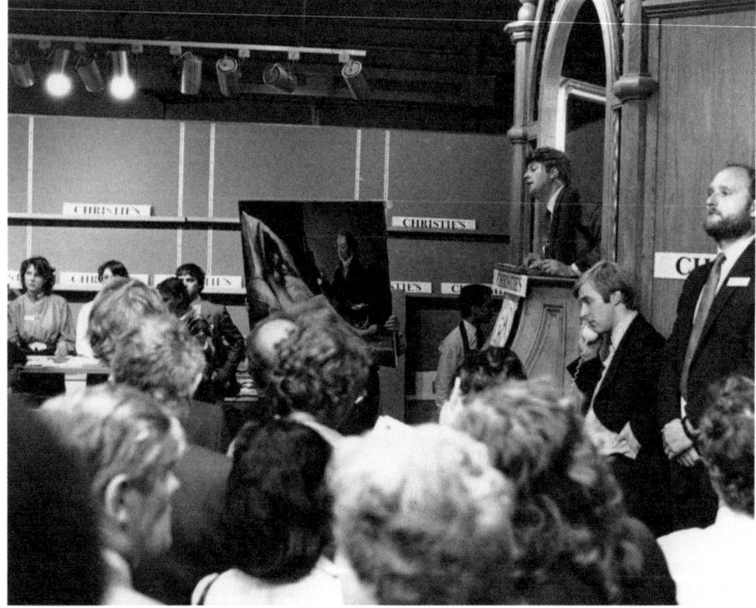

LEFT: Paintings by Tom Keating were sold at one of several auctions of his work held by Christie's in the 1980s.

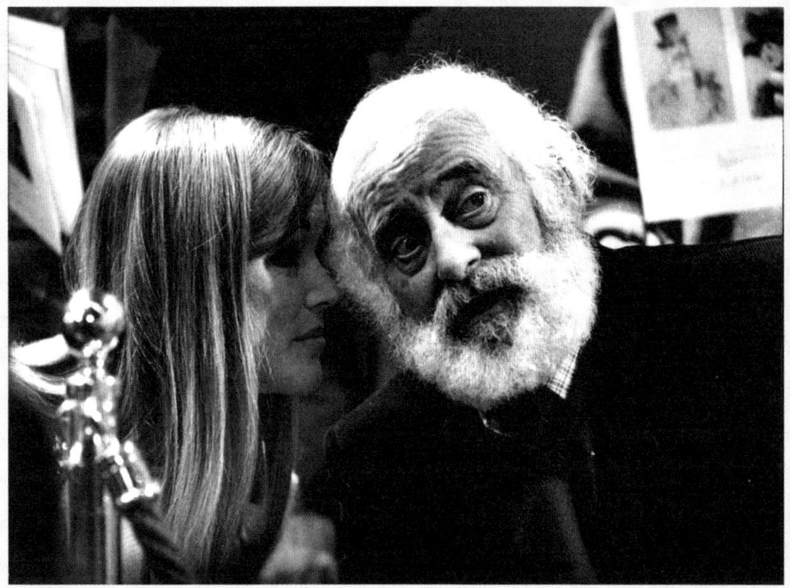

KEATING'S FAKES

Although the exact number of Keating's fake drawings and paintings is not known, this is generally believed to be a close estimate.

Number of works	Artist emulated
Over 100	Cornelius Krieghoff
c. 80	Samuel Palmer
40–50	Constantin Guys
30–60	Edgar Degas
c. 20	J.M.W. Turner
12	Amedeo Modigliani
8–9	Édouard Manet
6	Camille Pissarro

In addition, while numbers are less certain, Keating is thought to have created multiple forgeries of the following artists:

- Rembrandt van Rijn
- Francesco Guardi
- Alfred Sisley
- Georges Rouault
- Thomas Rowlandson
- Hans Holbein the Elder
- Hans Holbein the Younger
- David Teniers the Younger
- Thomas Girtin
- Edvard Munch
- Henri Matisse
- Richard Wilson
- Henri de Toulouse-Lautrec
- Tintoretto
- Peter Paul Rubens
- Albrecht Dürer
- George Stubbs
- Francisco Goya
- John Linnell
- Paul Klee

In the 1970s, verified by Keating as being his own work, a smaller number of fakes were listed by the police, art dealers and journalists as being definitely by him. This list included works mimicking the following artists:

Cornelius Krieghoff	8	Edvard Munch	5
John Constable	9	Auguste Renoir	4
Edgar Degas	7	Amedeo Modigliani	4
Constantin Guys	44		

Plus one or two works emulating each of the following:

- Rembrandt van Rijn
- Francesco Guardi
- Thomas Gainsborough
- Francisco Goya
- John Linnell
- Henri Fantin-Latour
- Henri de Toulouse-Lautrec
- Émile Bernard
- Raoul Dufy
- Wassily Kandinsky
- Frank Moss Bennett.

CHAPTER 5

Forger of the Century

Over several decades, Wolfgang Beltracchi (b. 1951), his wife Helene (b. 1958), her sister Jeanette Spurzem and colleague Otto Schulte-Kellinghaus sold hundreds of forged paintings to collectors and auction houses as works of art by significant artists.

Along with their elaborately constructed stories about the artworks having been lost during the Second World War and their creation of false authentication papers and photographs, the forgeries of works by modern artists including Max Ernst, Fernand Léger, Kees van Dongen and Heinrich Campendonk fooled many. However, they were all made by Beltracchi himself.

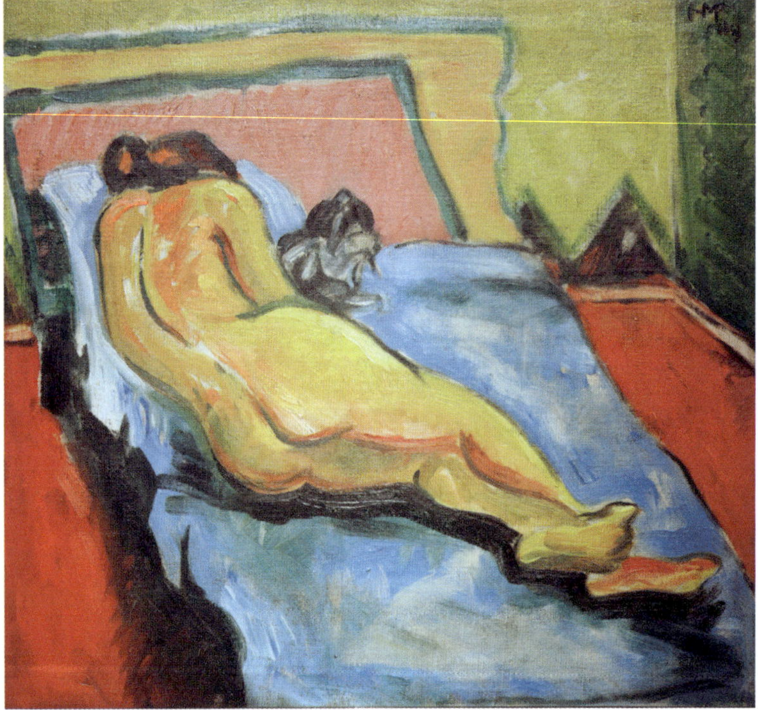

LEFT: *Reclining Nude with Cat*, attributed to Max Pechstein, dated 1909. Believed to be by Beltracchi, this painting was sold in 2003 by the Lempertz auction house in Cologne. It was said to depict Charlotte (Lotte) Kaprolat, who later became Pechstein's wife.

Making a profit

Beltracchi was born Wolfgang Fischer in a village in Westphalia in west-central Germany. His father was a house painter and restorer of churches who supplemented his income by producing cheap copies of paintings by Rembrandt, Picasso and Cézanne. At the age of 14, the boy stunned his father by painting an accurate copy of a mother and child from Picasso's Blue Period, and he soon surpassed his father's artistic abilities. Three years later, in 1968, he enrolled in an art academy in Aachen, although in the end he missed most of his classes. Instead, he dropped out: grew his hair, bought a Harley-Davidson motorbike, smoked hash and took LSD with US soldiers stationed at a nearby NATO base on their way home from Vietnam. For the next decade, he did little. He spent 18 months on a beach in Morocco and lived in a commune in Spain. He wandered around Barcelona, London and Paris, buying and selling paintings at antique markets; then he lived on a houseboat in Amsterdam, earning money by staging psychedelic light shows at a nightclub. He still painted a bit and in 1978 three of his works were accepted for a prestigious art exhibition in Munich. One day, he bought a couple of winter landscapes by a little known 18th-century Dutch painter for $250 each. He had noticed that winter scenes from that period sold for five times the price if they contained ice skating figures. So Beltracchi carefully painted skaters into the paintings he had found, then resold them for a considerable profit. Soon he was buying old wooden frames, painting his own ice-skating scenes in the 18th-century style and fitting these into the old frames. Describing them as the works of old masters, he made a handsome profit.

For a short time in 1981, with an estate agent from Düsseldorf, Beltracchi formed an art dealing firm, Kürten & Fischer Fine Arts GmbH, but he hated the business and his partner soon forced him out on the grounds of negligence. Instead, he began producing and selling more forgeries. By then, he had moved from painting old masters to copying early 20th-century French and German artists, partly because it was easier to find pigments and frames from that period. He worked arbitrarily – producing a forgery here and there when he needed money. He recalled later: 'Sometimes I'd paint ten works in a month, and then go for six months without doing any.' One of his favourite artists to forge was the German Expressionist Johannes Molzahn, who had escaped the Nazis in 1938, settled in the USA, then returned to Germany in 1959 for the last six years of his life. Fischer created and sold about twelve 'Molzahns' for up to $45,000 each. One was even bought by Molzahn's widow.

In the mid-1980s, he also began creating counterfeit paintings in the style of Heinrich Campendonk, who had also fled the Nazis

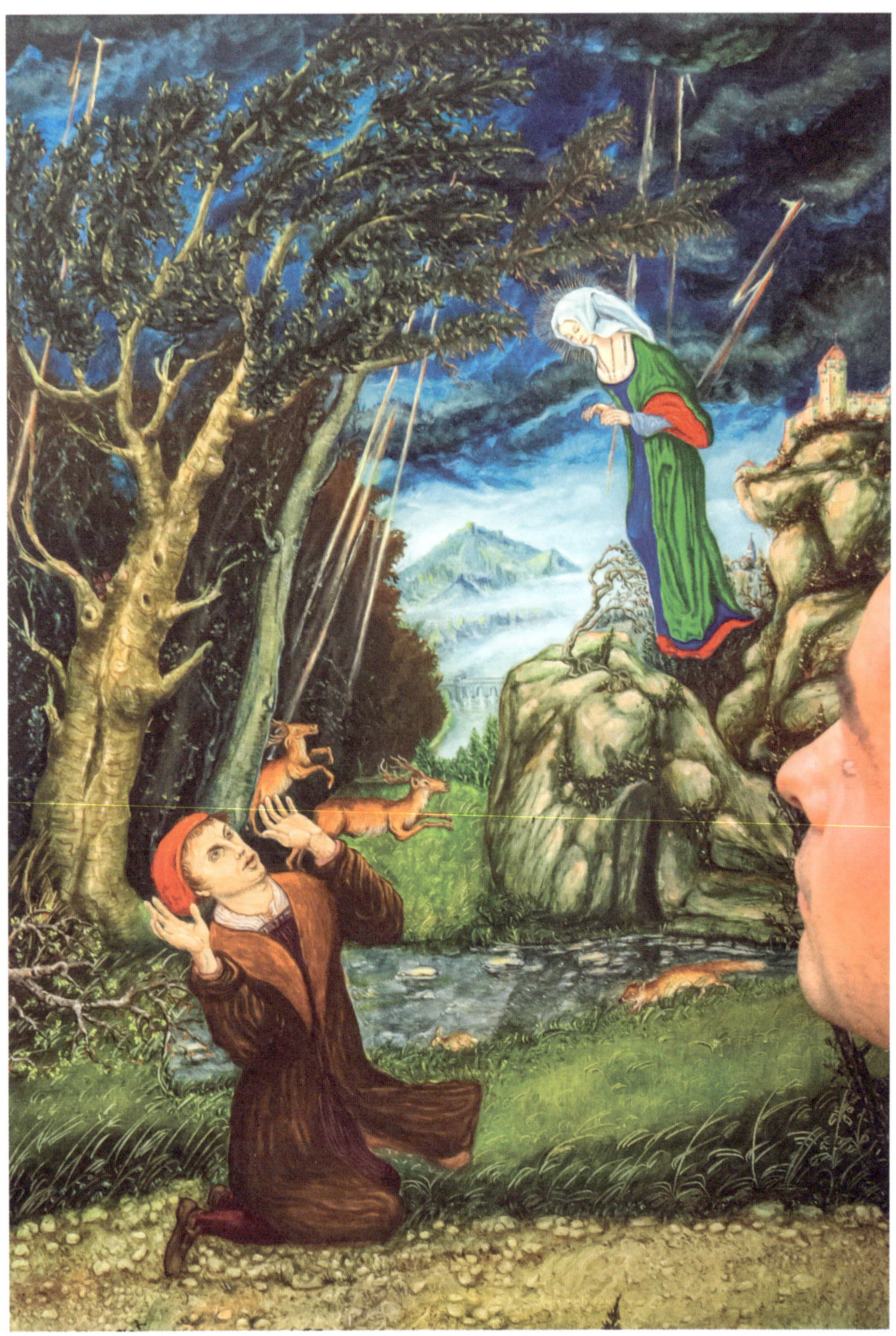

during the war. At that time, while he sat in an artists' café, Beltracchi met Otto Schulte-Kellinghaus, whom he later called Count Otto, who knew little about art but was keen to be involved in Beltracchi's schemes. In February 1992, he met Helene Beltracchi. Helene was living with her boyfriend, and Beltracchi (still called Fischer at the time) was sharing a large house he had bought and restored with his ex-girlfriend and their four-year-old son. At the time, he was not producing forgeries but writing and filming a documentary about pirates, which he hoped to sell to European television. With the money he had earned from his forgeries, he had bought the house, was paying for the filming of the documentary and had also bought an 80ft (24m) boat and hired a five-man crew as he was preparing to sail around the world, from Majorca to Madagascar to South America, as he filmed the documentary. Helene worked for the man who was backing the documentary. She first met Beltracchi in an editing trailer and disliked him. 'I thought the guy was a real big mouth, a lunatic,' she later recalled. However, she soon realized that

OPPOSITE: *Luther meets the Holy Anna*, painted in 2017 by Beltracchi. This painting was displayed in the exhibition 'Really Fake. Cranach and his Copyists' in Wittenberg, Germany, in May 2018.

BELOW: *Man, Horse, Cow*, Heinrich Campendonk, c. 1918. One of Beltracchi's favourite artists to counterfeit, Camperdonk was a German painter, printmaker, and stained-glass designer who first gained prominence when he worked with the German Expressionist group Der Blaue Reiter, which formed in 1911.

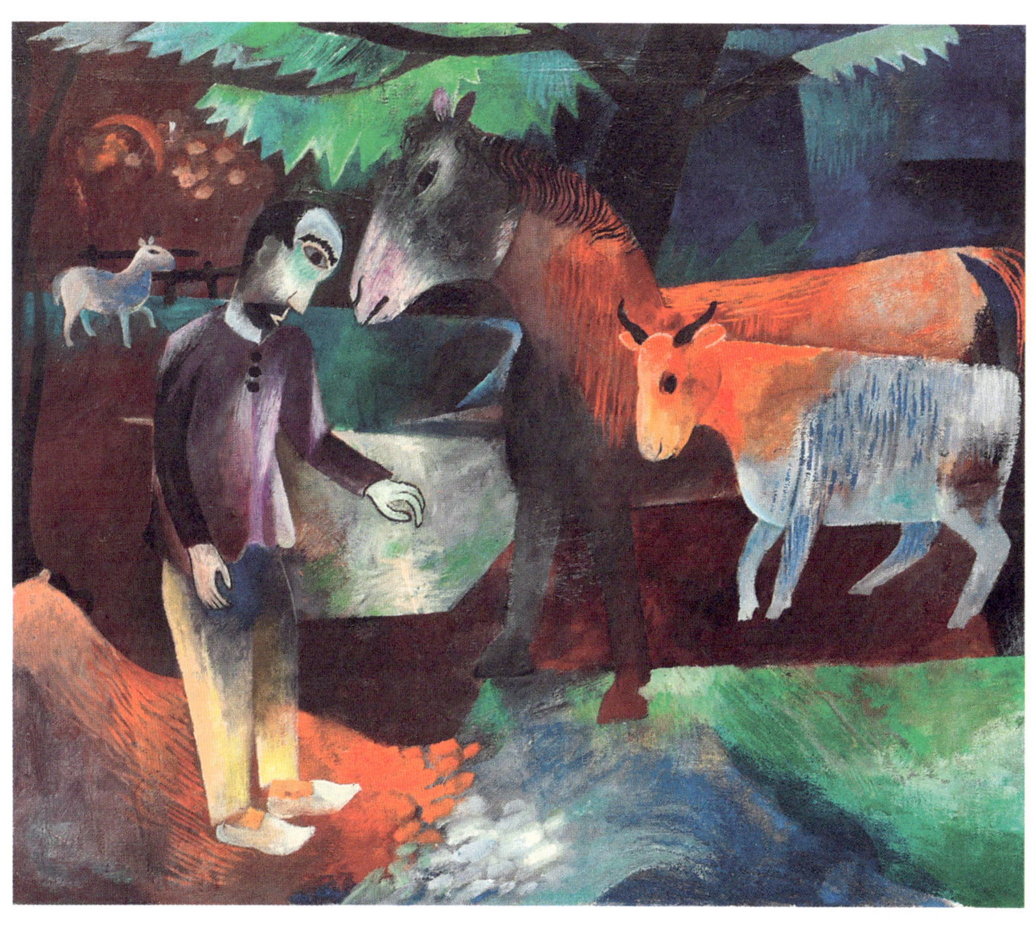

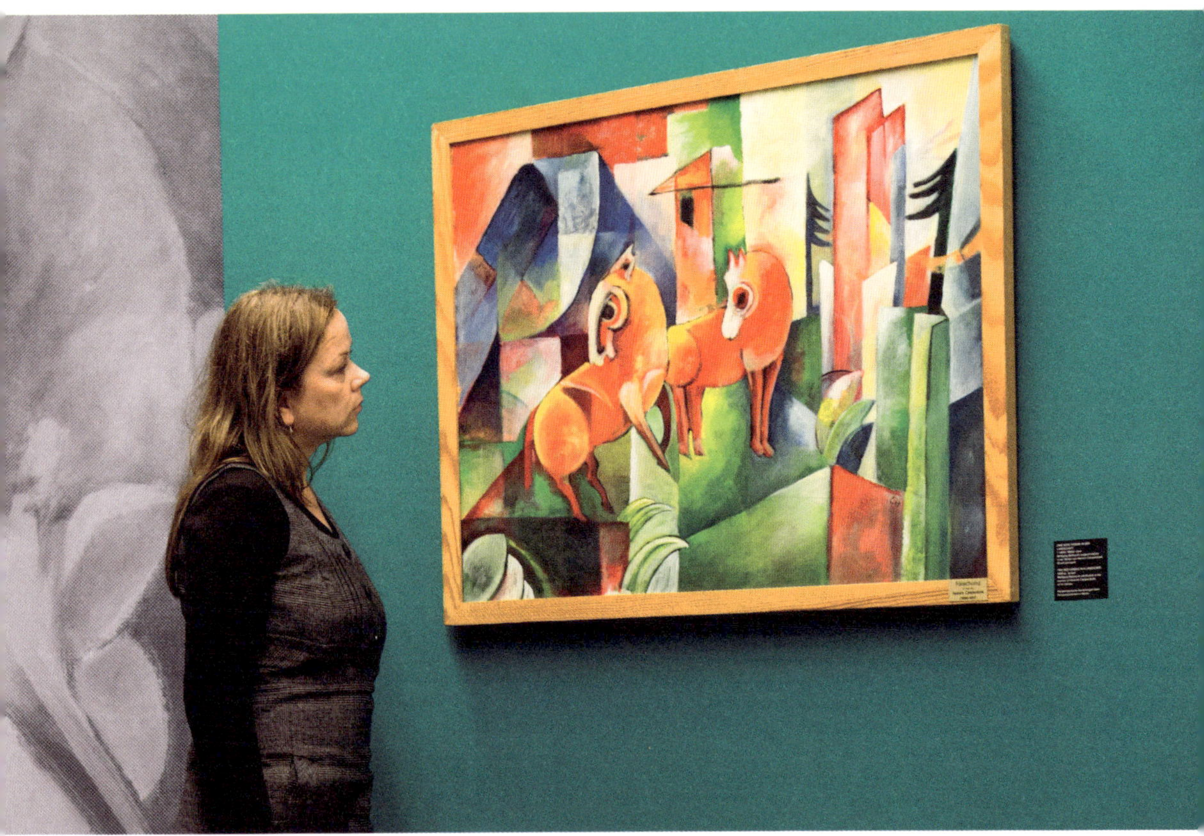

he was intelligent, educated and a perfectionist. She split up with her partner and moved in with Beltracchi; the couple married in February 1993. The pirate documentary was not completed and ended acrimoniously. Fischer changed his name to Helene's surname and their daughter, Franziska, was born nine months later.

ABOVE: In November 2014, at Moritzburg Art Museum, a woman is seen looking at a forgery of Heinrich Campendonk's artwork *Two Red Horses in the Landscape* painted by Beltracchi.

Helene

Early in their relationship, Helene learned about Beltracchi's secret career. At his home in Viersen, she noticed paintings by several famous 20th-century artists on the walls. When she asked him if they were all actually real, he replied, 'They're all mine . . . I made them.' She agreed to become his accomplice. Almost immediately, she notified Lempertz, a high-end auction house in Cologne, that she had a painting for sale by the early 20th-century French Cubist Georges Valmier. 'It was hanging on the wall, and they sent their expert,' Helene remembered. 'She looked for a few minutes, said it was wonderful, and then asked, "How much do you want for it?"' They accepted 20,000 deutsche marks, which was a modest amount. A few years later it sold at auction in New York for $1 million.

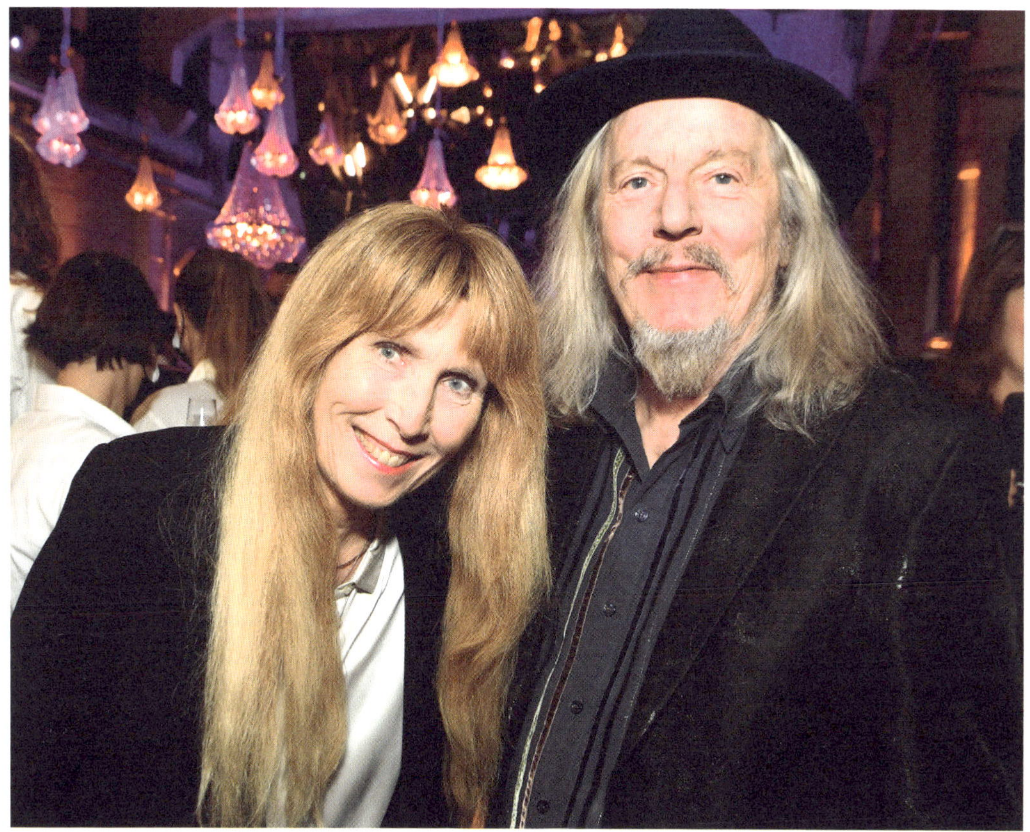

ABOVE: Wolfgang and Helene Beltracchi in Zurich, Switzerland, in November 2021.

Helene loved her exciting new life. She recalled feeling that it was like being in a film, as she felt detached from it. 'It was another person – an art dealer, whom I was playing,' she said. She could not believe how easy it had been to deceive the auction house.

Three years later, Helene introduced the art world to the 'collection' she claimed to have inherited from her recently deceased industrialist grandfather, Werner Jägers, who had been born in Belgium but made his fortune in Cologne. Jägers was indeed Helene's maternal grandfather. She stated that he had abandoned her grandmother after the Second World War, and she had had only a single brief meeting with him shortly before his death in 1992. The story she told gallery owners and collectors was that one of Jägers's friends in the 1920s and 1930s had been a well-known Jewish art dealer and collector named Alfred Flechtheim. In 1933, just months after Adolf Hitler came to power, Flechtheim fled into exile in Paris, and the Nazis seized his galleries in Düsseldorf and Berlin. Just before this, Helene said Flechtheim sold many works at bargain prices to Jägers, who hid them in his country home in the Eifel mountains, near Cologne, safe from Nazi plundering.

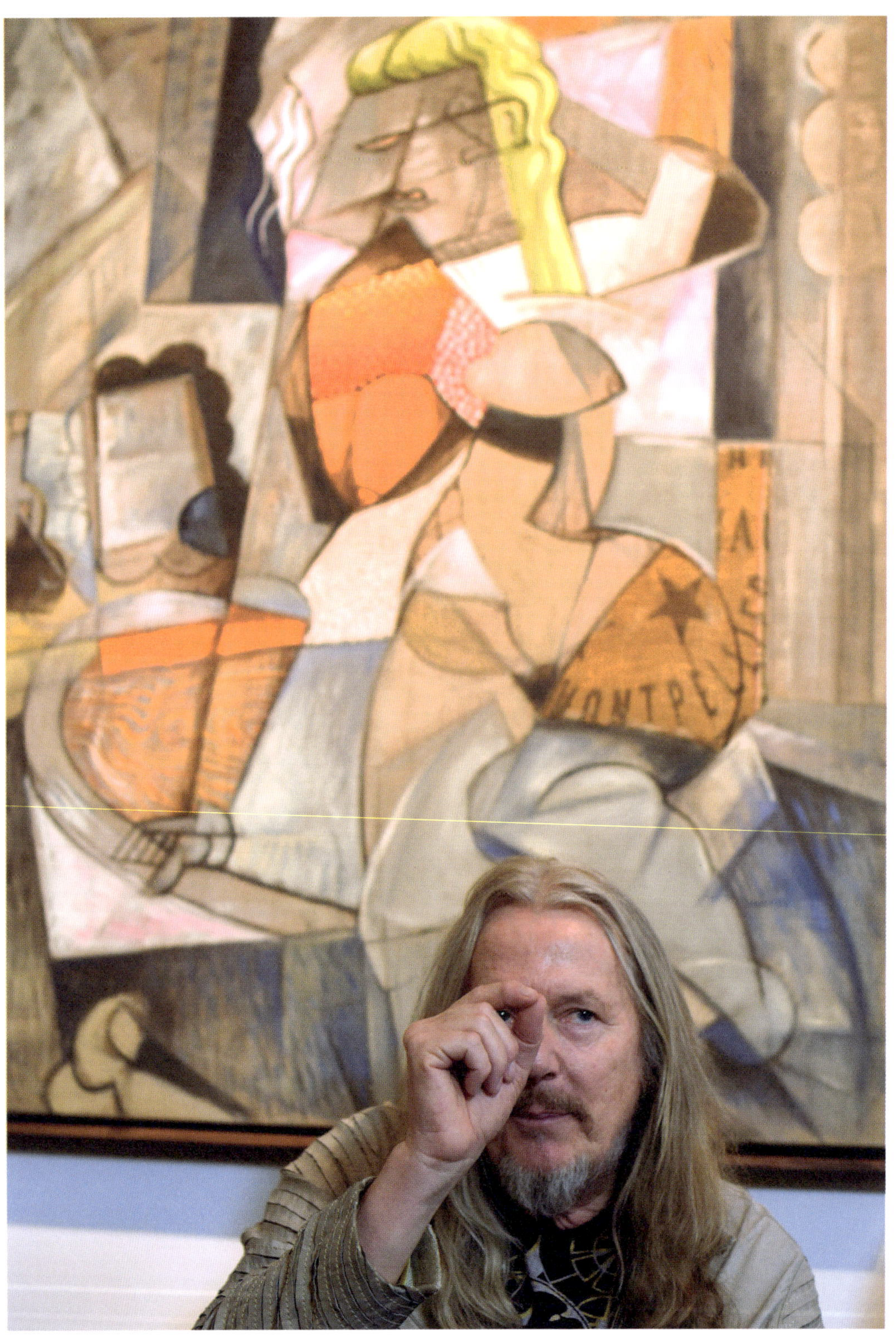

The Beltracchis took a photograph of Helene pretending to be her own grandmother, printed it on pre-war paper, and stuck fake labels on the backs of each artwork's frame. They had stained these with tea and coffee to create a patina of age and added a caricature of Flechtheim. The Beltracchis did not realize it, but Flechtheim never put stickers on his paintings.

Beltracchi's methods

It is estimated that Beltracchi forged over 300 paintings, making millions of dollars in profits over 20 years. His forgeries were exceptionally well executed, as he used a range of techniques, including ageing canvases, using authentic-looking materials and paying meticulous attention to research and detail. The Beltracchis took what they called 'cultural trips', travelling to places where the artists he was imitating had painted, or to see original works in museums around the world. They also studied any of the artists' letters and diaries they could find and conducted other forms of research. So although his paintings were largely from his imagination, Beltracchi often gave them titles of works that were already known but considered lost, which filled in gaps in artists' histories without raising suspicion. The couple bought old picture frames and canvases at markets and second-hand shops, and even

OPPOSITE: Beltracchi speaks in front of one of his paintings at the art gallery 'art room9' in Munich, Germany, in 2015.

BELOW: In August 2017, Beltracchi demonstrated his skill as he painted his work *A Group Picture of the Blue Riders* in Munich.

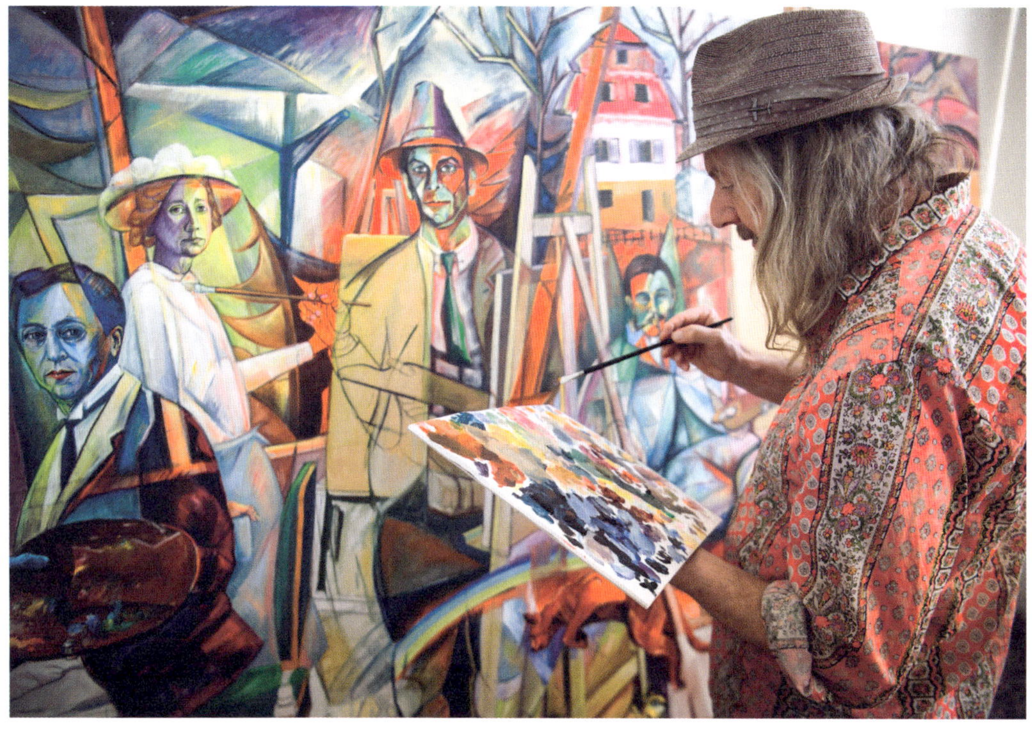

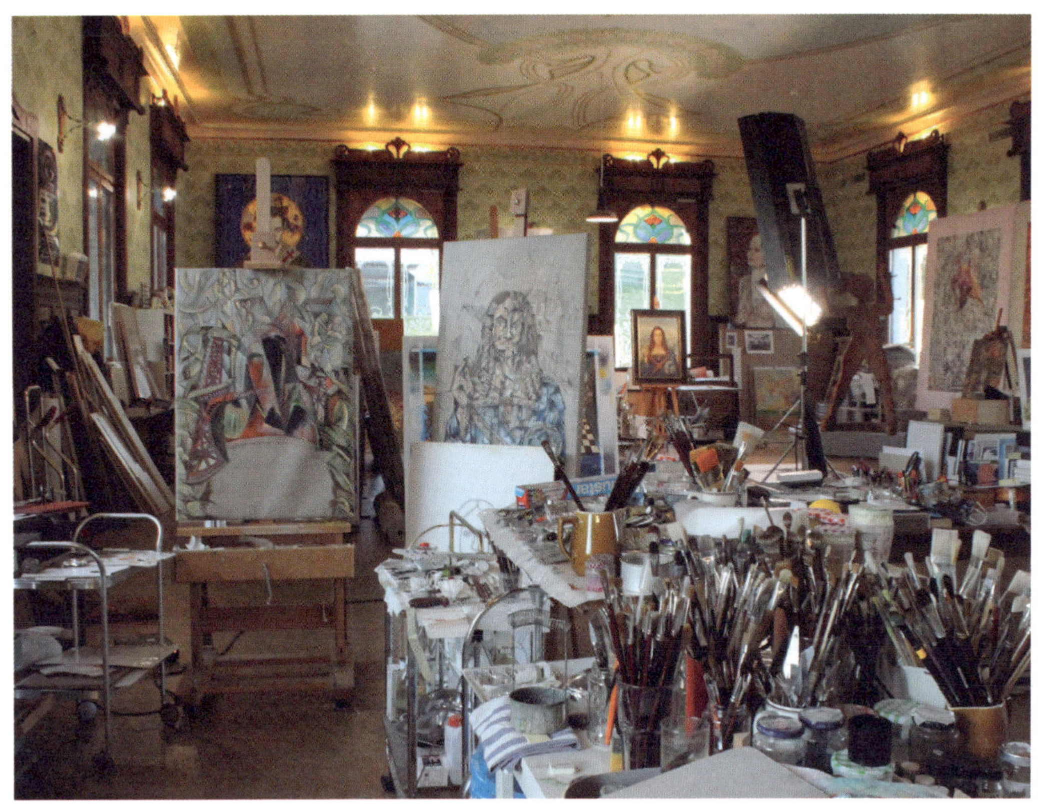

ABOVE: Beltracchi's studio, Lake Lucerne, Switzerland, 2021.

used a camera from the 1920s to take old-looking photos of their creations as evidence of historical provenance. They sold the forged paintings to unsuspecting art dealers and collectors, often with fabricated provenance documents to help make the works appear genuine. The couple were aided by Helene's sister Jeanette and Otto Schutte-Kellinghaus, but Beltracchi never interacted with clients, and their method was also dependent on ensuring that clients never asked for a scientific analysis in order to prove the provenance of the works they were buying.

Beltracchi's proficiency even deceived Werner Spies, a renowned expert on Max Ernst and former director of the Pompidou Centre in Paris. He went to Beltracchi's house to see *The Forest*, which he was informed had been painted by Ernst in 1927. He analysed and authenticated it. In 2004, the same painting was sold for €1.8 million to a Swiss art dealer. It subsequently passed to a Paris gallery, Cazeau, which in turn sold it to publishing tycoon Daniel Filipacchi for $7 million. Ultimately, Spies authenticated seven paintings by Beltracchi as works by Max Ernst. Less than a decade later, Spies was convicted in France for having incorrectly authenticated a fake Max Ernst painting.

Two mistakes

By the turn of the millennium, Beltracchi was making up to seven-figure sums for each of his paintings. He did particularly well when imitating the works of lesser-known Expressionists and Cubists, but he gradually moved into forging the paintings of more illustrious artists such as Fernand Léger and Max Ernst. Although he could sell these for higher prices, they were also more likely to attract closer inspection. After decades of this process, fabricating evidence and meticulously covering their tracks, two mistakes eventually exposed the Beltracchis.

One day, experts noticed that there was a sticker on the back of a painting from the Flechtheim Collection, but they knew Flechtheim had never used stickers on his paintings. So, working in coordination with pre-eminent art experts, the German police began finding more paintings with counterfeit 'Flechtheim' labels. They eventually contacted Werner Jägers's family and learned that his art collection, supposedly the source of the Beltracchis' 'long-lost masterpieces', was bogus.

On another occasion, Beltracchi ran out of the zinc he used to create white paint, and instead of his usual product he bought a zinc pigment from a Dutch manufacturer. Beltracchi did not investigate, but it contained titanium, and the next year his *Red Picture with Horses*, signed Heinrich Campendonk and dated 1914, sold at auction for a record €2.8 million. Unexpectedly, the buyer demanded that the auction house provide an authenticity certificate, which it did not have, so the buyer submitted the work for chemical analysis in Munich. The analysis revealed traces of titanium, a substance that had not been used as a white pigment until after the painting was said to have been made. The Beltracchis' business began to unravel.

Assuming identities

After the biggest operation that Berlin's art fraud division has ever conducted, with police teams sweeping across Germany, early in the morning of 27 August 2010, five police vans surrounded the Beltracchis' car as they were leaving their luxury home in Freiburg. Their trial began a year later on 1 September 2011 at the Cologne Regional Court. The prosecution's case was damaged by the lack of evidence to prove that Beltracchi had painted the fakes. By the end of October, the judge announced that the sides had reached a deal and terminated the proceedings, dismissing almost 200 prosecution witnesses and outraging police investigators. In a long, rambling confession, Beltracchi described his youthful indulgences in 'drugs and rock 'n' roll', attacked the 'greed and arrogance' of the art market and admitted that the deception had been 'great fun'. Among other

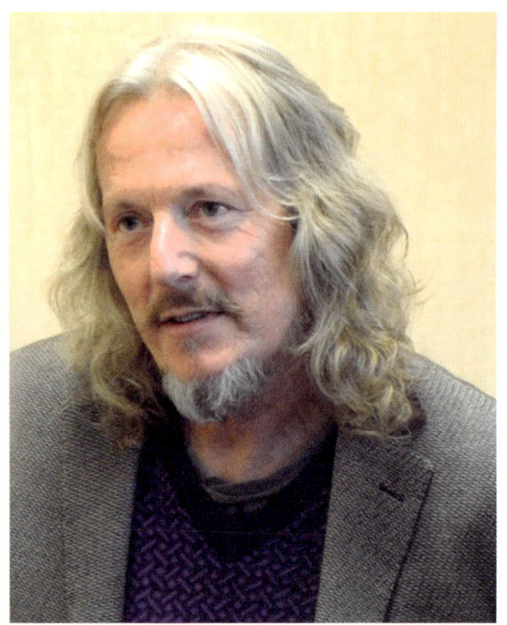

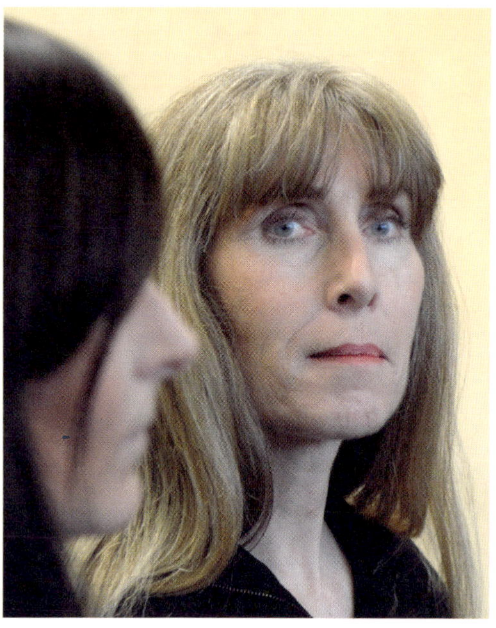

ABOVE: Wolfgang (left) and Helene (right) Beltracchi at their trial.

charges, he was convicted of fraud, money laundering and tax evasion, and he was sentenced to six years in prison. Helene was sentenced to four years, although both were released early. They were also required to pay €35 million in damages.

Since his release from prison, Beltracchi has continued to work as an artist, creating new paintings that openly acknowledge his history as a forger. He has also authored books and given lectures about his experiences in the art world. He frequently appears at speaking events; in 2021 he released a series of NFTs (NFT art, or non-fungible token art, refers to digital artworks that are uniquely authenticated and owned using blockchain technology) and he has appeared in a documentary. His first NFT was a digital recreation of Salvator Mundi, a painting said by some to have been painted by Leonardo da Vinci. The entire series was a group of seven digital works 'by' artists including Picasso and van Gogh.

He said he immersed himself completely in the artists' worlds as he assumed their identities, even describing feeling so close to the 17th-century painter Hendrick Avercamp that he felt like his brother. According to those who have interviewed the couple, they believed their crimes were victimless. Beltracchi said that he only made art that he believed to be beautiful, and that the owners appreciated them as much as the art market profited from them. However, those who have been deceived do not feel the same. As well as private collectors, an unknown number of galleries and museums fell victim to the fraud, with many possibly still displaying his forgeries.

The reputations of various experts were damaged, with one historian suing (unsuccessfully) for damages after he mistakenly authenticated a forgery. Auction houses including Sotheby's and Christie's were also defrauded, with Christie's even featuring one of the fakes on the cover of an evening sale catalogue.

Today, critics are divided about how clever Beltracchi actually was. Some say that he is a genius, but others declare that his greatest talent is as a self-promoter, and that at least some of his work was the result of meticulous duplication rather than artistic creativity. Overall, Beltracchi's case highlighted the weaknesses in the art market and authentication process, where forged works can easily be passed off as genuine. His story has been the subject of several books, documentaries and even a feature film, showcasing the complexity and scale of his elaborate fraud. The case has led to increased scrutiny and authentication measures within the art world, although the problem of detecting high-quality forgeries remains a persistent challenge.

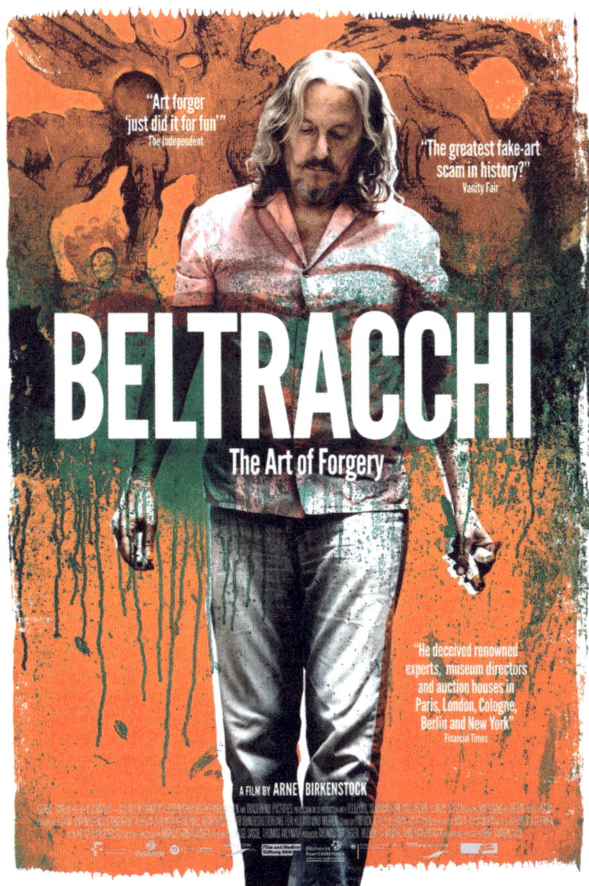

LEFT: The promotional poster for the 2014 Arne Birkenstock documentary about Beltracchi called *Beltracchi: The Art of Forgery* (German: *Beltracchi—Die Kunst der Fälschung*).

CHAPTER 6

The Faker's Handbook

Showing an early aptitude for drawing and painting, Eric Hebborn (1934–1996) maintained that over his career he created more than a thousand forgeries.

Yet only a few of these works have been exposed as fakes. Some have been displayed in locations such as the National Gallery of Denmark and the Morgan Library & Museum in New York, and some have passed through some of the finest auction houses in the world.

Over his career, Hebborn claimed to have forged the work of many different, exceptional artists, including Anthony van Dyck (1599–1641), Giovanni Battista Piranesi (1720–1778), Jean-Baptiste-Camille Corot (1796–1875) and Peter Paul Rubens (1577–1640).

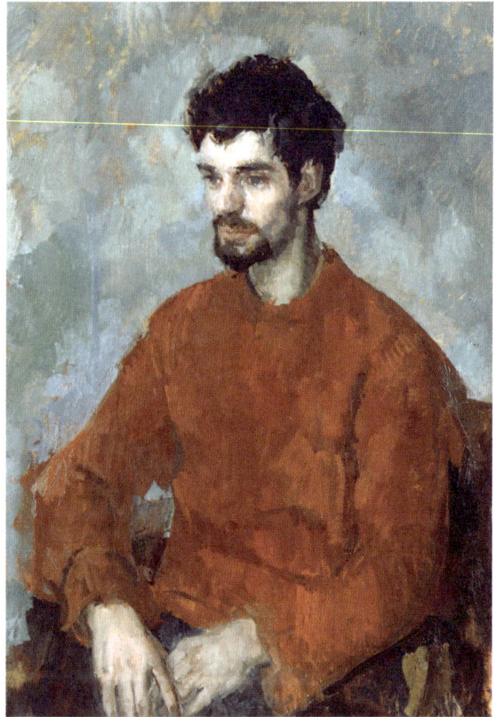

LEFT: Portrait of Eric Hebborn by Peter Greenham. Greenham was one of Hebborn's teachers at the Royal Academy, described by Hebborn as 'retiring, courteous and amiable'. Hebborn, meanwhile, was one of Greenham's best students. This portrait was probably painted during Hebborn's final year at the school, and exhibited at the Royal Academy in 1959.

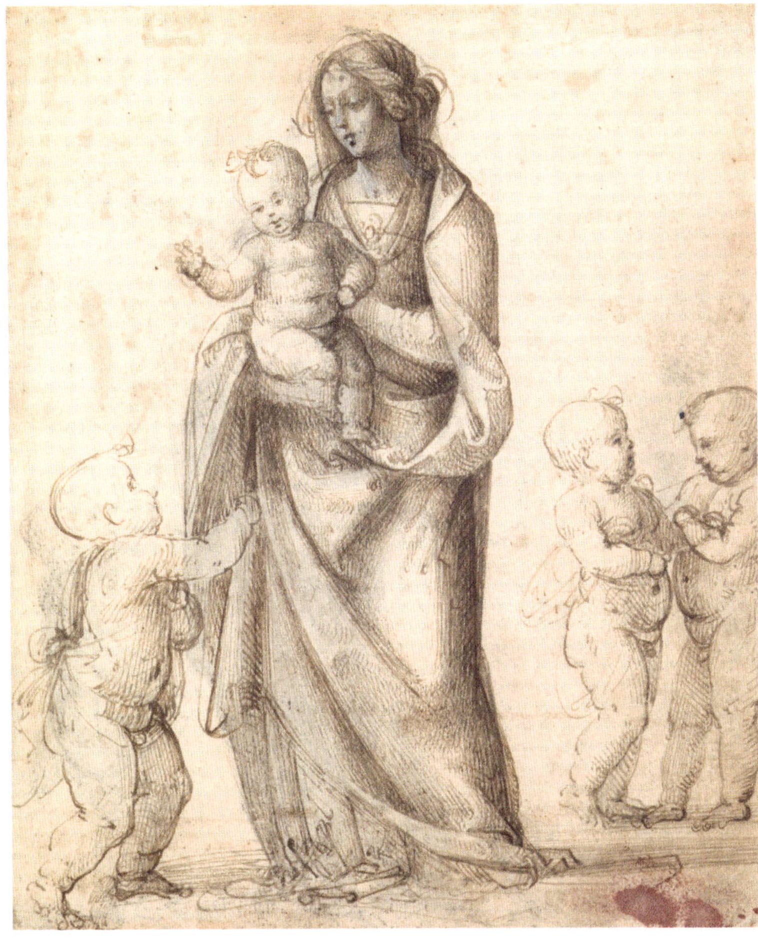

LEFT: In pen and brown ink, white gouache and black chalk, Fra Bartolomeo drew this image of the *Madonna and Child with the Infant Saint John the Baptist* in 1505–06. His drawing style was sensitive and delicate, and just the type of work that Hebborn enjoyed emulating.

Prize winner

Born in South Kensington, London, Hebborn first exhibited his own artwork at the age of 15. Soon after that, he attended Chelmsford and Walthamstow Art Schools and finally studied art at London's prestigious Royal Academy. There, he won the Hacker Portrait prize, the Silver Award and the British Prix de Rome in engraving, which was a two-year scholarship to the British School at Rome, in 1959. While there, he came to know several artists and art historians, including Anthony Blunt, who became an art advisor for Queen Elizabeth II and was later revealed to be a Russian spy. Blunt remarked that a couple of Hebborn's drawings looked as if they were by Nicolas Poussin.

On his return to London from Rome, Hebborn was hired by an art restorer who instructed him both to restore paintings and to alter and improve them. However, he soon fell out with his boss and left. He and his lover Graham David Smith often visited a junk and

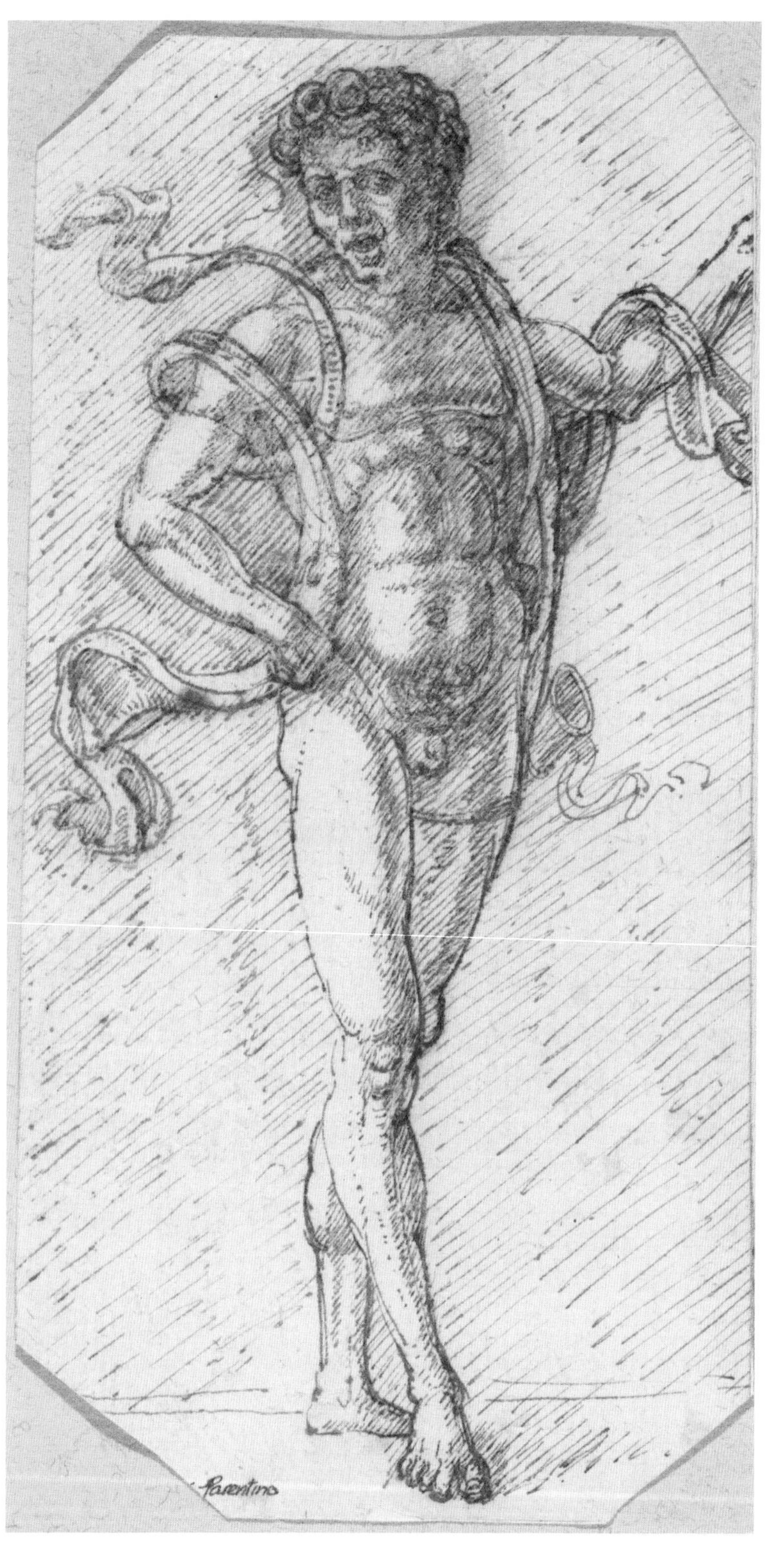

LEFT: Also known as Bernardo Parenzano, Bernardo Parentino was a Renaissance artist born in Venice but mainly active in Padua. This is *Standing Male Nude* in pen and brown ink by Hebborn and described by the National Gallery of Art in Washington, DC, USA, where the artwork is held, as a 'Parentino Imitation'.

antique shop near Leicester Square, and they became friends with one of the owners. Hebborn began helping out by rearranging and cataloguing the prints in the shop, and as he did so he learned about paper, its history and its uses in art. On some of these old sheets of paper, he made his first pencil drawing forgeries after Augustus John (1878–1961). Meanwhile, even though he had been so successful at the Royal Academy, he struggled to find a market for his own work, and he began to copy the style of artists such as Corot, Giovanni Benedetto Castiglione (1609–1664), Andrea Mantegna (c. 1431–1506), Van Dyck, Poussin, Rubens, Jan Brueghel the Elder (1568–1625) and Piranesi. He studied the work of these artists and more, regularly visiting, among others, the British Museum in London and the Gallerie degli Uffizi in Florence. Then he drew what appeared to be preparatory drawings for some of their major paintings or painted imitations of their works.

Confessions of a master forger

In 1963, Hebborn and Smith moved to Italy, where they opened Pannini Galleries. There, Hebborn exhibited both authentic artworks and his forgeries, which he sold to renowned art dealers, collectors and experts. He and Smith developed personal and professional relationships with a number of significant people in the London art world, including dealers Hans Calmann and Christopher White, a specialist in old master drawings at Colnaghi, the oldest commercial art gallery in the world. Founded in 1760, by the late

TEST-PROOFING

Hebborn combined his own artistic skill with materials that would withstand forensic testing. So along with his talent for mimicking the styles and techniques of a wide range of artists, he used ingredients such as eggs to make tempera paint, milk as a fixative, breadcrumbs as erasers, chalk, potato, ink, coffee, tea, olive oil, gelatin and flour to make pastes and glues. On his stove, he heated, combined and hardened pigments, creating the aged appearance of craquelure. He made his own inks because modern inks contain varnish to make them shine. He made carbon black ink with charcoal soot and a binder of oil, glue or gum. He made iron-gall ink, dark brown bistre with burnt wood, and sepia with cuttlefish ink. He used old paper from books made prior to 1798, as previously all paper had been made with rag, while after that year it was made with wood pulp. Sometimes he dipped a reed pen in sulphuric acid and drew on paper to simulate areas that would be eroded more than others where oak gall ink had been used. He cut and used his own quills from bird feathers. For his paintings, he analysed and reproduced the artists' individual palettes. For example, for Titian he used flake white, genuine ultramarine, madder lake, burnt sienna, malachite, yellow ochre, red ochre, orpiment and ivory black, and for Frans Hals he used flake white, yellow ochre, red ochre and charcoal black. He aged his forgeries using various other techniques to make them appear authentic and to fool experts and collectors, and he also recommended drinking alcohol while producing forgeries in order to be relaxed and create fluid lines.

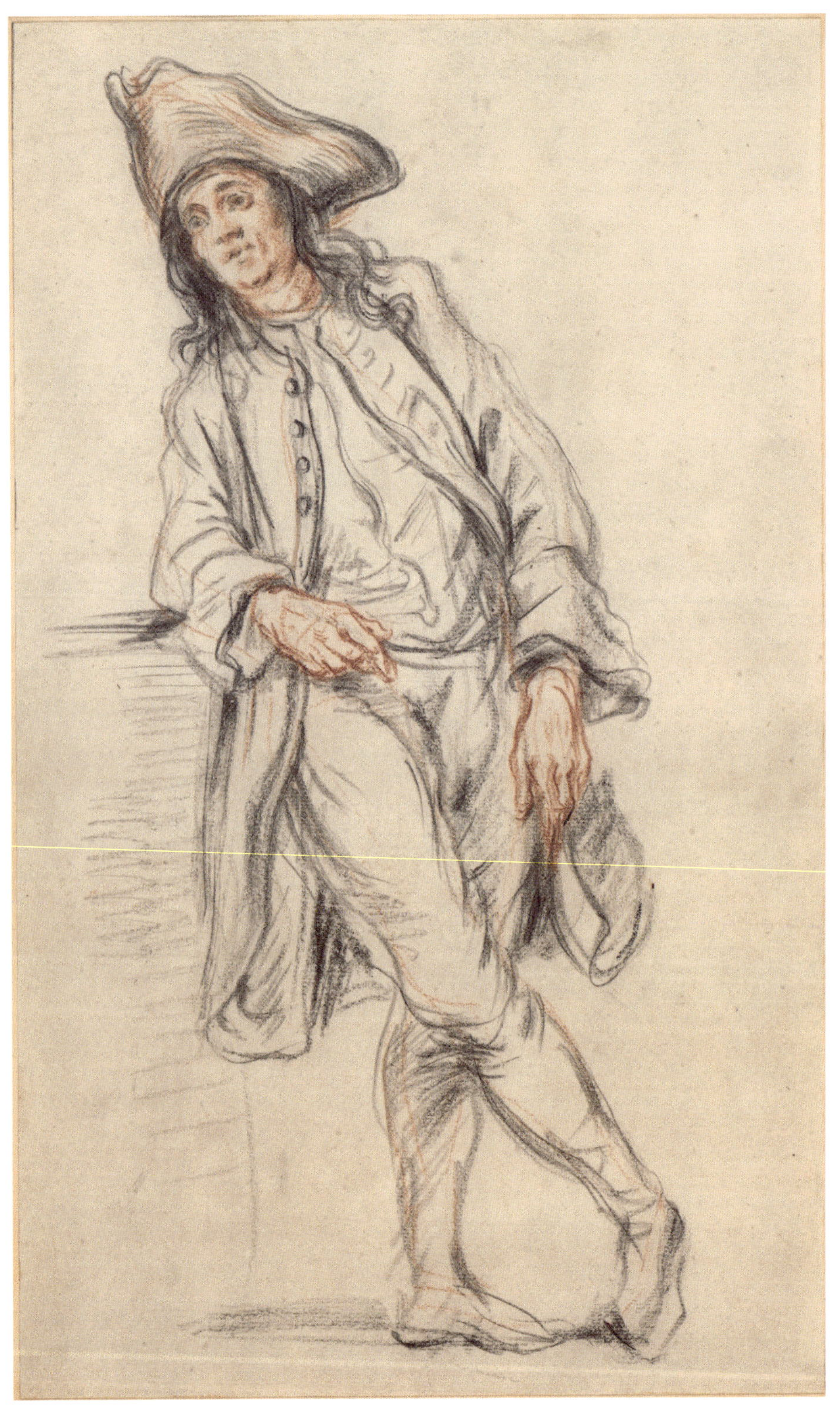

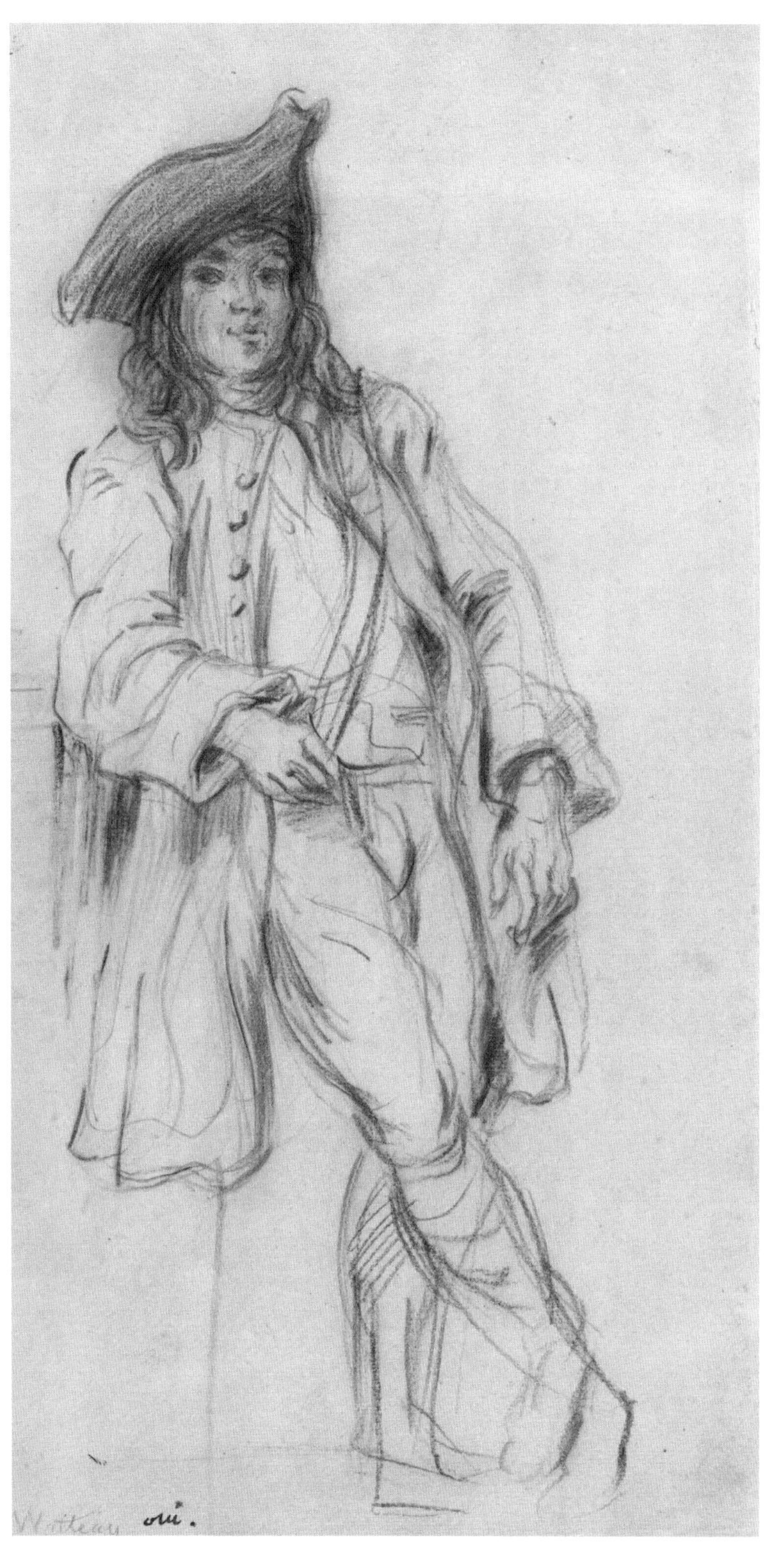

OPPOSITE AND LEFT: These two drawings, in black and red chalk laid on paper, were drawn by Eric Hebborn in the 1970s in imitation of drawings by French Rococo painter and draughtsman Jean-Antoine Watteau.

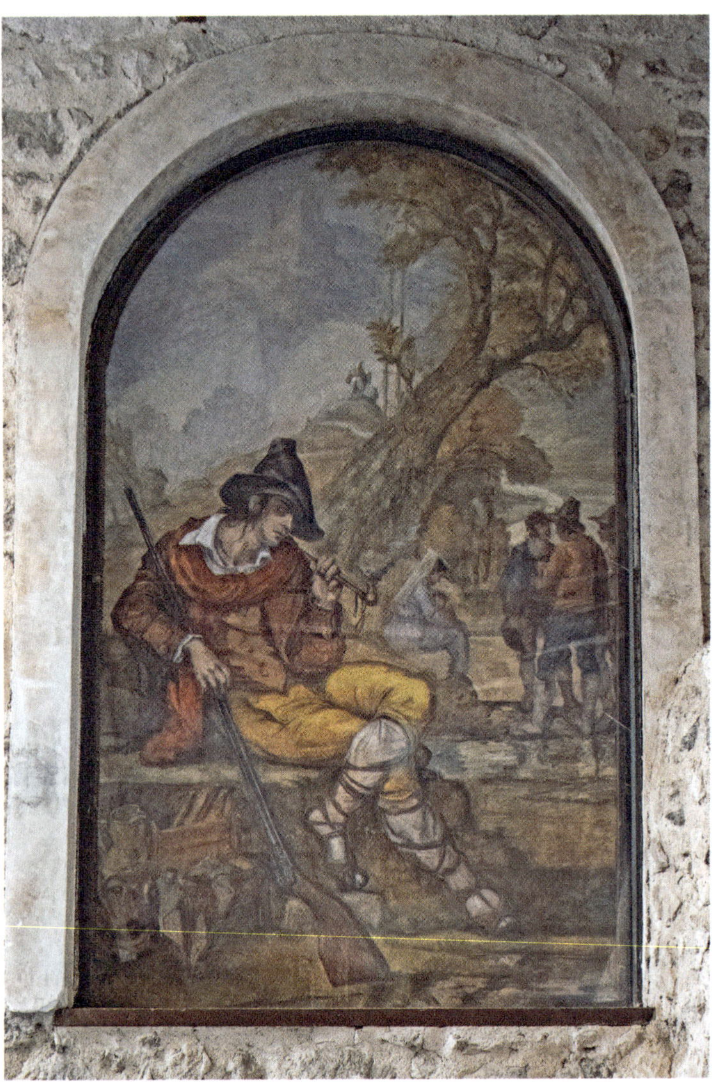

LEFT: In the church in Cervara di Roma (31 miles east of Rome), Our Lady of Graces, this large painting by Hebborn has pride of place. Painted in 1984, it depicts bands of brigands from the past and was inspired by villagers' stories.

19th century it was established across the world as a prominent trader in old master paintings, prints and drawings, and was selling these to some of the greatest collectors and museums worldwide. Respected art historians declared Hebborn's drawings and paintings to be authentic, and they were sold for tens of thousands of pounds through art auction houses, including Christie's and Sotheby's.

Then, in 1978, Konrad Oberhuber, a curator at the National Gallery of Art in Washington, DC, was examining two drawings he had bought for the museum from Colnaghi. The drawings were by 15th-century artists Savelli Sperandio and Francesco del Cossa, but Oberhuber noticed that they had identical artistic styles and both drawings had been executed on the same type of paper. He told a fellow curator at New York's Morgan Library & Museum, who noticed similar issues with a drawing there. They contacted Colnaghi and after 18 months the gallery issued a statement about their concerns over old master drawings purchased from Hebborn, although they did not openly name him.

Over the next ten years, Hebborn sold more than 500 drawings and paintings, but in 1984 he admitted to a number of forgeries. Like so many of the forgers in this book, he believed he had done nothing wrong. He was never charged with any crime and in 1991 he appeared in a BBC documentary. His book, *Drawn to Trouble: Confessions of a Master Forger*, was published that year. He simply criticized the expertise in so many respected galleries and auction houses that accepted his works and sold them to some of the most prominent art institutions in the world.

In *Drawn to Trouble* he wrote about his ability to deceive supposed art experts who were eager to accept his forgeries for the sake of profit. Five years later, in early 1996, Hebborn was found lying in a street in Rome having been hit with a blunt instrument. His skull was fractured, and he died a few days later in hospital. No one has ever been arrested in connection with the crime. Many of his artworks are alleged to hang in renowned collections, but this continues to be debated.

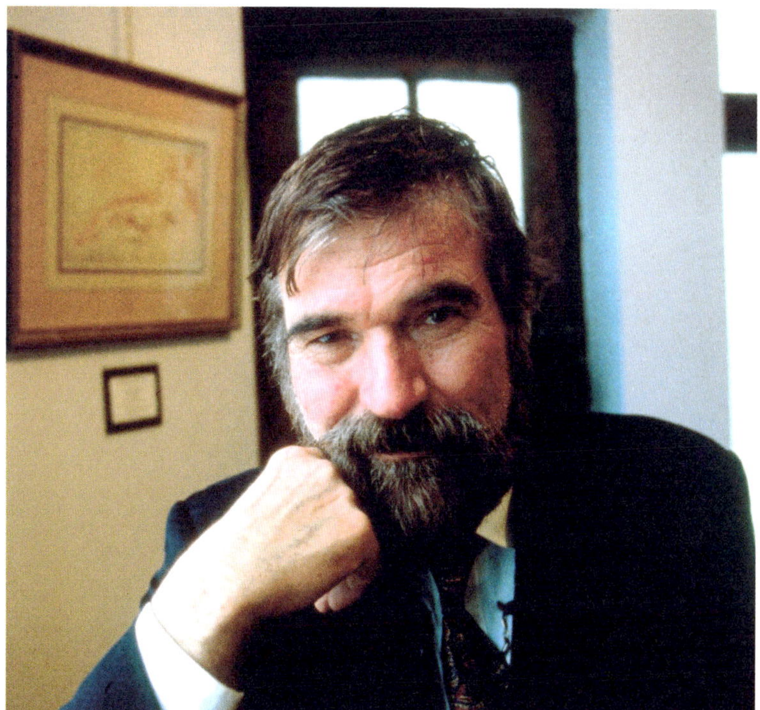

LEFT: Eric Hebborn in 1991, aged 57. In a TV documentary, he insisted, 'I'm not a crook, I'm just doing what people have always done during the history of the world. [Forgeries] should be enjoyed for what they are, rather than being questioned for what they're not.'

CHAPTER 7

The Art World is Rotten

One of the most productive art forgers in the world, Robert Driessen (b. 1959) specialized in creating forgeries of work by numerous artists, especially the Swiss Alberto Giacometti (1901–1966), for over 30 years.

Allegedly, he and his gang made more than €8 million. Personally, he probably made at least €3 million. Currently, he lives on a tropical island, Koh Samui in Thailand, running a café by the sea far away from Europe.

Auctioneer

Born in Arnhem in the eastern Netherlands, Driessen had a difficult childhood. When he was 16, he left school and home. At school, his artistic talents had been encouraged by his teachers, and knowing a little bit about art history from his antique dealer father, he began painting for a living. It was hard to make ends meet and by the time he was 19 years old, he considered himself to be a 'failed' artist. Then he met a German art dealer who was looking for someone who could paint landscapes. Driessen said he could. The dealer provided him with small and large panels, already primed and ready for the oil paints that Driessen would use. Initially, he produced typical Dutch scenes that were especially popular in Germany. They featured classic Dutch elements, including windmills, canals, fishing boats and figures. The dealer was pleased but wanted Driessen to work faster and to produce copies of the works of the 19th-century Dutch Romantic painters Paul Gabriël, Hendrik Willem Mesdag and Johan Hendrik Weissenbruch. A routine was established, with the dealer coming to Driessen's home every fortnight to collect the paintings he had produced and pay him on the spot. When asked, Driessen recalled, 'I had never had so much money in my pockets before and in such a short period of time.' With the money he was earning, he

OPPOSITE, ABOVE: *Summer Day*, painted by Johan Hendrik Weissenbruch, 1903.

OPPOSITE, BELOW: *Sunny Day, a Mill on a Watercourse*, painted by Paul Gabriël, between 1860 and 1903. These are both examples of paintings by the Dutch masters that Driessen emulated.

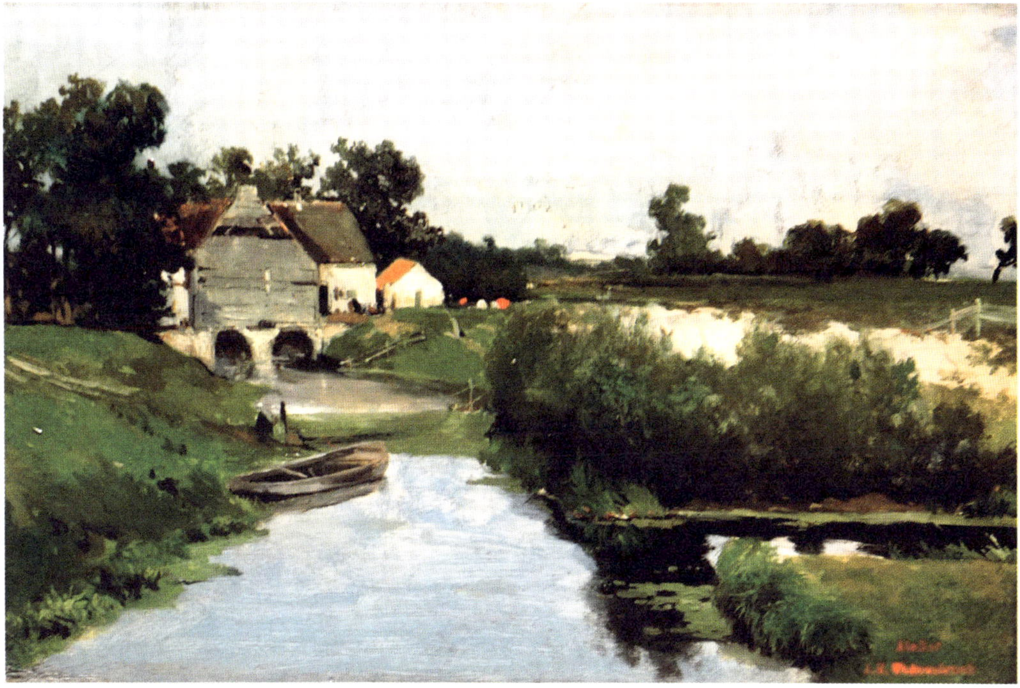

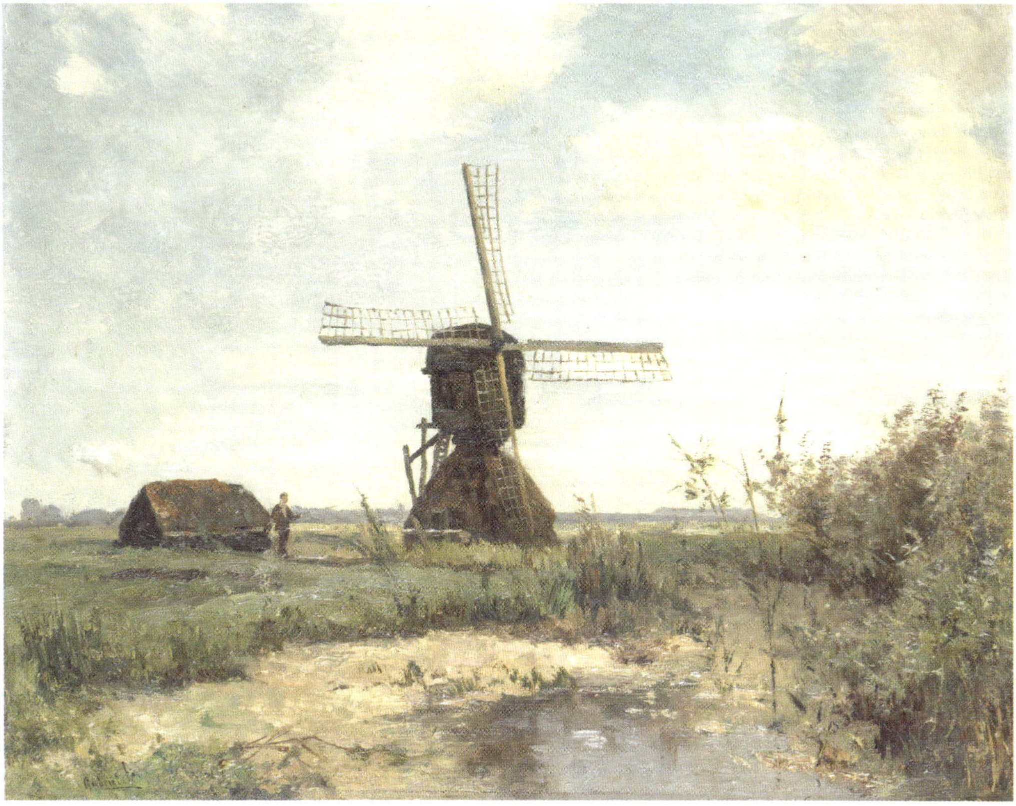

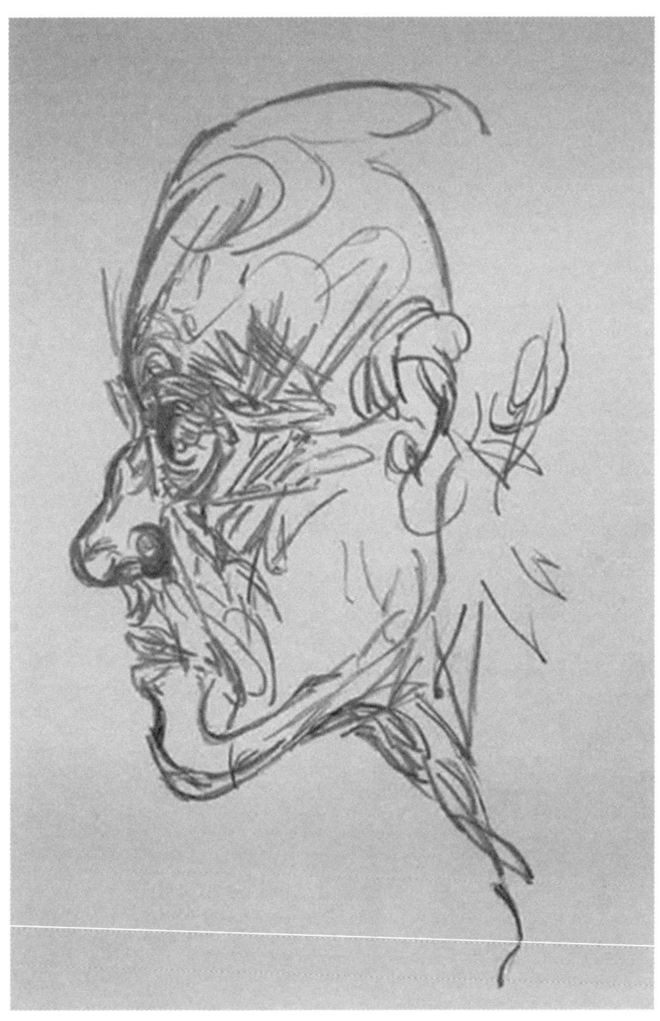

LEFT AND BELOW: During the late 1980s, Driessen began producing sculptures. He was particularly inspired by Giacometti's works and has since made many drawings in Giacometti's fluid, gestural style. These were made in the mid-1990s on paper from the 1950s.

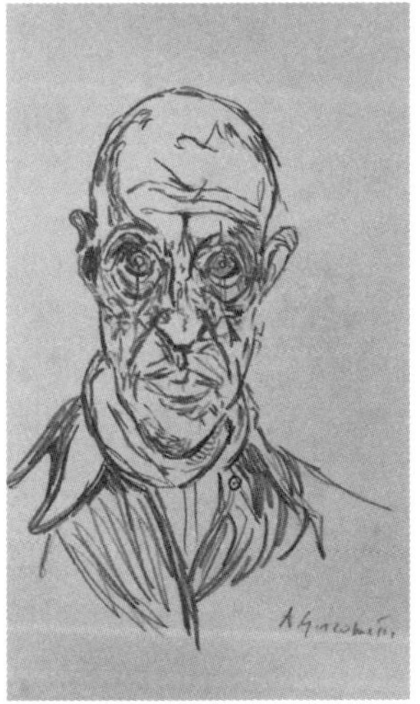

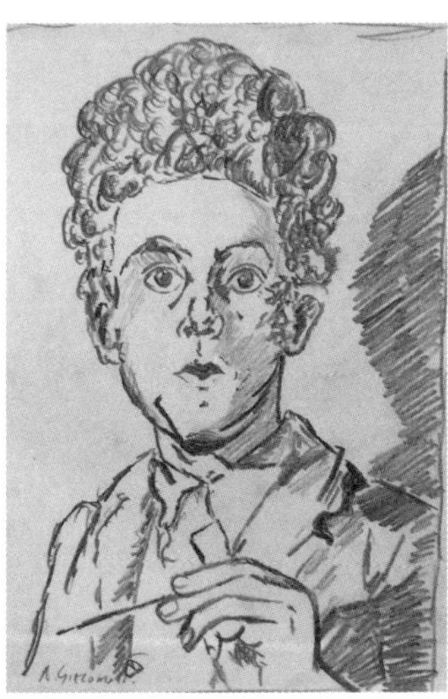

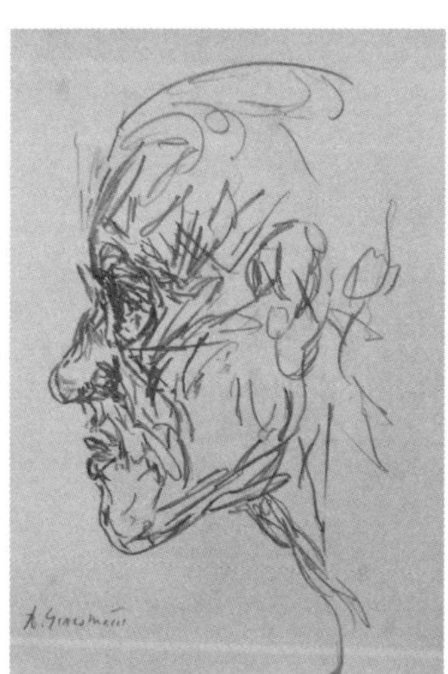

took himself off on a trip around Asia. He loved it so much that on the plane on his way back, he decided to further his art career. Back in the Netherlands, he became the youngest arts and antiquities auctioneer in the country, frequently selling his own artworks that were copies, adaptations and interpretations of paintings by 20th-century Expressionist artists including Emil Nolde, August Macke, Wassily Kandinsky and Karl Schmidt-Rottluff, under the artists' names to enhance his work. He visited museums and galleries, read books, papers and articles, and generally immersed himself in the art he was emulating. Sometimes he copied original works back to front and sometimes he created new paintings by using a combination of elements from several images.

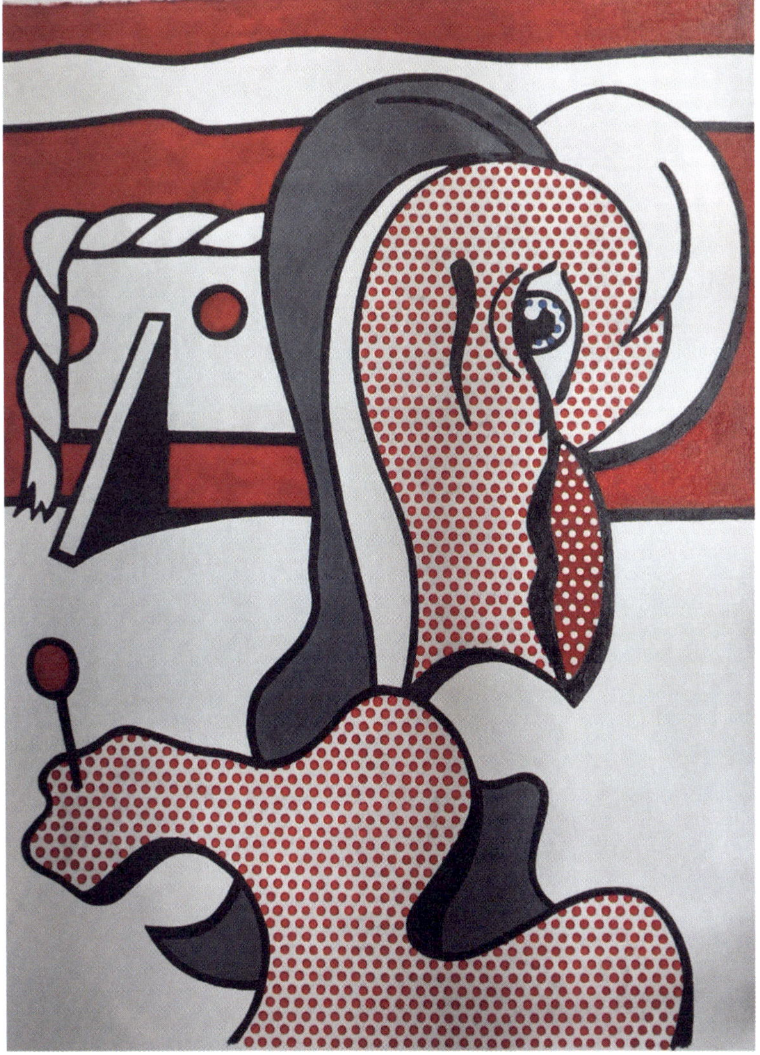

LEFT: *Woman with a Lollipop*, created by Driessen in tribute to American Pop artist Roy Lichtenstein. It was painted on the same canvas, with the same paint and dimensions as Lichtenstein's 1977 painting of the same title.

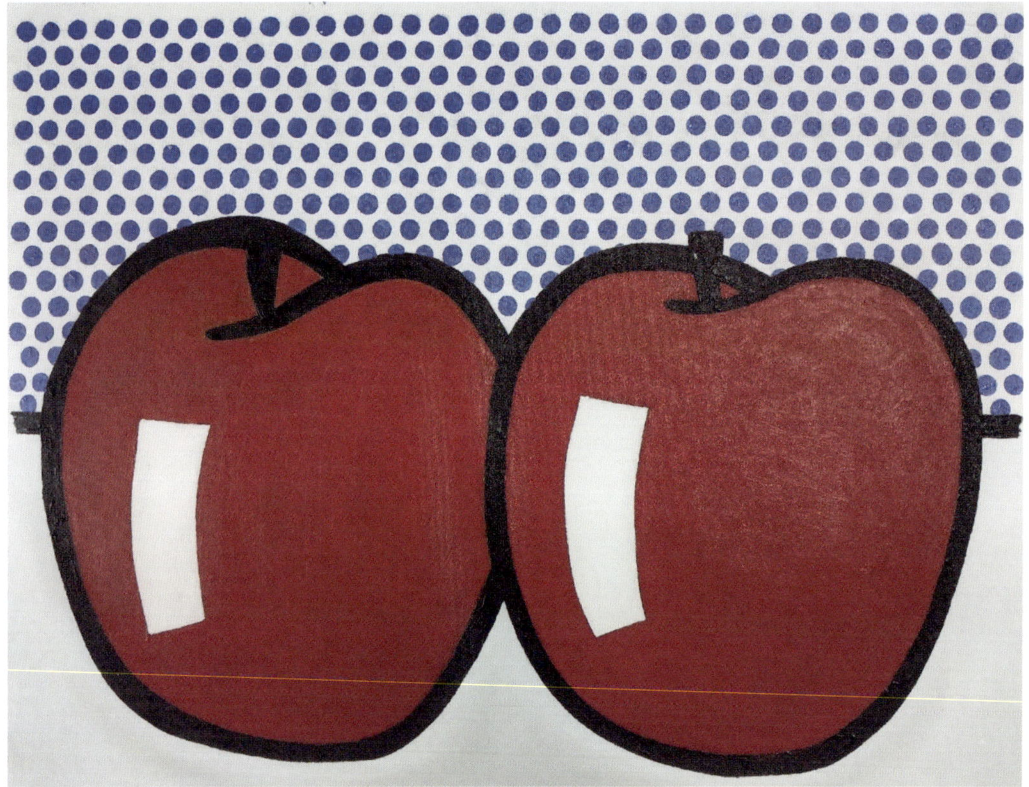

BELOW: In the signature comic book style of Lichtenstein, Driessen made this exact copy of his 1972 painting *Two Apples*, using the same paint, canvas and dimensions.

A number of dealers began buying his work. One of them was Michel van Rijn, who later became known as the most successful art smuggler in the world. The dealers also asked for certain elements to be included and Driessen worked to order, estimating that he probably produced more than a thousand paintings in total. He reflects, 'I knew that I was forging art. The dealers knew that they were buying forgeries. But we didn't talk about it. I assume that they sold the forgeries as authentic paintings.'

Painting and sculpture

Driessen says that after a few years, during the 1980s, he stopped doing auctions. He decided to just make art: paintings, watercolours and, for the first time from 1987, sculpture as well. He rented a big house in the Dutch countryside with eleven bedrooms, six bathrooms and three studios on the top floor, 10km (6 miles) from the German border. His car was a costly BMW 7 Series. Completely self-taught, he had one studio for his painting, one for watercolours and drawings, and the third for his 'new passion' of sculpting. He said he had never worked with clay or sculpting wax, but after a few experiments he suddenly had a female torso in the style of Aristide Maillol (1861–1944). 'I liked that. I monogrammed it with the letter R and left it to dry. I had heard of a bronze foundry not far away, in Brummen near Arnhem, so I took it there and surprisingly they liked it . . . We agreed on a price which I thought was cheap and I could pick it up three weeks later.' The caster, Roel Maaskant, showed Driessen how to cast bronze. Driessen said, 'What a beautiful profession, I thought, an art form in itself.'

BELOW: *Seated Youth*, created by the German artist Wilhelm Lehmbruck in 1917, made of composite tinted plaster.

Some of Driessen's first bronze sculptures that he made with moulds were sold to an art dealer in The Hague for 17,000 Dutch guilders (about €7,700). He went on to forge many more bronzes after taking many photographs of well-known works of art in museums and galleries. To sell some of these works, he bought an ad in the art journal *Weltkunst*. His first potential buyer arrived in Arnhem by helicopter. The second was one of Germany's great gallery owners, Michael Werner, who paid €42,500 for a copy of a sculpture by Wilhelm Lehmbruck (1881–1919). Werner put the work in the garden of his gallery in Trebbin, south of Berlin. Driessen recalls that Werner was enthusiastic about the sculpture when he bought it, but later dismissed it as an 'atrocious forgery'.

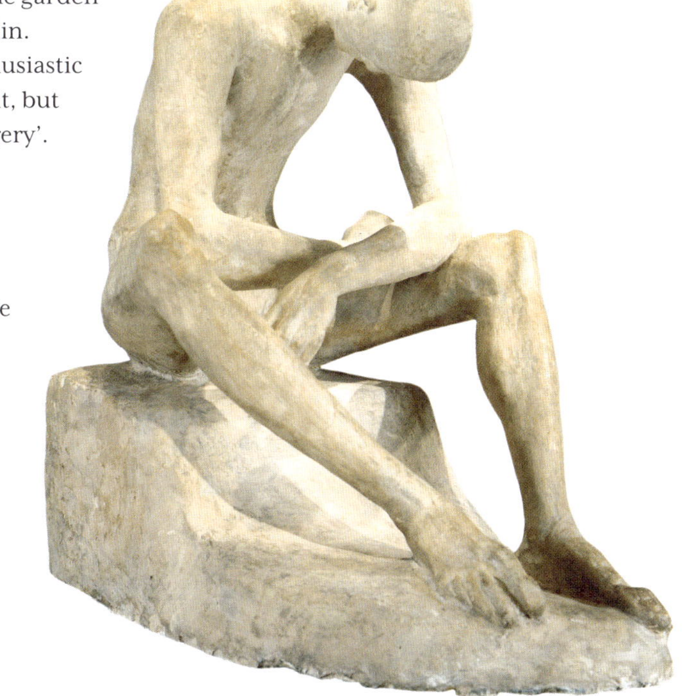

In 1998, Driessen produced his first 'Giacometti'. Having long been an admirer of the Swiss artist's work, he studied his style, signature and the foundry stamp. Then he made a thin plaster figure 2.7m (8ft 10in) tall and entitled it *Annette* after Giacometti's wife. Until one of his dealers found a buyer, Driessen kept the plaster figure in his attic; then he had the bronze cast. Within a relatively short time, several men visited him. They included a Dutch art dealer, an antique dealer from the south-western German city of Mainz, and a

ALBERTO GIACOMETTI

Swiss sculptor, painter, draughtsman and printmaker Alberto Giacometti has become the most expensive sculptor in the world. His face is featured on the Swiss 100-franc banknote, and his sculpture *L'Homme qui marche I (Walking Man I)* of 1960 sold at Sotheby's in 2011 for $104.3 million. *L'Homme au doigt (Pointing Man)* of 1947 sold for $141.3 million in 2015 at Christie's in New York, making it the most expensive sculpture ever sold.

When he was 20, Giacometti left his native Bergell and travelled to Paris. Friends with all the great artists and writers of the time, including Max Ernst, Joan Miró, Pablo Picasso, Jean-Paul Sartre, Simone de Beauvoir, Man Ray and Igor Stravinsky, he became one of the most important sculptors of the 20th century, particularly famed for his figures that posed philosophical and existentialist questions about the human condition, perception, alienation and anxiety. Embodying the notion of the suffering human figure after the Second World War, his spindly, solitary figurative sculptures are instantly recognizable. Experts believe that he may have produced approximately 500 unique works, but no one knows for sure exactly how many he made as he worked incredibly fast and rarely kept records of how many artworks he created.

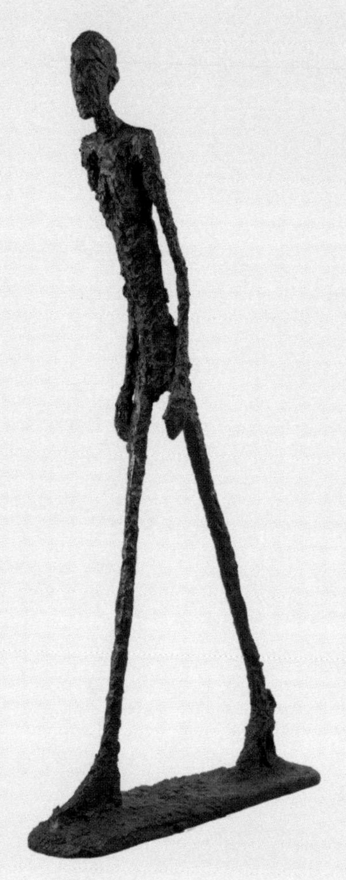

Greek man who was living in Germany. One took out a brown envelope, from which he counted out 250,000 deutsche marks (around €130,000), all in newly printed 1,000-mark bills, and offered it to Driessen. They asked him to make more Giacomettis.

Because there is no definitive catalogue of Giacometti's work, just an incomplete database, it was relatively easy for Robert Driessen to add some new works to his *oeuvre*. It was also fairly easy from a technical perspective. 'It isn't difficult to make Giacomettis,' Driessen has reflected. He says it took him about 30 to 40 minutes to make the small figures. He made his own models based on Giacometti's style, had them cast, and then stamped them with the seals of the foundries Giacometti had used.

Boom and bust

Three weeks later, the dealer from Mainz returned to Driessen, paid him a further 6,000 deutsche marks (€3200) and left with

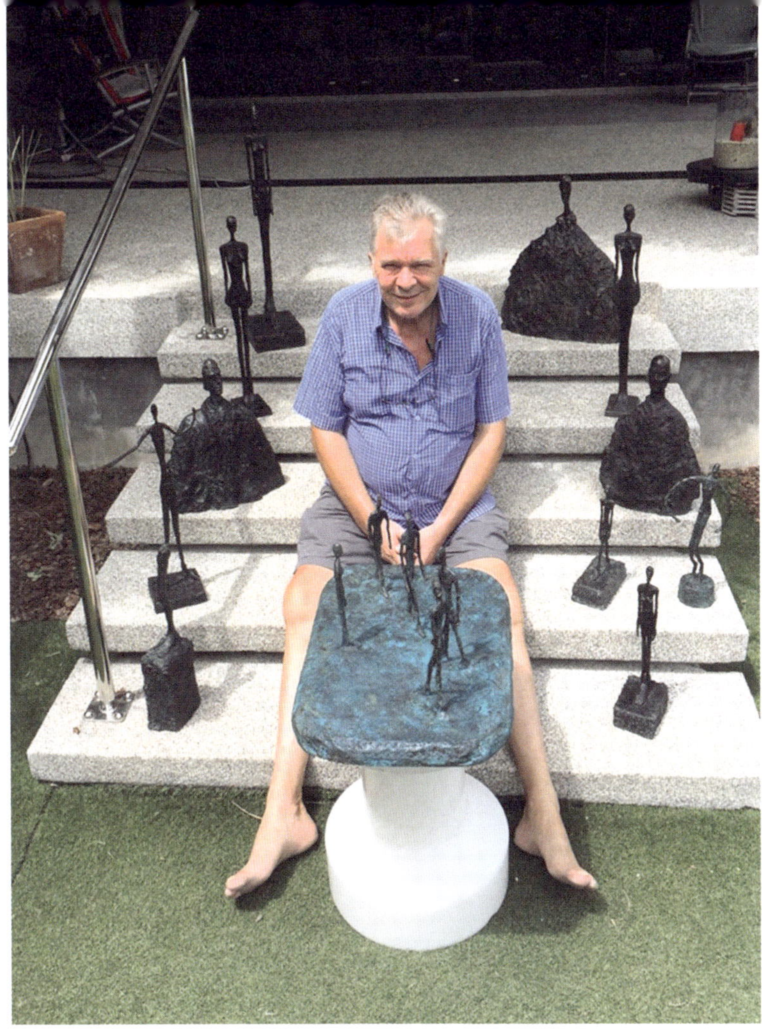

LEFT: Robert Driessen sitting amongst some of his own 'Giacomettis'.

12 Giacometti bronzes, all smaller than 40cm (15¾in) tall. The same dealer kept ordering more. At one point, he told Driessen that he intended to open a gallery in Portugal's Algarve region, so he wanted 1,500 Giacomettis. Driessen managed to make 1,300. Although he worked alone at first, eventually he had to hire two assistants to keep up with the casting.

Soon, Driessen was introduced to the German art dealer's partner and the trio became a working network – or cartel. Driessen made the works, the dealer was the strategist, and the partner handled sales. Their business thrived for ten years. Among many other buyers, a billionaire in Wiesbaden, near Frankfurt, bought 49 fake Giacomettis for €3.5 million. Investment manager Peter Hans Schuck from Stuttgart paid at least €3.7 million for 18 forgeries. However, an attempt to sell about 300 sculptures to two New York galleries for €50 million failed when the potential American buyers became suspicious.

In 2005, to escape the cold European winters, Driessen, his wife and their son emigrated to Koh Samui, an island in Thailand where he bought a café. Before leaving, he burned all his photos of the forged works of art. In Koh Samui, he rented a large villa, and his dealers continued to send money to his bank account from Germany. At first, he still made regular trips to the Netherlands to produce more forgeries. Then, in February 2009, the police detained his German dealer for two hours at Frankfurt Airport, and for ten days, when Driessen drove to the Netherlands from Frankfurt to work, the police watched him. When he became aware that he was being watched, as a precaution he did not visit the foundries where his work was cast but instead flew back to Thailand. Early the following month, he received a text message from his German art dealer: 'I'm transferring the money to your account, make sure you don't come to Germany.' That August, both art dealers and two assistants were arrested at Frankfurt Airport by a mobile police unit while they were attempting to sell five Giacometti forgeries for €338,000 in cash. Their 'buyers' had been undercover investigators. Police searched the gang's warehouse in Mainz, and along with other forged artworks they discovered 831 bronzes and 171 plaster figures in the style of Giacometti stored in several rooms in the basement.

The case went to court in Stuttgart. One of Driessen's dealers was sentenced to nine years' imprisonment, and the other was sentenced to seven years and four months. Driessen, not being a German citizen, could not be extradited from Thailand. However, on 4 July 2014, he returned to Amsterdam to visit his now ex-wife on her birthday – and was arrested. He was tried and sentenced to five years and three months in prison, although he served just two years and eight months in total.

After his release, Driessen discovered that on average he had been paid less than a fifth of the price his dealers had sold his artworks for. The police destroyed more than a thousand of his forgeries.

FORGING BRONZE SCULPTURE

Bronze sculptures are expensive and complex, and the path from a wax or plaster figure through a latex mould to the finished sculpture is a long one. Because recasting is relatively easy, and because castings of an artist's work are often made after their death, sculptures can often be forged more easily than paintings. It can be difficult to prove how many genuine castings of a sculpture exist, sometimes because foundries make copies or cast more than the artist commissioned. Consequently, there are both authentic and replica sculptures that are identical to each other.

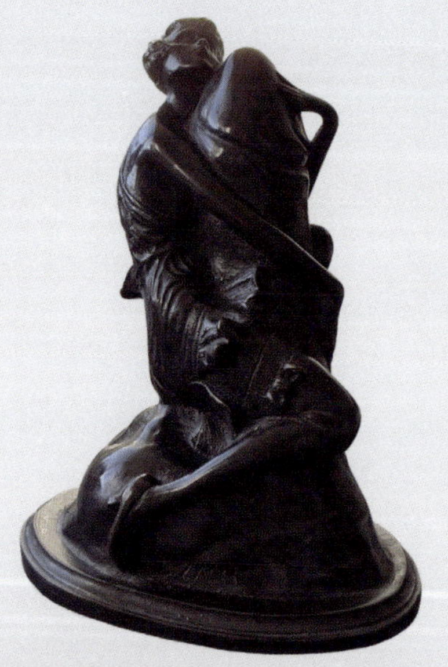

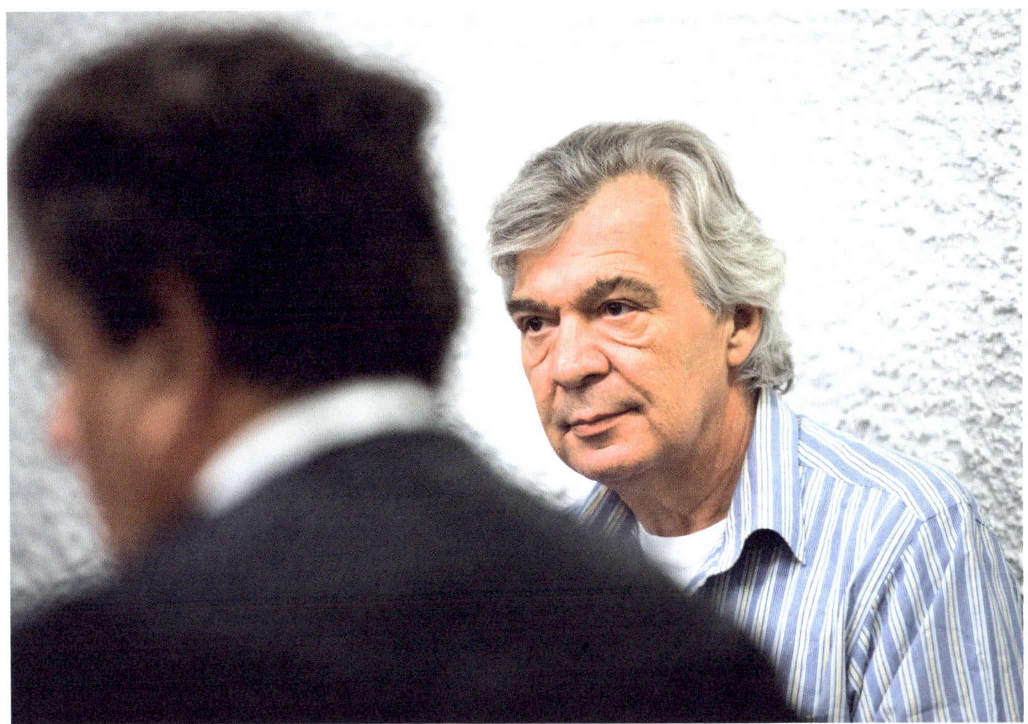

Driessen says that he watched a television report on the destruction of his works on YouTube, but he was not particularly upset by it. Neither does he feel guilty about what he did, or feel sorry for his victims. He maintains that the art world is corrupt and that a few people are making a lot of money dishonestly. He also said, 'Anyone who believes he can buy a real Giacometti for €20,000 deserves to be duped. The art world is rotten.'

ABOVE: Robert Driessen in 2014 in Stuttgart. He was charged with gang and commercial fraud, accused of forging several Giacometti sculptures with other accomplices between 2003 and 2009 and selling them for around €8 million.

CHAPTER 8

A Legal Forgery

Despite his forgeries and false identities, Mark Landis (b. 1955) was technically guilty of no crime, as no money changed hands for his artworks.

For over 20 years, under several different aliases, including a Jesuit priest, American painter Mark Landis donated artworks to more than 50 museums across the USA. He even gave about six copies of the same work to different museums.

Born in Norfolk, Virginia, Landis now lives in Laurel, Mississippi. As a child, he travelled a lot with his family because of his father's different postings in the US Navy. Among these were Hong Kong, the Philippines, Cap Ferrat, London, Paris and Brussels. On their travels, they collected museum handbooks. 'There was no TV in hotel rooms in the 1960s, and I would entertain myself by copying the pictures in these books,' Landis recalled.

In 1968, the family returned to the United States, settling in Jackson, Mississippi, but three years later Landis's father was diagnosed with cancer and died the following year. At the death of his father, 17-year-old Landis suffered a nervous breakdown. He was treated for 18 months in a Kansas hospital, diagnosed with schizophrenic, paranoid and psychotic disorders and catatonic behaviour. Art therapy helped him somewhat. It also revealed his talent for copying, and he found he could produce reproductions of paintings at an astonishing speed.

Small museums

Always better at art than his peers, Landis took art classes at the Art Institute of Chicago and then in San Francisco, where he also worked on repairing damaged paintings. He studied photography because he believed he already knew how to draw and paint. After leaving college, he bought an art gallery, but it was unsuccessful. In 1988, at the age of 33 he went back to live with his mother and stepfather in Mississippi. He had already started to copy other artists' works and donate his forgeries, and, he said, in commemoration of his father and to please his mother, he donated some paintings that he had

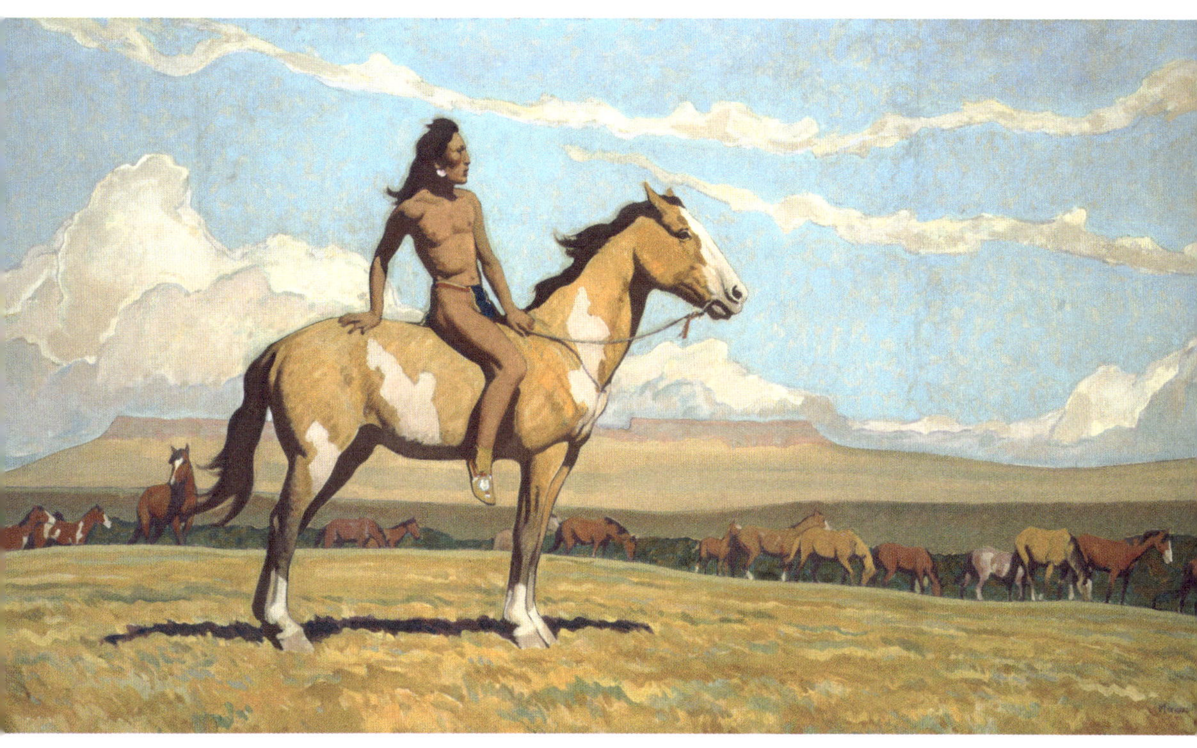

copied by American artist Maynard Dixon (1875–1946) to a museum in California. He commented, 'I put Maynard Dixon's name on [the paintings] because that's what the museum wanted.' Indeed, what inspired Landis to pretend all of his works were by other artists was because museums would only want paintings by listed, valuable artists. '[Dixon] was a cowboy artist, so I went to the library and checked out some books of photographs of American Indians and copied a bunch of them. I knew the museums wanted cowboy pictures, so that's what I did.'

ABOVE: *The Pony Boy*, painted in 1920 by American artist Maynard Dixon, known for his paintings that focused on the American West. Landis said he put Dixon's name on his paintings because that is what the museums wanted.

The museum seemed delighted with the gift, and this first success gave Landis the confidence to repeat the deed. For more than two decades, he produced and gave all kinds of paintings to institutions across the USA, including more than 50 museums. He copied artists including Dixon, Picasso, Marie Laurencin (1883–1956), Jean-Antoine Watteau (1684–1721), Honoré Daumier (1808–1879) and Walt Disney (1901–1966). He generally donated to fairly small museums, as they did not have large resources or methods of analysis used by larger, more well-known museums. He also gave art to hundreds of churches. When he gave his works, he assumed various characters, including Jesuit priest Father Arthur Scott, Father James Brantley (his stepfather's name), Stephen Gardiner, Mark Lanois (he exchanged the 'd' in his actual surname for an 'o'),

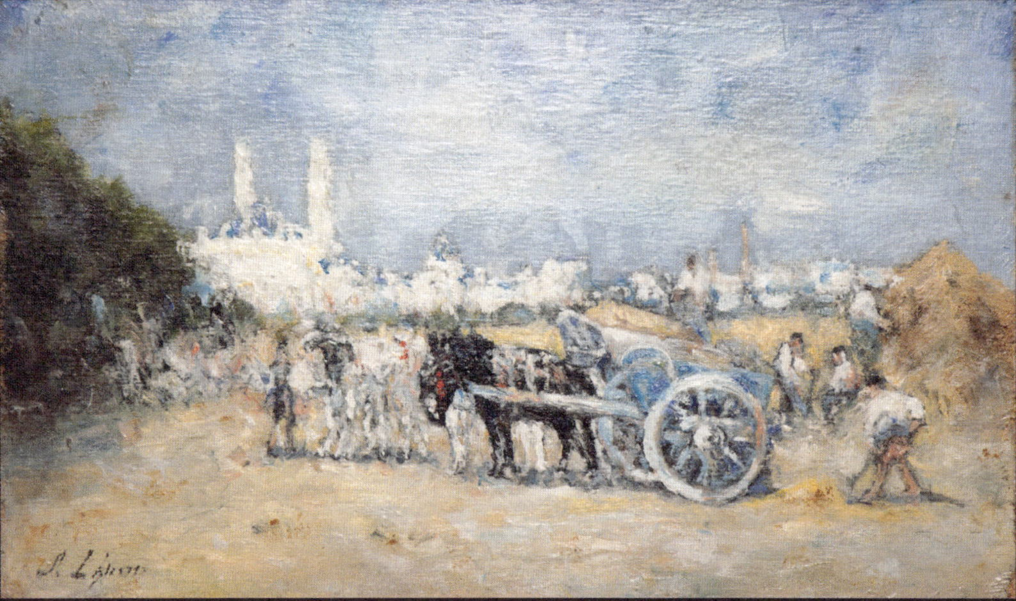

Untitled painting, in the style of Stanislas Lépine, painted by Mark Landis in oil on board.

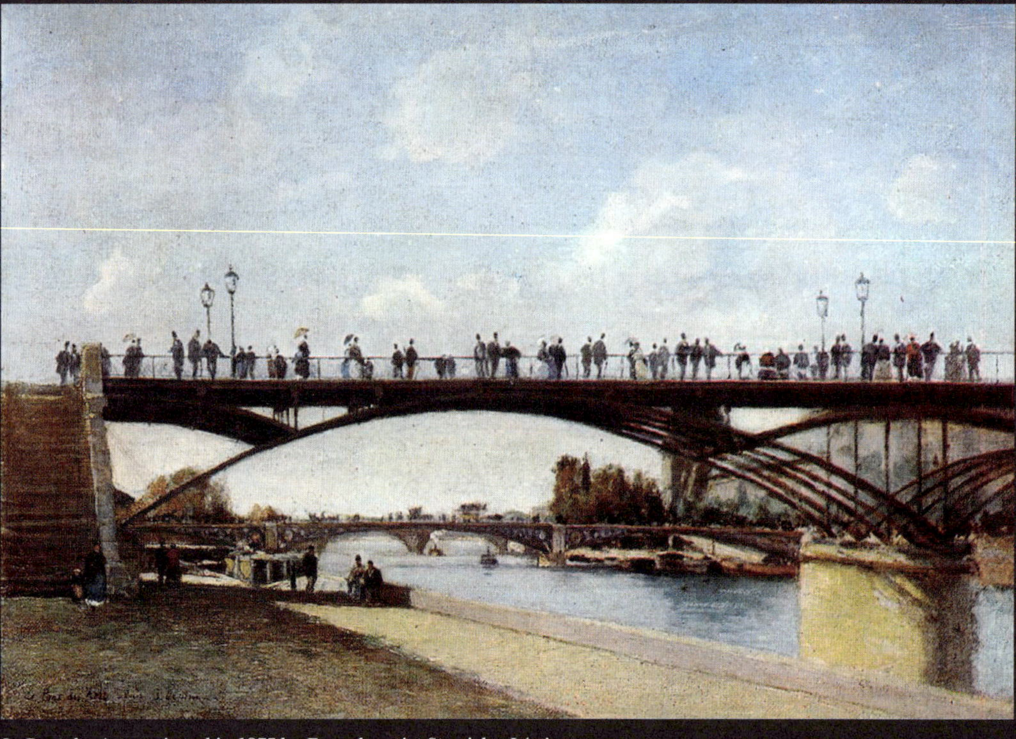

Le Pont des Arts, painted in 1875 by French artist Stanislas Lépine, who specialized in landscapes, especially views of the Seine.

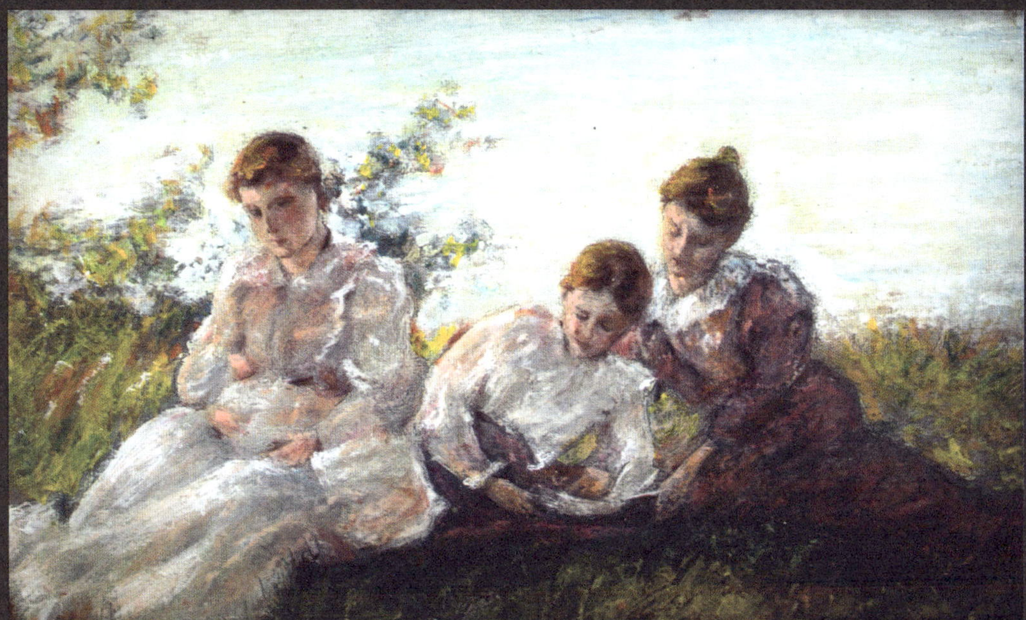

Three Women Seated on a Lawn, Mark Landis, c. 2000, in the style of Charles Courtney Curran.

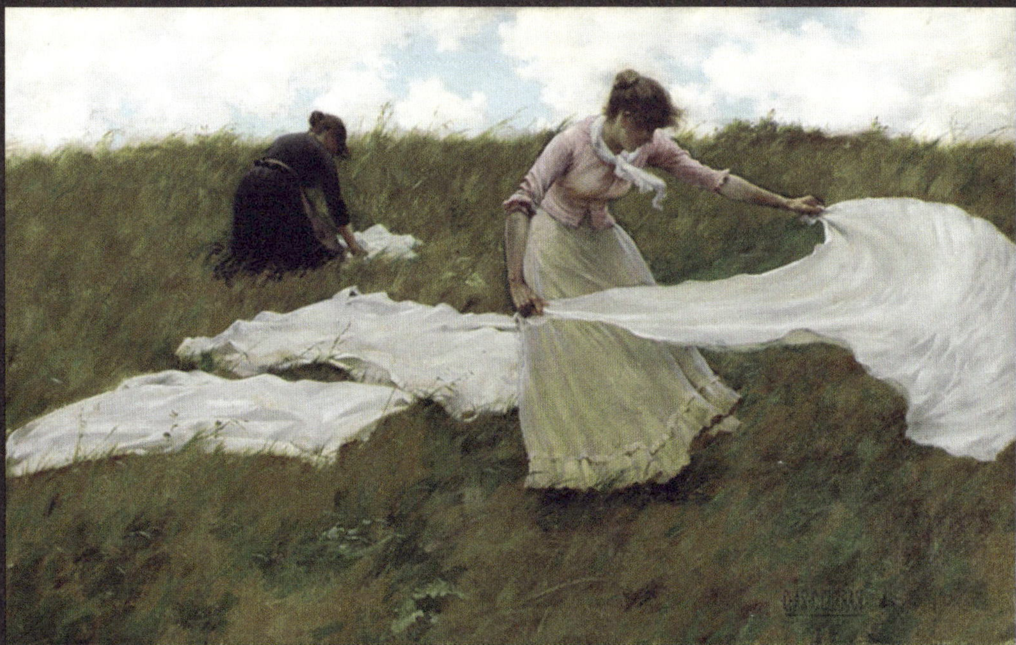

A Breezy Day, painted by Charles Courtney Curran, 1887, depicts a lively laundry day in the country.

Martin Lynley and John Grauman. While not taking any money, instead working sporadically in animation and newspaper illustration, selling portraits and doing painting repairs to make ends meet, Landis nonetheless derived huge personal satisfaction from knowing that his art had fooled the experts. During that time, he also painted original artworks of his own and sold some through Narsad Artworks, which sells work by artists with mental illness.

Landis constructed scrupulous back stories for all his alter egos, and he was fortunate that the people he donated to rarely questioned or examined his paintings too closely. Later, he reflected that he did not spend much time on them, nor did he treat them with any chemicals or substances, or use special materials to make them seem authentic or to withstand any tests. They usually took just a couple of hours, using cheap materials like felt-tip pens. 'All that really counts is what it looks like,' he explained. 'You know, when you go to a museum, you don't put it under one of those giant microscopes that they have down in the basement.' He also reflected: 'I like acrylics. And magic markers and coloured pencils. It's what it looks like that counts. I know everybody's heard about forgers that do all these complicated things with chemicals and what-have-you, but I don't have that kind of patience. I buy my supplies at Walmart or Woolworth – discount stores – and then I do it in an hour or two at most. If I can't get something done by the time a movie's over on TV, I'll give up on it.' He added: 'I always paint by my window with a TV. I couldn't do anything without a TV on. I got the idea of being a philanthropist from watching TV and the idea of wearing a priest's outfit from a movie, *The Swan*. The uncle in it was a priest.'

Discovered

In 2007, Landis offered several artworks to the Oklahoma City Museum of Art. They included a watercolour by French Fauvist painter Louis Valtat, a harbour scene by French Neo-Impressionist Paul Signac, a self-portrait by Marie Laurencin, a 19th-century landscape by Stanislas Lépine and a drawing by Daumier. The museum's registrar, Matthew Leininger, examined the works and discovered that an extremely similar painting by Signac had been offered to the SCAD Museum of Art in Savannah, Georgia. At first, though, he decided that Landis must simply be a really eccentric art collector. His gallery framed the Valtat and put it on display next to a Renoir. However, he investigated further and found a press release from SCAD that mentioned the donation of the Signac and a self-portrait by Laurencin. The press release gave Mark Landis's real name. Alert and suspicious now, Leininger investigated further. Eventually, after a lot of probing and researching, he discovered that

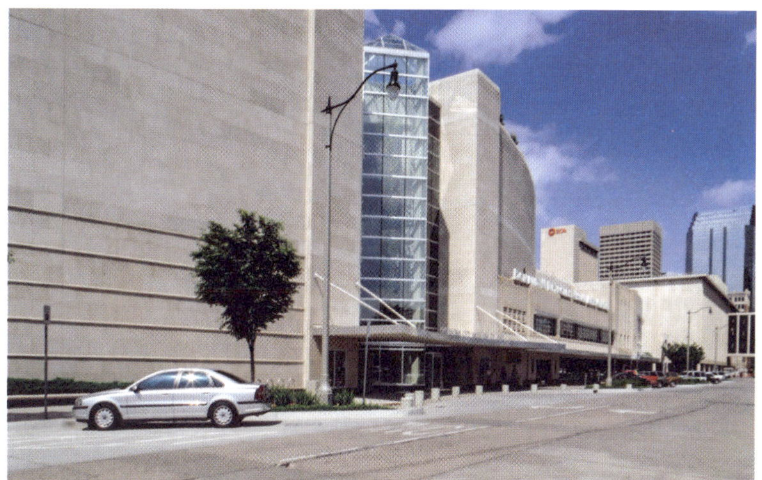

LEFT: In 2007, Landis offered several artworks to the Oklahoma City Museum of Art.

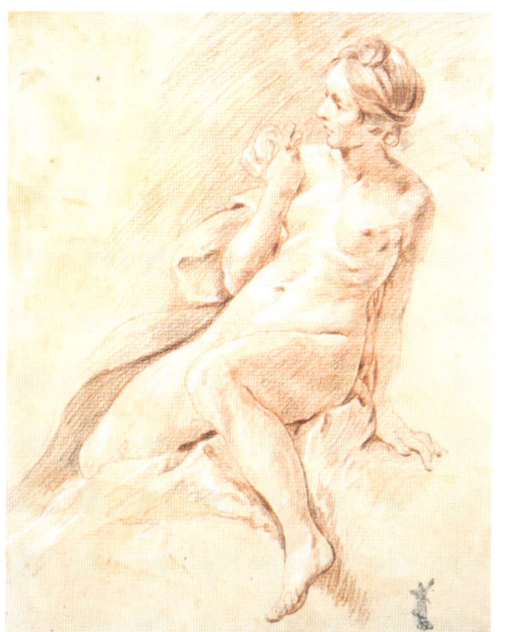

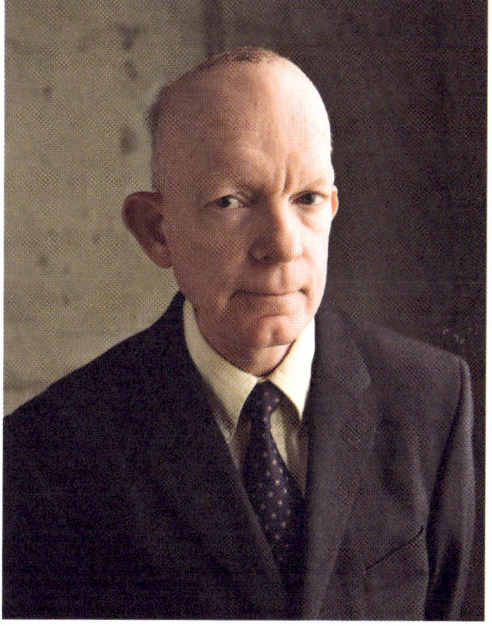

ABOVE: This drawing of a nude in the style of an 18th-century academic drawing was one of the works Landis gave to the Oklahoma City Museum of Art. As he gave it, he said that he wanted to donate artworks from his collection before undergoing heart surgery.

ABOVE: After years of donating his paintings to galleries and museums, Mark Landis's paintings are now on display in museums such as the Art Institute of Chicago under his own name.

Landis had used numerous identities to donate his fake paintings and drawings, resulting in the duping of more than 50 museums in 20 states across America. While he didn't inform the authorities, Leininger immediately warned the other museums.

Then, in September 2010, Landis went to the Paul and Lulu Hilliard University Art Museum in Lafayette, Louisiana, under his Jesuit guise of Father Arthur Scott. He donated a painting by American artist Charles Courtney Curran (1861–1942). Mark A. Tullos Jr, the museum director, asked the registrar, Joyce Penn, to inspect the painting. She examined it under ultraviolet light. The colours glowed as if they were made in the 21st century rather than the 19th. Next, an examination through a microscope revealed that the painting had probably been made over a photocopy of the original, that the artist had probably projected the photocopy on to a board and painted over the outline. Two months later, *The Art Newspaper* published an article about the affair, and other publishers followed. The earliest donation of a forged artwork by Landis they discovered was in 1987, and they tracked his fraudulent operations from that time.

Yet despite these revelations, Landis continued to produce forged works and donate them to unsuspecting galleries. His productivity even intensified. He reflected that his need to donate art to museums was like a calling: 'I don't think it's a calling like a priest or a rabbi has a calling, but since 1985, I felt an impulse to give away pictures. I'd watched so much TV and learned about philanthropists – wealthy people who gave to others – so I gave a picture away, and I was treated with so much respect and deference and friendship. Those are things I had never experienced before. I really liked it, and I got addicted to it.' He had admired the philanthropists who would donate valuable paintings and endow art museums ever since he was a teenager. In July 2011, he tried to donate artworks to a gallery under the name of Father James Brantley. Leininger heard of it and contacted him, but he did not reply. So Leininger sought advice from a former FBI agent who specialized in art crime, who told him that because no money had changed hands for the forgeries, Landis had not broken the law, even though his activities were fraudulent. Because, apart from a few gifts from curators, he did not gain economically from his actions, and because he gave his artworks to specialists who had the expertise to detect his forgeries but did not, he was protected in the eyes of the law.

Later, Landis explained that he thought a priest would be trusted, and that he 'liked being a priest and being kind to people. I remember once I was at a bus station and saw a family who had

OPPPOSITE, ABOVE:
In 2008, Landis took a briefcase full of art to the Oklahoma City Museum of Art, including this watercolour in the style of Paul Signac.

OPPOSITE, BELOW:
Sailboat at a Pier, 1920s, painted by Paul Signac – this was the type of simple watercolour sketch that Landis copied.

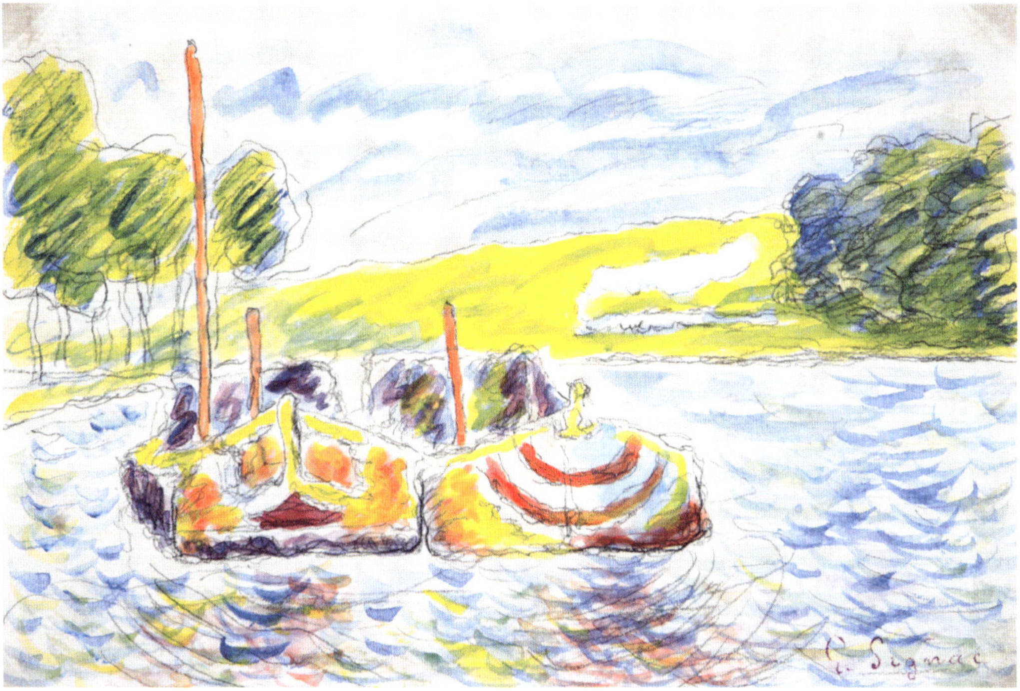

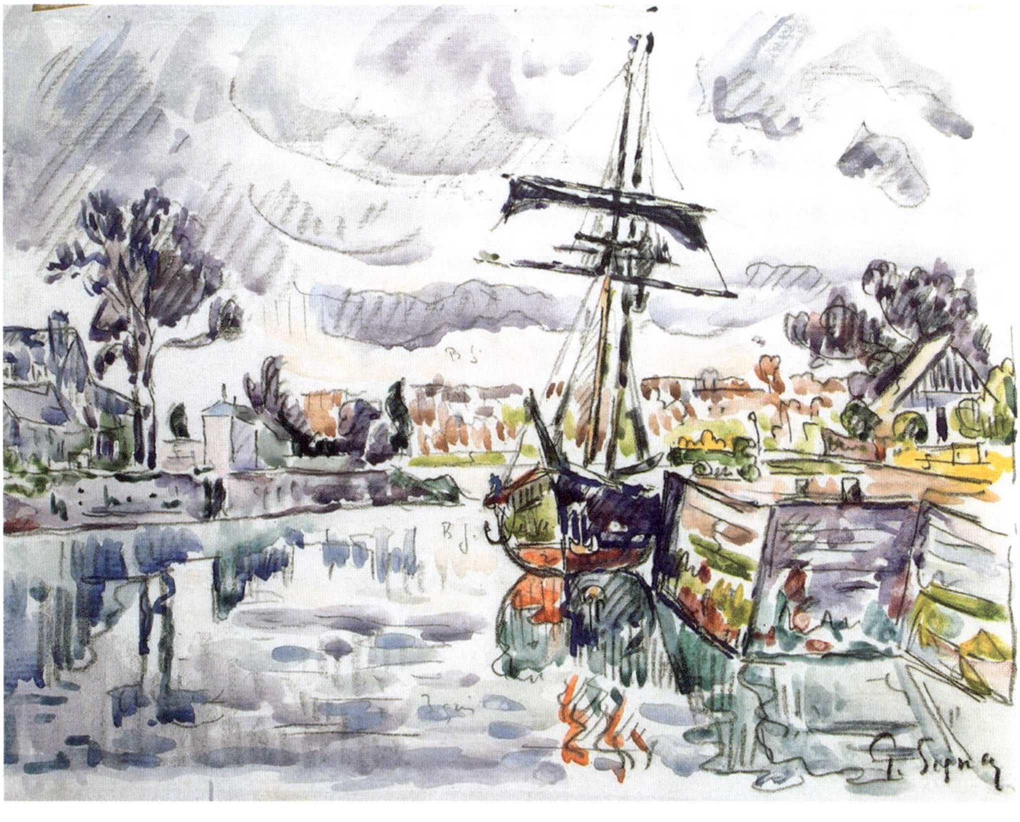

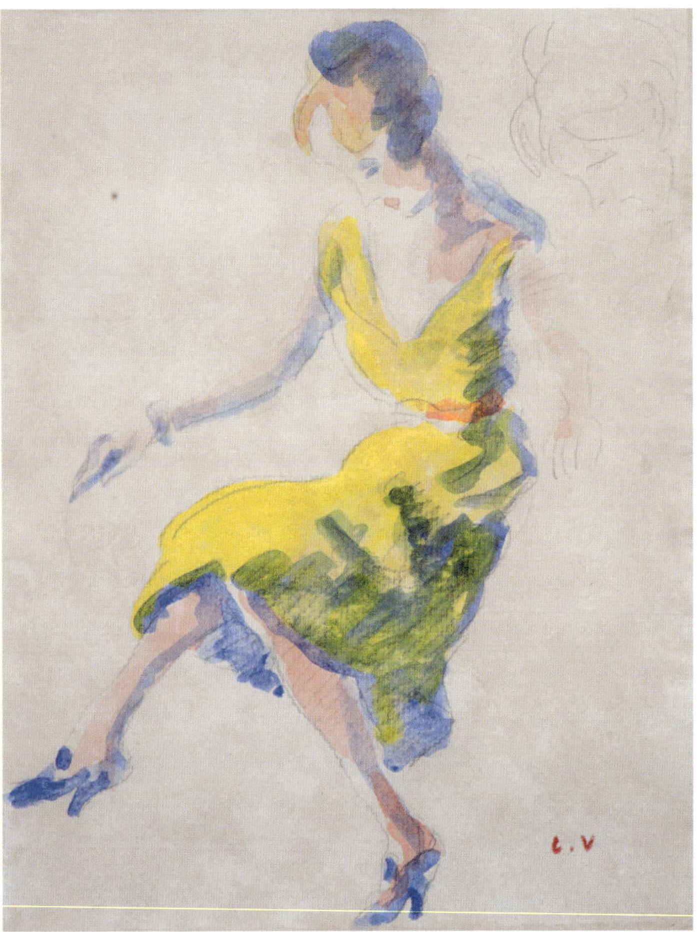

everything they owned tied up in boxes, so I watched all their things for them when they wanted to go off and do something. Then, when they came back, I gave them a blessing and sent them on their way. I've also comforted people at airports, with marital problems and so forth.'

ABOVE: Before Landis visited the Oklahoma City Museum of Art in 2007, he sent this watercolour, allegedly by French artist Louis Valtat, explaining that he wanted to give the work in memory of his late father, Lieutenant Commander Arthur Landis Jr.

Faux real

It is still not clear why so many institutions were so easily fooled by the artworks Landis produced. He believes it is because his works, for the most part, looked 'superficially authentic'. It also seems that he carefully analysed what each museum collected and wanted, and so he was sure that they would accept his work because it would fit well in their collections. His deceit embarrassed dozens of experts but he has said that he does not feel bad about it: 'I'm like Pinocchio. You let your conscience be your guide. If something's really wrong, you kind of know. I wasn't worried about being prosecuted.'

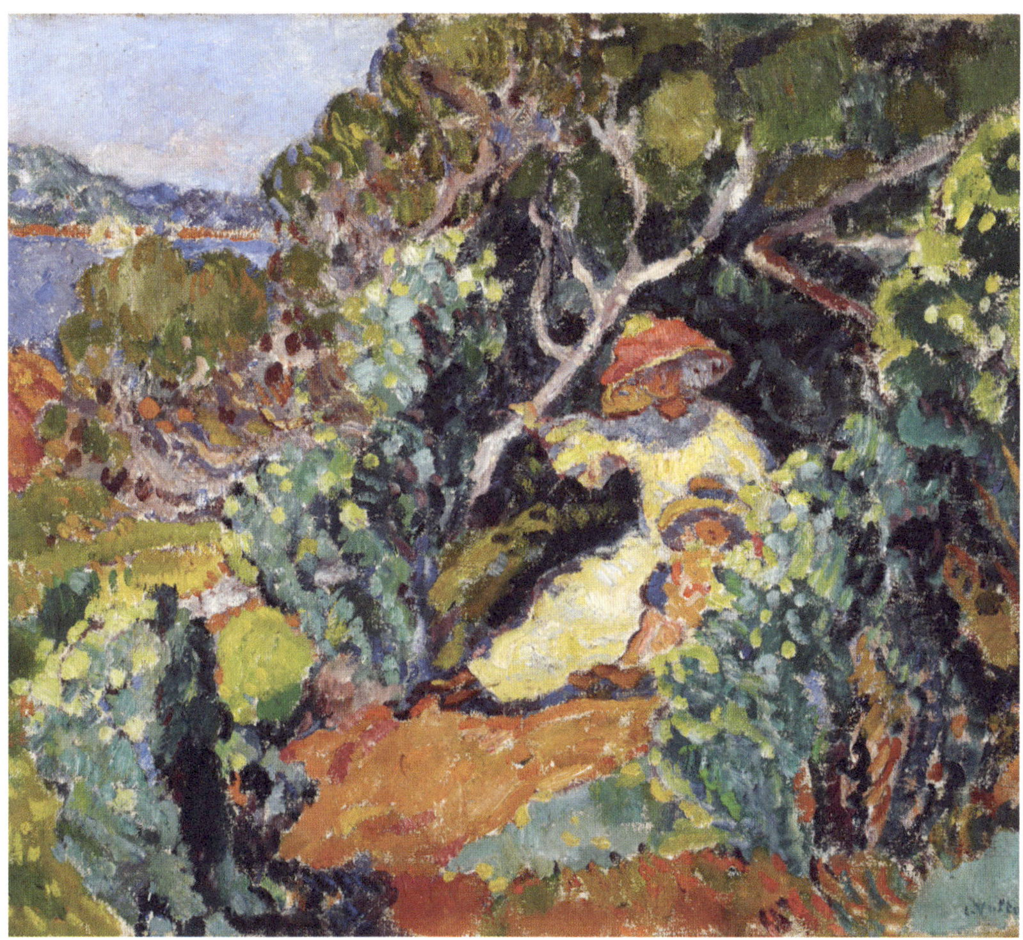

After his deception had been discovered and publicized, on April Fool's Day in 2012, the University of Cincinnati held an exhibition of approximately 60 forged artworks by him, curated by Leininger and called *Faux Real*. Landis was the guest of honour. It was the first time the two men had met, and Landis apologized for any problems he had caused. A decade later, an exhibition called *Creative Conscience* opened in New York City, aiming to separate Landis's art from his story as a forger and presenting it instead on its own artistic merit. Yet even now, it is not much clearer exactly why he produced – and is possibly still producing – all his forgeries and sought to fool so many art experts. In conversation, Landis said that he feels no resentment towards the art world at all. Officially, he harmed no one but, unofficially, he destabilized and damaged the art world.

ABOVE: *In the Sunshine*, painted in 1898–1910 by Louis Valtat, a French painter and printmaker associated with the Fauves ('Wild Beasts'), who were named for their loose painting styles and bold use of colour. They first exhibited together in 1905 at the Salon d'Automne in Paris, and Landis was fond of painting in this style.

CHAPTER 9

The Garden Shed Gang

Over a 17-year period, between 1989 and 2006, and with the assistance of his brother and elderly parents, Shaun Greenhalgh (b. 1961) sold many of his forged artworks around the world to museums, auction houses and private buyers. His forgeries were more diverse than any other in the history of art crime.

Overall the Greenhalgh family earned at least £825,000 from Shaun's forgeries, deceiving many experts, including several at highly respected institutions such as Tate Modern, the British Museum, the Henry Moore Institute, and auction houses Bonhams, Christie's and Sotheby's. It is likely that many more of the forgeries are still on display or in archives in various locations, considered by those around them to be original works by more skilful and famous artists.

'I felt so insignificant'

Growing up in Bolton in the north of England on a poor council estate, Greenhalgh had a natural artistic talent but was never formally trained. His first source of income came from selling pot lids and clay pipe busts that he made at school and sold at local flea markets, telling buyers they were antique and that he had dug them up. As a child, he said he often visited Bolton Museum: 'It kind of inspired me when I was little; I was always there. It was my second home in the school holidays.' He also visited Rome with his parents, where he became inspired by the work of Renaissance artists Sandro Botticelli, Pietro Perugino, Luca Signorelli and Raphael. He compared himself to them, saying, 'I felt so insignificant.' He would later emulate them.

One day, when he was in Bolton Library, he saw a pile of sheets of old paper on a table. They were being stripped from Victorian binders, to be replaced by acid-free covers. Many were watermarked with dates from the mid- to late 1800s. 'I asked if I could have some sheets, I think they were going to be thrown away,' he recalled.

The librarian told him to help himself. 'So I rolled the bundle up and went. At the time I thought they were just valuable in their own right.' He later used one of the sheets for a copy of a drawing by Degas that he sold, but that was much later.

At the age of 16, he left school with no qualifications. Needing to earn money, he tried his hand at several jobs, including an antiques dealer, which required him to go to London, where he was shown some unpublished research papers. In them, he saw at first hand 'what the experts look for and what ticks the boxes in the mind for authenticity'.

In the early 1980s, Greenhalgh met an art restorer whom he said he knew simply as Tom. When Tom discovered that Greenhalgh could paint, he commissioned him to produce copies of old paintings, for which he then fabricated provenances and sold at a profit. Eventually, Greenhalgh began to feel exploited and fell out with Tom. Independently, he developed and honed his own creative skills, working with oil paints, pastels and watercolours, as well as reliefs and various methods of sculpture using a wide range of materials. Yet despite his best efforts, no galleries were interested in his work. After trying repeatedly with no success, he became resentful towards the entire art world, and along with other members of his family, he devised a plan.

Replicating with precision

Using art books, photographs and catalogues, and a large variety of materials, Greenhalgh began creating a diverse range of forgeries of both modern and ancient art, including paintings, drawings, busts, sculptures, reliefs and metalwork. Undertaking scrupulous research, he followed up each artwork with fabricated authentications. To do this, he invented histories and provenances, or a fake documented history of ownership. The whole Greenhalgh family became adept at creating these fake documents and stories to support the authenticity of his forgeries, including counterfeit letters from the assumed artists or from invented owners of the works. He produced everything from 'ancient' Egyptian sculpture to a Renaissance 'masterpiece' and 19th-century watercolours to a mid-20th-century statue by Barbara Hepworth.

Greenhalgh's artistic talents were remarkable. He could replicate numerous artistic styles and techniques with precision, creating convincing copies of artworks by many different artists spanning different periods and places. He and his family conducted extensive research on the artworks he replicated. They studied the materials, techniques and historical contexts to ensure that their forgeries appeared authentic. He often used old materials and techniques to make his imitations appear aged and genuine. This attention to detail helped to convince experts of the legitimacy of the artworks. Generally, he focused on unfamiliar or disregarded works of art rather than the more well known; this avoided attracting too much scrutiny and attention.

As several experts and institutions examined the aesthetic qualities of Greenhalgh's works rather than conducting thorough scientific and historical analysis, the forgeries went undetected for a long time. Greenhalgh was a fast worker too. He once boasted that he could create a watercolour that looked as if it had been painted by American artist Thomas Moran (1837–1926) in half an hour. He claimed to have completed a statue that replicated an ancient Egyptian Amarna sculpture in three weeks. However, he needed his family's help. He was shy and did not like to use the telephone, so his mother, Olive, phoned potential buyers, and his father, George, met them face to face. They were an ordinary looking couple. George, in particular, was a mature, respectable-looking man in a wheelchair. Their story was that they owned the artworks as family heirlooms. Greenhalgh's older brother, George Jr, managed the money.

BELOW: *The Faun* was created by Shaun Greenhalgh and successfully passed off as a work by Paul Gauguin, selling at Sotheby's for £20,700 in 1994. Three years later it was bought by the Art Institute of Chicago and described by them as one of their most important acquisitions in the last twenty years.

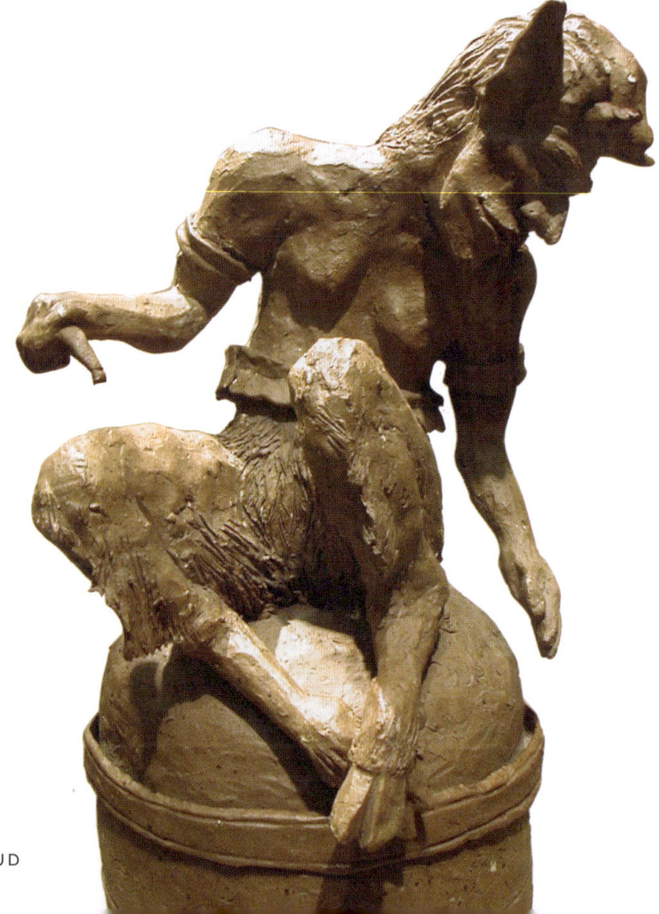

They also conjured up other members of the family to generate notions of legitimacy for the forgeries. These included Olive's father, who allegedly had owned an art gallery, a great-grandfather who it seemed had had the foresight to buy well at auctions, and an ancestor who had apparently worked for the mayor of Bolton as a cleaner and was given a Thomas Moran painting. Their business began to thrive and Greenhalgh produced artwork after artwork with broad scope.

Catalogue of artworks

Although not all his artworks are known, those that been verified are extensive and varied. The following are just some of the works known to have been made by Greenhalgh. In 1989, he created 'The Eadred Reliquary', a small purportedly 10th-century silver vessel that he said contained a relic of the True Cross of Jerusalem. He presented it to the University of Manchester, turning up soaking wet, claiming that he had found it in a river in Preston. Although the university concluded that the vessel was a fake, experts were unsure about the wood and bought it for £100. The following year, a still-life painting 'by' Samuel Peploe, a Scottish Post-Impressionist painter, supposedly inherited from Olive's grandfather, sold for £20,000. However, when paint began to flake off, the buyer cancelled the cheque. In 1992, private buyers bought an 'ancient Roman' silver plate for £100,000 and donated it to the British Museum in London, where it was displayed as genuine. Within a year of this, a sketch and a watercolour 'by' Thomas Moran were acquired by Bolton Museum. The Greenhalghs donated the sketch and the museum bought the watercolour for £10,000. In 1994, a ceramic sculpture 'by' Paul Gauguin, *The Faun*, was authenticated by the Wildenstein Institute (a French art institute that published catalogues

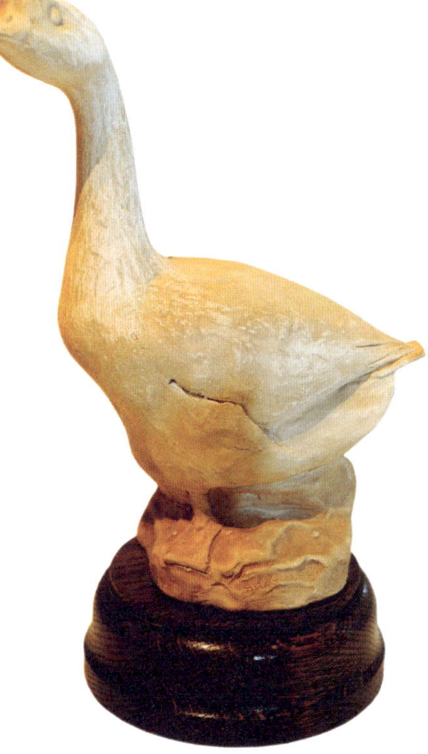

RIGHT: Copy of a sculpture of a goose by Barbara Hepworth, made by Shaun Greenhalgh, which was shown at the 'Fakes and Forgeries' exhibition at the Victoria and Albert Museum in London in 2010, put on by the Metropolitan Police Service Art and Antiques Unit.

raisonnés and scholarly inventories of artists including Monet and Gauguin) and sold at a Sotheby's auction for £20,700 to the private London dealers Howie & Pillar. Three years later, the sculpture was bought by the Art Institute of Chicago for $125,000 and remained on display until October 2007.

In 1995, the Greenhalghs tried to sell an 'Anglo-Saxon' ring through Phillips Auctioneers in London. However, it was determined by the British Museum to be a fake. During that same year, numerous sketches 'by' Thomas Moran sold in New York. Paintings by L. S. Lowry (1887–1976) were claimed by the Greenhalghs to have been owned by Olive's gallery-owner father. They forged letters from Lowry, inserting their names to make it look as if the family had been great friends with him. As Lowry was such a solitary figure, this could have seemed feasible. In 1999, George Greenhalgh withdrew two gold 'Roman' ornaments from Christie's when the auction house wanted to undertake a scientific analysis on them. The sculpture of a goose 'by' Barbara Hepworth was claimed by the Greenhalghs to have been given to the family in the 1950s 'by the curator of a museum in Leeds'. It was later sold to the Henry Moore Institute in Leeds for £3,000.

Mistake

The purchase of *The Amarna Princess* made headlines around the world. The Bolton Museum considered it a 'coup', as the statue was alleged to be worth even more, closer to £1 million. Extra security was installed and the museum's Egyptian curator, Angela Thomas, speculated, 'It may even be the case that this will lead on to us getting further funds to do more.'

Using the same provenance as *The Amarna Princess*, the Greenhalghs tried to

THE AMARNA PRINCESS

In the winter of 1999, Greenhalgh produced what has become known as *The Amarna Princess*, an alabaster sculpture allegedly depicting the daughter or wife of the ancient Egyptian Pharaoh Tutankhamun. In his 2015 book, *A Forger's Tale: Confessions of the Bolton Forger*, Greenhalgh states: 'By my mid-teens, I had tried a lot of sculptural styles, but I always seemed to end up back with the Egyptians.' In 1998, Greenhalgh had bought the 1892 sale catalogue of the contents of Silverton Park, Devon, the home of George Wyndham, 4th Earl of Egremont. Although Wyndham was not known as a collector, his ancestors had been, and a great number of art and antiquities had been acquired by his family. So he had amassed a large collection in his newly built mansion at Silverton, and among the lots in the sale were a group lot comprising 'a draped figure of a female, five marble statuettes and eight Egyptian figures'. The vagueness of the catalogue description played into Greenhalgh's hands. He created a statuette that he said 'was made to be sold at auction, there were some dealers I knew that I had dealt with [them] before and I wanted to get them back. They kind of ripped me off and it was kind of planned for them.' The figurine was a torso dressed in a fine diaphanous pleated gown. Her head, feet and arms had gone. 'My inspiration for her was a beautiful red granite version in the Louvre,' Greenhalgh reflected.

In 2002, the statuette was presented to Bolton Museum for a valuation. It stood at just 50.8cm (20in) tall, and the Egyptologist identified it as an Amarna Period torso of a princess. In 2003, Bolton council bought it for £440,000.

perform a similar scam again to support their ownership of what they claimed to be a 2,700-year-old Assyrian frieze. George suggested the family would be willing to part with their prized artefact for £500,000, but on closer inspection, the experts noticed that the carving of a bearded horseman leading two horses that was supposedly part of a documented bas-relief presented to the Assyrian king Sennacherib featured atypical harnesses, and even more significantly, contrary to the family's usual meticulousness, they misspelled several of the words in cuneiform, the ancient Mesopotamian script.

The museum contacted Scotland Yard's Art and Antiques Unit, which began an 18-month investigation into 84-year-old George Greenhalgh, his 83-year-old wife, Olive, and their 47-year-old son Shaun, an antiques dealer. Detectives were astonished by what they found at the Greenhalghs' end-of-terrace council house in Bolton. These included many forged artworks in original materials, along with detailed 'histories' removed from obscure archaeological records and historical texts. They also found evidence of tools and materials for making sculptures and paintings, and two further completed copies of *The Amarna Princess*. They discovered that the ancient Assyrian relic had been produced in three weeks by Greenhalgh using DIY tools from a local store.

BELOW: George, Olive, and Shaun Greenhalgh convinced the Bolton Museum to buy the fake statue, *The Amarna Princess*.

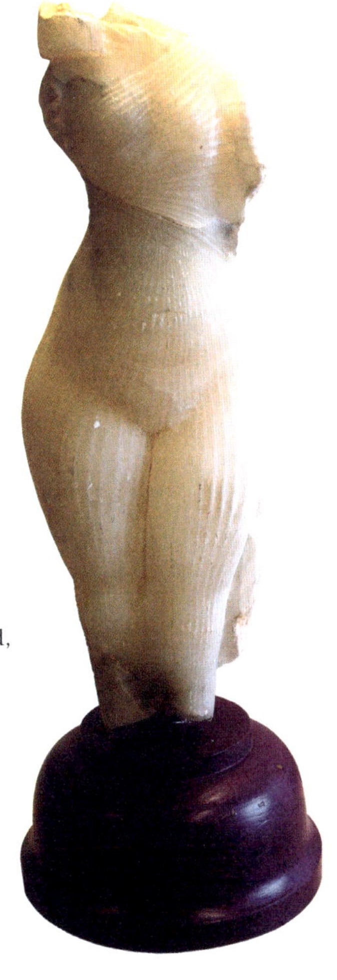

After admitting fraud and money laundering at the subsequent trial at Bolton Crown Court in 2007, Shaun Greenhalgh was sentenced to four years and eight months in prison. George and Olive were both given suspended sentences for their roles in the con. The family had assets of £404,250 confiscated by the court, and they were ordered to pay £363,000 to Bolton Museum. After the trial, Bolton Museum described itself as 'blameless', insisting that it had followed established procedure. The presiding judge vindicated the institution and any council staff involved, describing instead the 'ambitious conspiracy' and the sophistication of the deception.

Of the 120 forgeries which had been presented to art institutions, 44 were discussed during the trial. Yet Detective Sergeant Vernon Rapley from the Metropolitan Police Arts and Antiquities Unit observed: 'Looking at them now, I'm not sure the items would fool anyone, it was the credibility of the provenances that went with them.'

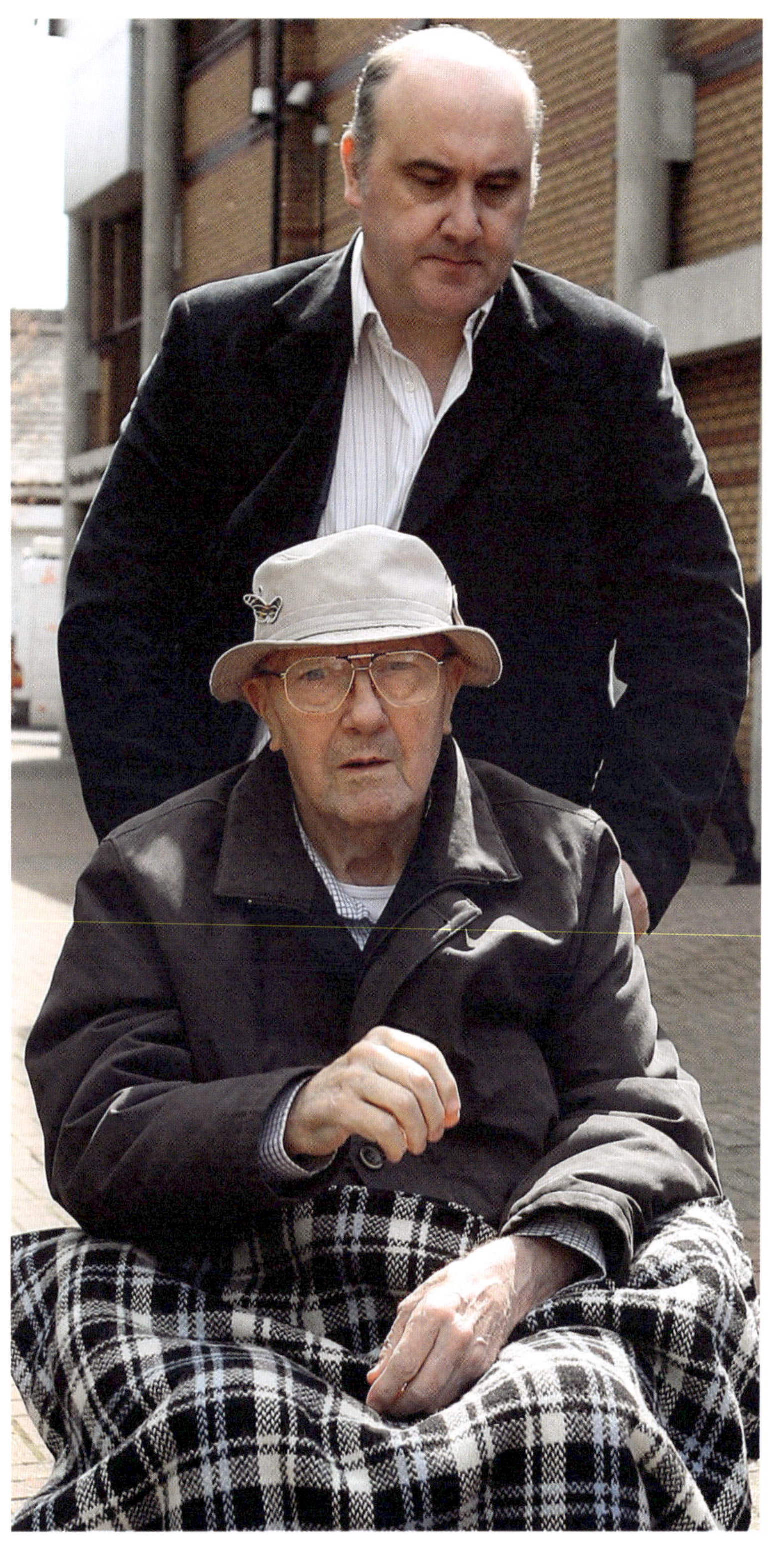

LEFT: Shaun Greenhalgh pushes his father George in his wheelchair from Bury Magistrates Court, Greater Manchester, where they were tried in 2008 over the fake Egyptian statue.

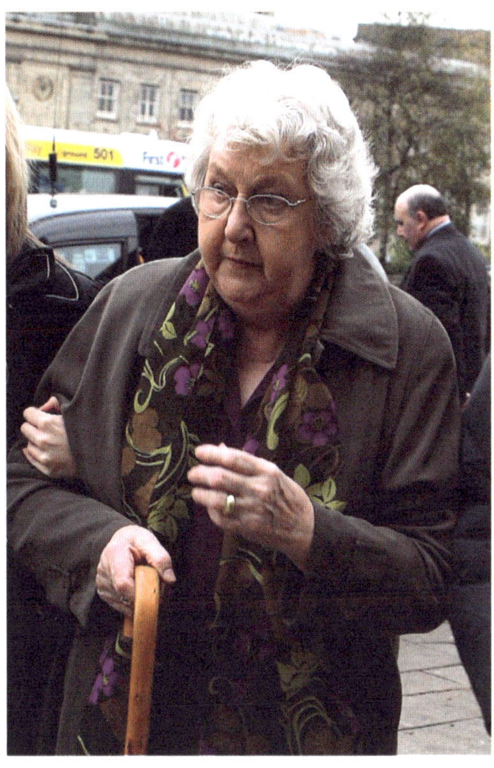

LEFT: Olive Greenhalgh, arrives at Bolton Crown Court to be sentenced, along with her husband and son, for defrauding galleries and antique dealers with counterfeit works of art.

Cottage industry

After the discovery of the fraud, the Greenhalgh family were described by the police as 'possibly the most diverse forgery team in the world'. They had established their elaborate cottage industry in South Turton, north of Bolton town centre. The Metropolitan Police built a mock-up of the shed where some of the artworks had been produced. Many of Greenhalgh's fakes, including *The Amarna Princess* and works professedly made by Barbara Hepworth and Thomas Moran, were displayed. After searching the house, police described what they saw: 'There were scores of sculptures, paintings and artefacts, hidden in wardrobes and in the garden shed. There were blocks of stone, a furnace for melting silver on top of the fridge, half-finished and rejected sculptures, a watercolour under the bed, a cheque for £20,000 dated 1993, and a bust of an American president in the loft.'

Had the Greenhalghs managed to sell all 120 artworks they had offered, it is estimated that they could have earned as much as £10 million. However, their bank records only went back six years, so the exact amount of money involved over the 17-year scam was never determined. What is known is that 'two Halifax accounts . . . one containing £55,173 and the other £303,646' were frozen pending a

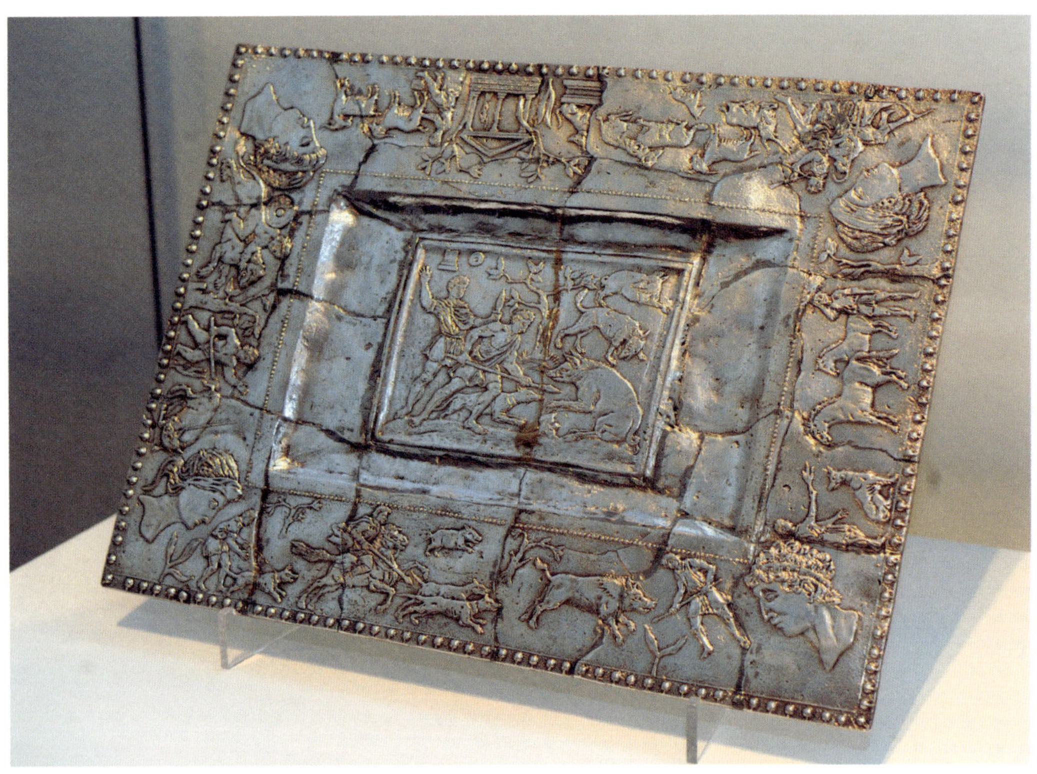

confiscation hearing in January 2008, and that Shaun Greenhalgh was convicted for 'conspiracy to conceal and transfer £410,392'. Estimates of the amount of money the family actually made vary from £825,000 to £1.5 million. Yet the family did not seem to make much use of the money they gained. They lived in a 'shabby' council house and possessed some basic but far from lavish belongings, including 'an old TV, battered sofa, and a Ford Focus', but not a computer. Detective Sergeant Rapley said that the conditions they lived in were 'relatively frugal', even 'abject poverty'. Olive Greenhalgh said she had never even travelled outside Bolton.

Shaun explained that as long as the provenance details seemed authentic, the dealers did not look into his works with too much detail: 'No matter how many mistakes, [dealers] were always blown away by the provenance. Often they hardly looked at the work.' He also said that he 'always had a tinge of guilt' about making forgeries. Although he was offered early release from prison, he declined. 'I've done the crime, I'll do the time,' he said. He wrote *A Forger's Tale* to avoid drawing portraits of other inmates' loved ones. In the book, he explained what really happened, and countered slanderous remarks that had been made by journalists against him and his family.

ABOVE: In 1991, George Greenhalgh claimed to have an item resembling the Risley Park Lanx — a large Roman silver dish (or lanx) discovered in 1729 in Risley Park, Derbyshire, England. In fact, Shaun made the item from melted Roman coins.

OPPOSITE, ABOVE AND BELOW: In 2010, the Metropolitan Police Service Art and Antiques Unit recreated Greenhalgh's workshop at the V&A Museum in London, England. These are two interior views of the recreated workshop – the garden shed – of Shaun Greenhalgh.

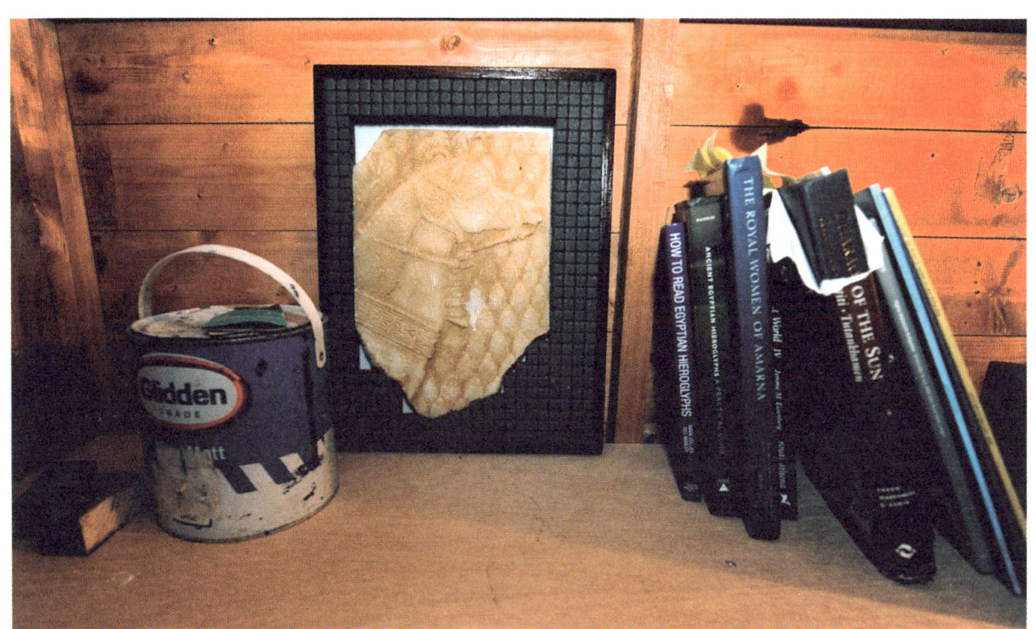
Glidden
HOW TO READ EGYPTIAN HIEROGLYPHS
ANCIENT EGYPTIAN HIEROGLYPHS A PRACTICAL GUIDE
THE ROYAL WOMEN OF AMARNA
OF THE SUN

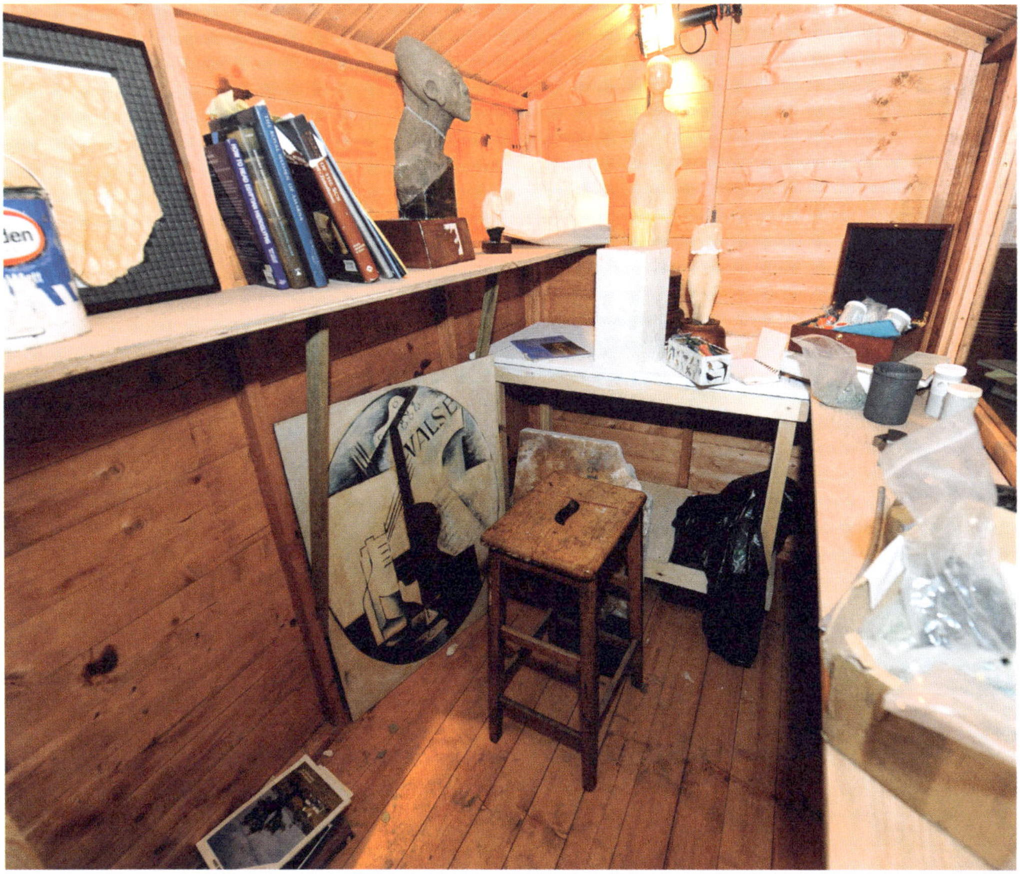

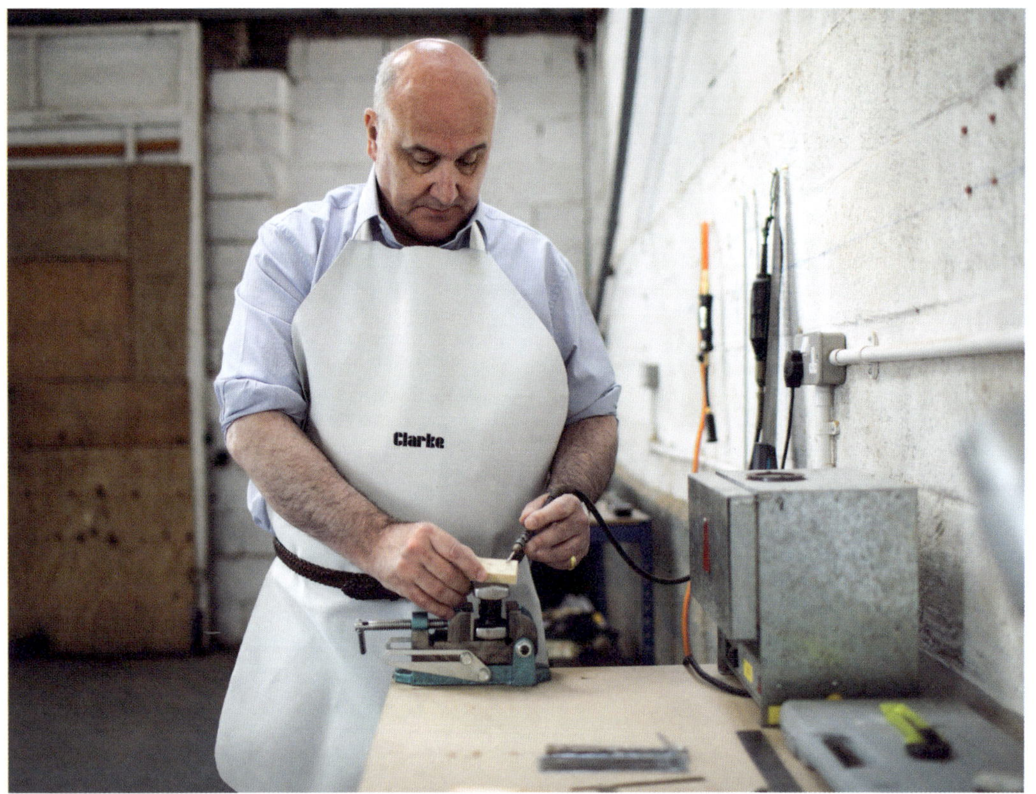

ABOVE: Shaun Greenhalgh at his studio unit in Darwen, Blackburn, May 2017.

While the major museums and auction houses tried to exonerate themselves from their mistakes, the general public was cynical and unimpressed by what they perceived as the experts' incompetence and the law's heavy-handedness. More enlightened experts later commented that the fakes were obvious. However, as many have said, it is almost certain that there are a number of forgeries still circulating within the art market. In 2011, *The Amarna Princess* returned to Bolton Museum to be displayed in an exhibition of fakes and forgeries.

Fame

In January 2009, BBC Two broadcast a dramatization of the Greenhalgh story called 'The Antiques Rogue Show', but following this, in a letter from his prison to the *Bolton News*, Greenhalgh complained about the depiction of himself and his family, calling the drama 'character assassination'. Three years later, he appeared in another BBC documentary called *The Dark Ages: An Age of Light*. Polish-British art critic and television documentary producer and presenter Waldemar Januszczak once bought a 'Gauguin' forged by Greenhalgh, but nevertheless later commissioned him to make a

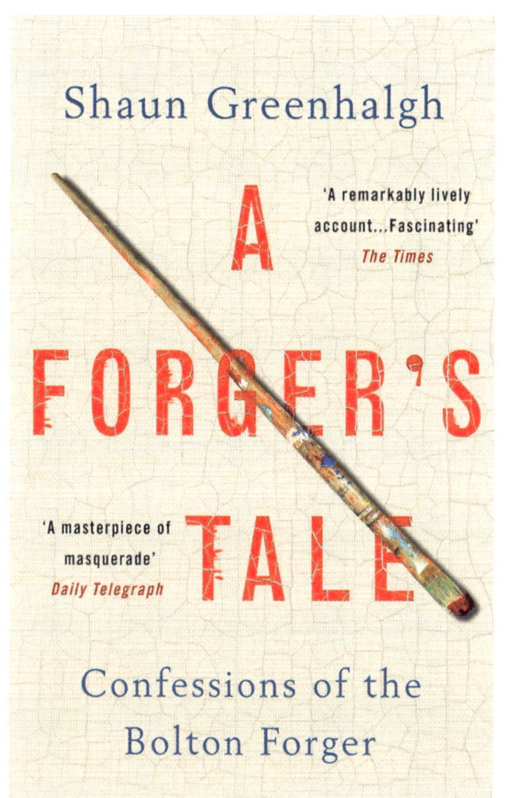

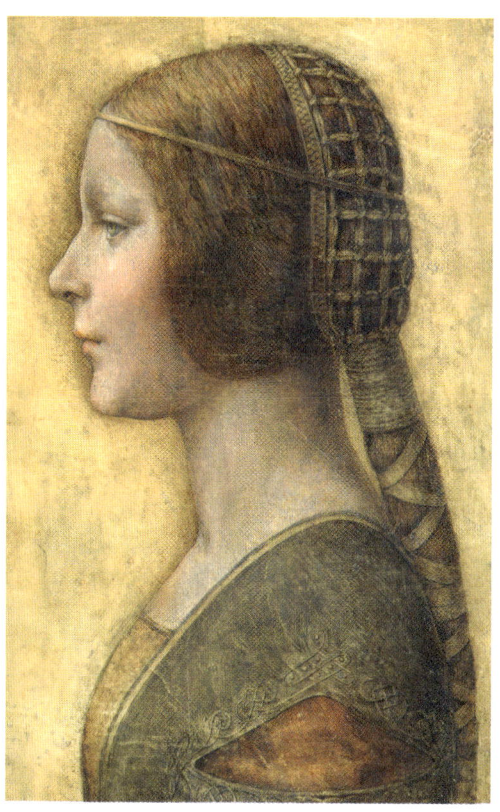

copy of an Anglo-Saxon brooch to be featured in a TV documentary. Other filmmakers, including the BBC, also commissioned him. In November 2015, as part of the publicity for *A Forger's Tale*, an article in *The Sunday Times* mentioned his claim that he created the 1495–6 ink and chalk drawing *La Bella Principessa* attributed to Leonardo da Vinci. In the book Greenhalgh wrote, 'I drew this picture in 1978 when I worked at the Co-op [supermarket]. The "sitter" was based on a girl called Sally who worked on the checkouts.' This claim has been dismissed by various experts. In October 2019, he appeared in the short documentary series *Handmade in Bolton*, in which he remade four objects from the past using traditional materials and methods.

ABOVE, LEFT: The cover of Greenhalgh's autobiography, which he wrote in prison and published in 2018. It was chosen as the *Observer*'s Best Art Book of the Year.

ABOVE, RIGHT: Leonardo da Vinci painted *La Bella Principessa* (*The Beautiful Princess*) in coloured chalks and ink on vellum in 1495–6. Greenhalgh claimed that he, not Leonardo, is the artist.

CHAPTER 10

The Last Word in German Art

German-born artist Lothar Malskat (1913–1988) became known for his convincing forgeries of works by famous artists such as Picasso and Chagall that he sold to galleries and collectors worldwide. His expertise in imitating various styles made him one of the more notorious art forgers of the 20th century.

Hailing from Königsberg, Germany (which became Kaliningrad, part of the Soviet Union, in 1946), Lothar Malskat worked as a church painter and restorer in post-Second World War Germany. He had studied art at the Kunstakademie Königsberg and there his professors praised him for his 'extraordinary, almost uncanny versatility'. Filled with optimism, he moved to Berlin seeking fame, but this eluded him.

Medieval restoration

In 1937, Ernst and Dietrich Fey were tasked with restoring murals in the Cathedral of St Peter in Schleswig. Professor Ernst Fey, Dietrich's father, was a respected art historian and restorer in Berlin, whose prestige was reinforced in the early 1930s by the rise of the Nazi party when he became friendly with the Luftwaffe commander-in-chief Hermann Göring. Accompanied by his son Dietrich, Professor Fey restored paintings in churches throughout Silesia – an area of Central Europe that lies mostly within Poland, with small parts in the Czech Republic and Germany. Ernst taught Dietrich his historical expertise and his ability to ingratiate himself with powerful patrons, but he lacked technical painting abilities. Just before the Second World War in the late 1930s, the Feys received several prestigious ecclesiastical commissions, but they were in urgent need of an assistant just when the young Lothar Malskat came asking for work. Professor Fey employed Malskat to whitewash his home, and after

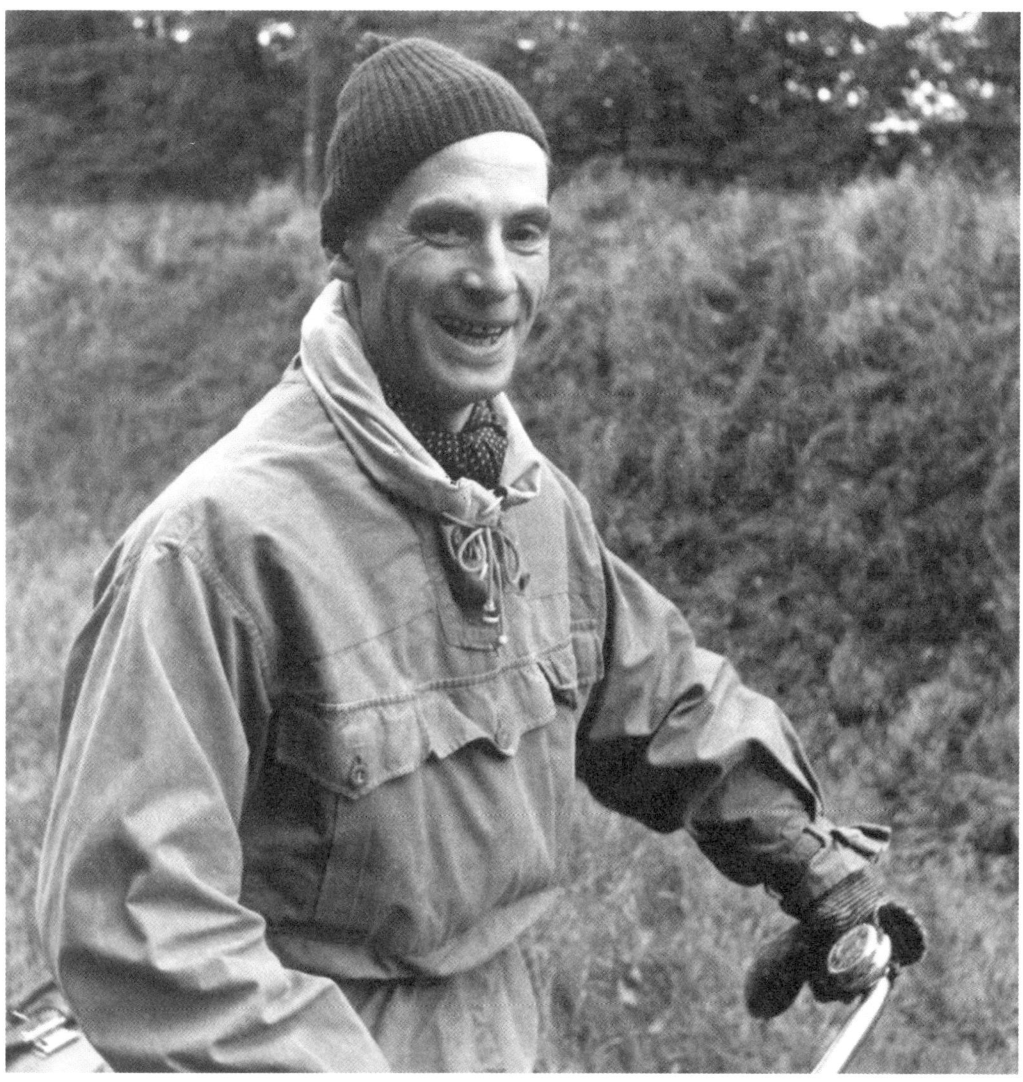

ABOVE: Lothar Malskat on his bike.

chatting to the house decorator and discovering his love of art, Ernst lent Malskat books on ecclesiastical art.

In the Cathedral of St Peter in Schleswig, Dietrich Fey had been asked to remove some heavy-handed restorations from 1888 and restore the medieval paintings to their former glory. However, as he scraped away the 19th-century paint, shockingly, he also accidentally removed most of the original work. Rather than admit what had happened, he asked Malskat if he could repaint the murals and pretend that these were the restored original works. Malskat made a good job of the medieval forgery, but he made several mistakes, including featuring turkeys, which were unknown in 14th-century Europe, and modelling the Virgin Mary's face on the contemporary

Austrian film star Hansi Knoteck. Nevertheless, the imagery was well received.

Fast forward to the end of the war, and Malskat returned from fighting. Ernst Fey had died, but in Hamburg he and Dietrich Fey set up a forgery studio. Fey took care of the business and sales aspects while Malskat produced forgeries of paintings and drawings by artists including Edvard Munch, Henri de Toulouse-Lautrec and Marc Chagall. Fey supplied Malskat with canvases and a list of artists' names he could sell, including Munch, Chagall, Toulouse-Lautrec, Rembrandt, Watteau, Corot and Picasso. The business flourished, and to keep up with orders from collectors in Frankfurt and Munich, Malskat had to work fast. He later reflected that he could sometimes copy an old painting in a day and do a Picasso in an hour, 'but what I liked best was to do new paintings in the style of the French Impressionists'. Fey sold the paintings to art dealers, who sold them on to the many buyers that emerged after the war. Most of the new collectors were inexperienced, and it was never made clear if any of the dealers knew that they were handling forgeries. People were aware by then that many works belonging to private, mainly Jewish, owners, had been looted by the Nazis, so these artworks appearing on the market after the Holocaust were rarely questioned. Malskat simply provided written guarantees that none of the works they were selling had been stolen. For all the transactions, he was generally paid a fifth of Fey's earnings.

In 1948, Fey was commissioned to restore damaged frescoes in the Marienkirche (St Mary's Church) in Lübeck, Germany. Built between 1265 and 1352, the building is an important medieval basilica and Fey naturally hired Malskat. The main problem with this restoration was that they had no photographic documentation of the original appearance of the frescoes. So Fey and Malskat restored what they could of the remaining frescoes and had to imagine what had been in the other areas. Malskat repainted apostles and saints who had previously been faint and incomplete, adding his own interpretations. He worked quickly with bold lines and bright colours, covering in days the areas that would have taken most artists and conservators months. By the summer of 1950, he had recreated all the 14th-century murals in the nave. During that time, only one expert seems to have managed to climb the 21m (70ft) scaffold uninvited: a doctoral student named Johanna Kolbe. Although she did not see Malskat at work or meet him, she was able to scrutinize the paintings with a magnifying glass at close hand, rather than with binoculars from far below. Shocked by what she saw, she told the local government that the paint was applied 'much too thickly' and also noted some idiosyncrasies in the nave, such as

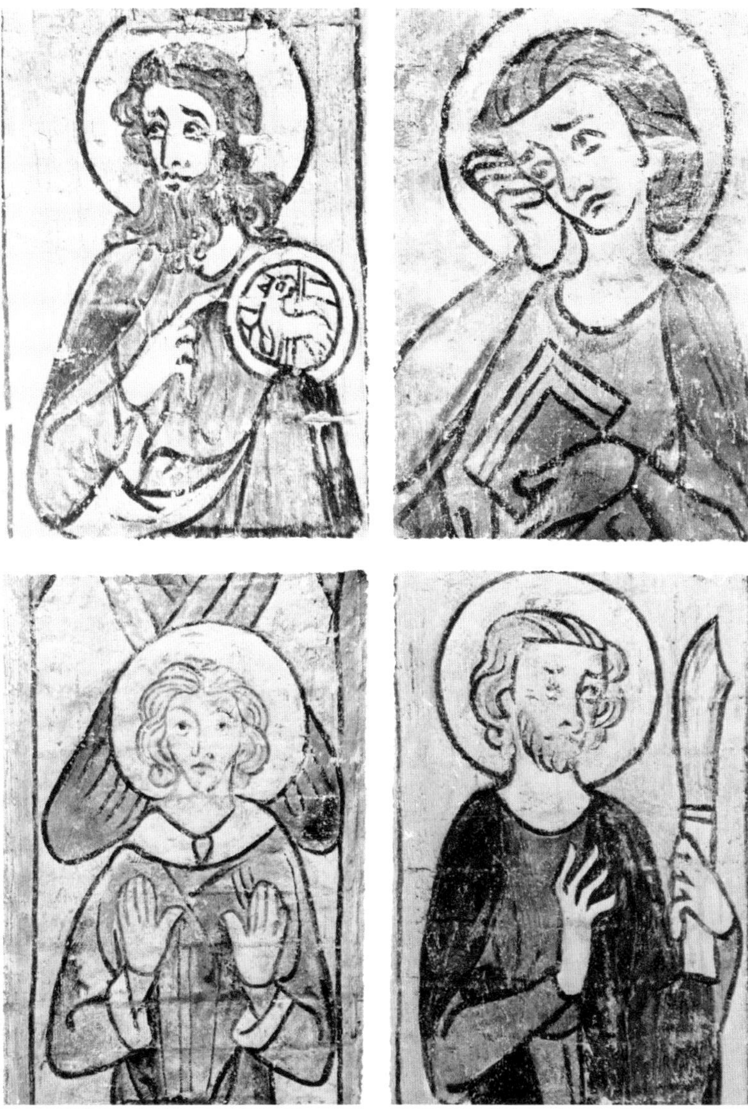

LEFT: Four seemingly old frescoes adorn the walls of Marienkirche in Lübeck, Germany. However, they are now generally believed to be expertly painted forgeries by Malskat.

the disappearance of Mary Magdalene's sandals. When he heard of this, Fey accused her of defamation and, worried about repercussions, she stopped talking about it. Meanwhile, while he was working, Malskat claimed to have discovered hidden medieval frescoes beneath layers of plaster and whitewash. He proceeded to paint them in full colour.

Resentment

When the restoration of the Marienkirche was finished in September 1951, scholars were shocked to see the previously unknown medieval frescoes. They were fresh and new-looking, and no one else had

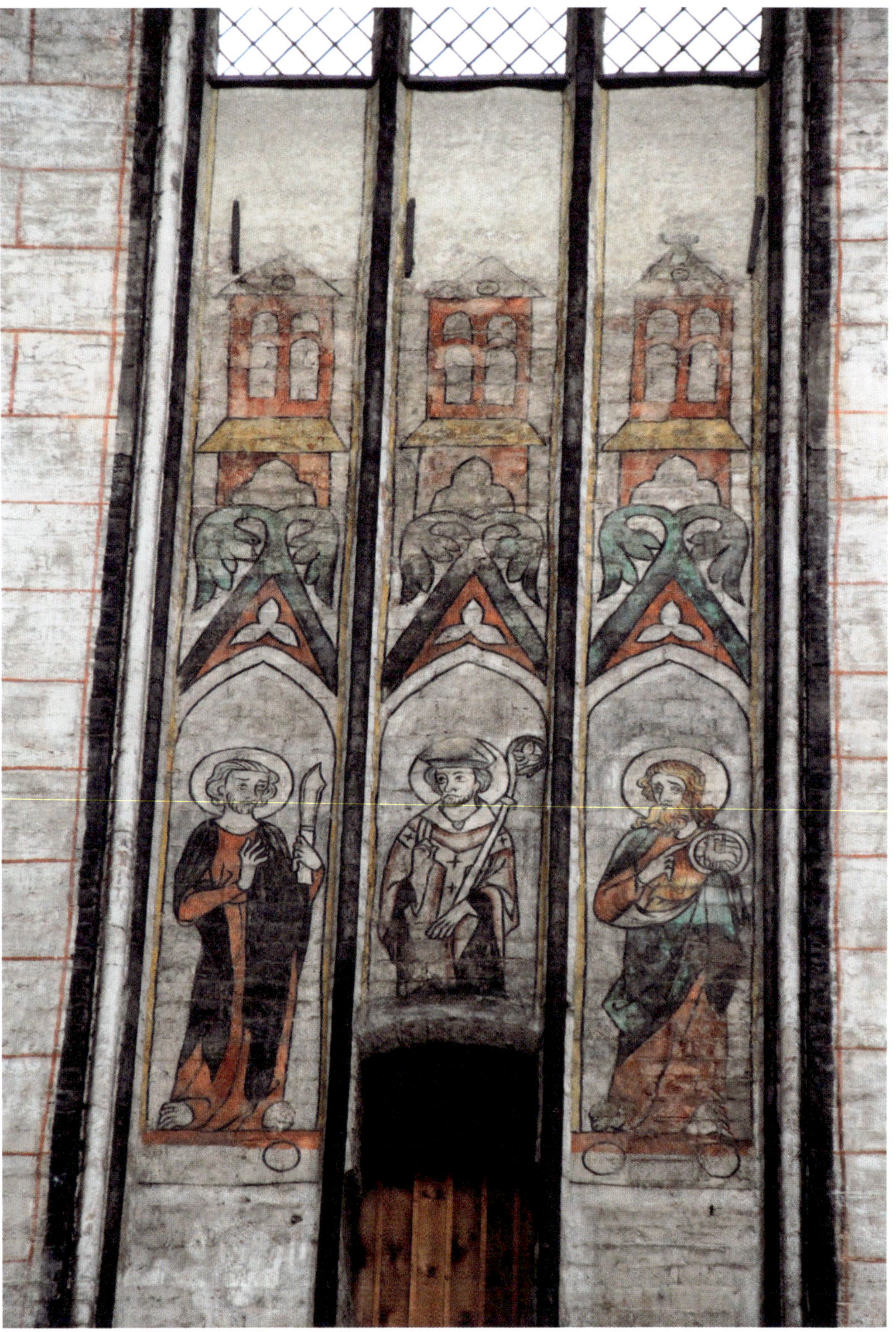

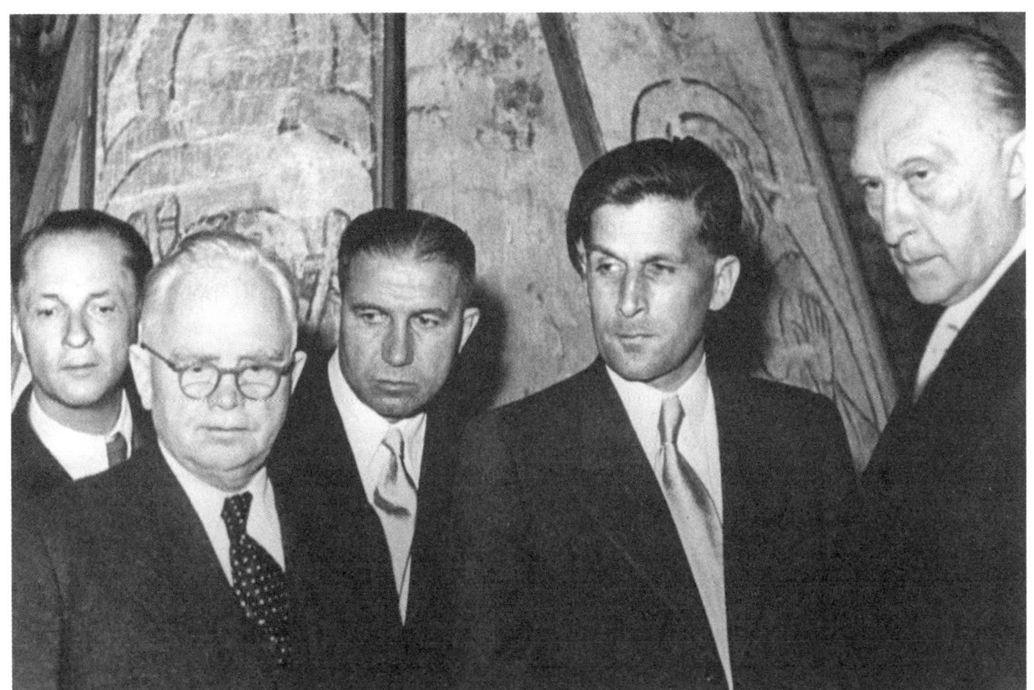

known about them. It was an uplifting occurrence after the darkness of the war. A huge press event celebrated the 700th anniversary of the founding of the church, and two million postage stamps were printed depicting the newly discovered frescoes. Around the world various magazine articles were published about the paintings. *TIME* magazine described them as 'a major artistic find', informing readers that 'the interior of the Marienkirche looks more as its original decorators intended than it has for five hundred years.' Over the following months, 100,000 people visited the church, boosting Lübeck's declining economy with revenue from tourism.

Meanwhile, Malskat was becoming increasingly resentful. While restoring the church, he and Fey had

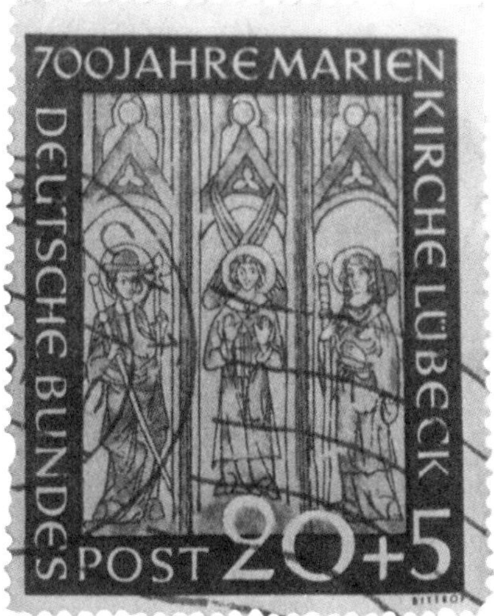

OPPOSITE: Malskat claimed to have discovered the supposedly Gothic frescoes in the clerestory zone of the choir when he was restoring the church. At the time, they were hailed as medieval masterpieces.

ABOVE: Dietrich Fey stands second from the right along with prominent politicians in the Marienkirche in Lübeck on its 700th anniversary.

ABOVE, RIGHT: This special stamp of the Deutsche Post (Bundespost) was made of the painting in the Marienkirche for the 700th anniversary of its inauguration.

frequently quarrelled. Fey had paid him just 110 deutsche marks a week out of the 88,000 deutsche mark budget for the project. When Malskat protested that he was doing all the work, Fey said that he was just an anonymous assistant, while he, Fey, had been commissioned for the work and was acclaimed and respected. Perhaps even more than the low pay, Malskat resented his anonymity. As he had worked in the church, he had become attached to the paintings, and he had marked some of the figures he painted with his initials. At one point he wrote, 'All Paintings in this Church are by Lothar Malskat', but Fey had this whitewashed immediately. So when he saw Fey take full credit for the murals and receive all the honours, including an additional 150,000 deutsche marks in restoration money, and be nominated for a prestigious university professorship in Bonn, he was livid.

Sueing himself

Eventually, he announced to the media that he had painted the frescoes himself. No one believed him. So he asked Fey to verify that he had fabricated the new section, but Fey denied all knowledge. So in May 1952, seething, he went to a police station and announced that the Marienkirche murals were fake, and that he had created the 'medieval' paintings on Fey's orders. Next, he hired a lawyer and told

BELOW: As part of the Committee of Inquiry in the Marienkirche in Lübeck, white-coated Professor Scheeper examines some of the controversial paintings. At the same time, Fey is leaving the scaffolding, and Malskat is setting up a camera.

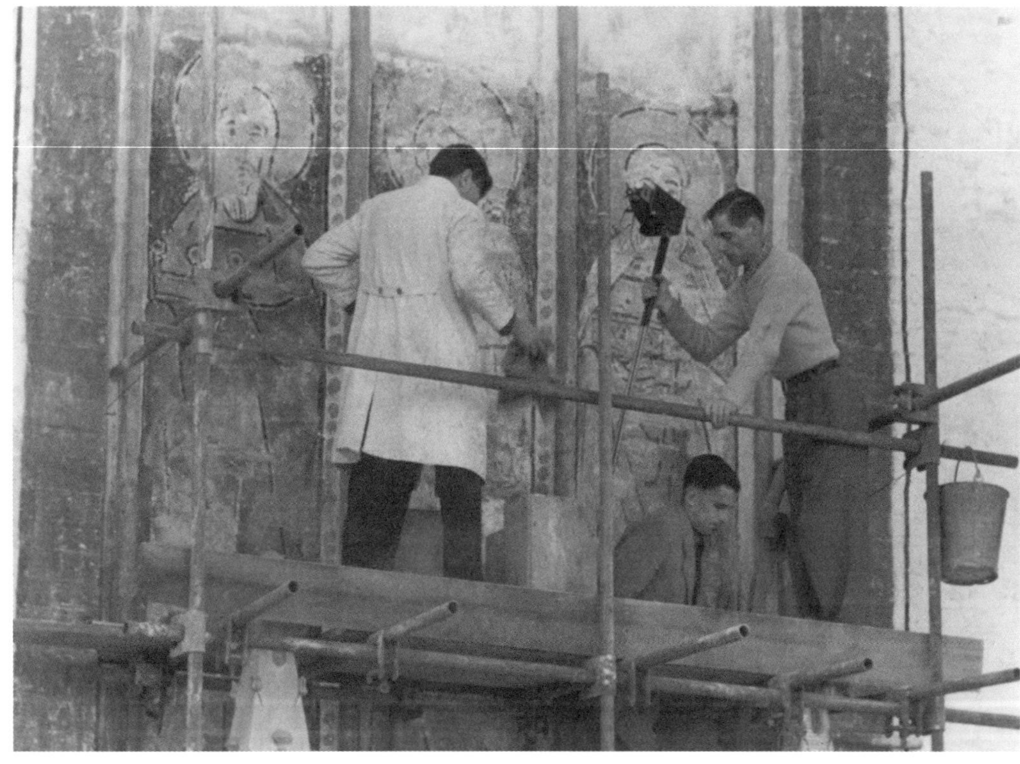

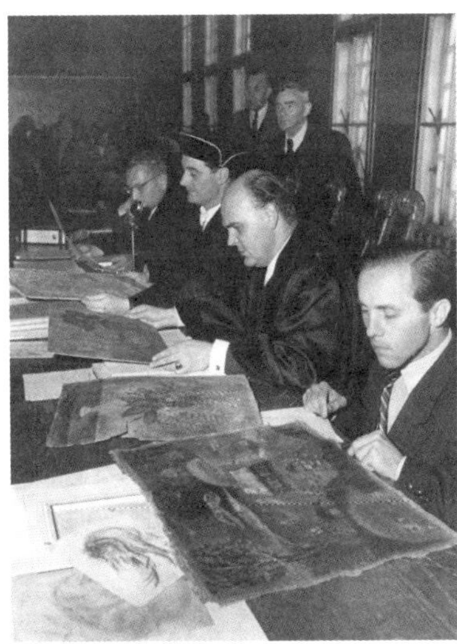
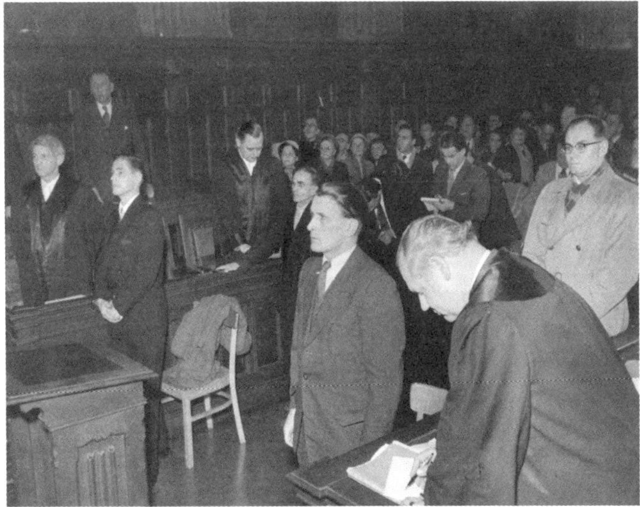

ABOVE: In May 1954, Malskat stood before the Second Criminal Chamber of the Lübeck Regional Court with presiding judge Dr Brammer and the assessors as they viewed the forged paintings. The verdict was announced in January 1955.

him about the counterfeit restoration work, and also about the fake paintings 'by' artists including Picasso, Munch and Rembrandt. Supplying the lawyer with evidence, he instructed him to file charges against both Fey and himself, legally compelling the police to act.

Two days later, Fey was detained while police searched his house. They found 7 paintings and 21 drawings that Malskat had made, including forgeries of Matisse, Degas and Chagall. A commission of experts was sent to examine the Marienkirche murals. In their report, they wrote: 'The twenty-one figures in the choir are not Gothic but painted freehand by Malskat. The painting described as old by the restorer, Fey, does not lie on the medieval layer [of mortar] but on a post-medieval laycr, and cannot, if for this reason alone, be considered original.' The report also established that the murals in the nave had been repainted. Then the Bishop of Lübeck, Dr Johannes Pautke, spoke: 'If the restorer Dietrich Fey has fraudulently succeeded in getting his work recognized as faithful restoration, this was possible only because of an extremely cunning deception which misled not only the church administration . . . but also curators and art experts.'

The trial began on 10 August 1954. Malskat showed a short film of the unpainted walls with no trace of medieval frescoes and pointed out that within them he had painted some portraits of people born long after the period, including the Russian mystic and faith healer Grigori Rasputin (1869–1916) and the actress Marlene Dietrich (1901–1992). When Malskat was asked why he admitted to the work, he told the court, 'Everybody raved about my beautiful murals, yet Fey got all the credit. Nobody even knew my name.' Once he had all their attention, he described how easy he had found imitating

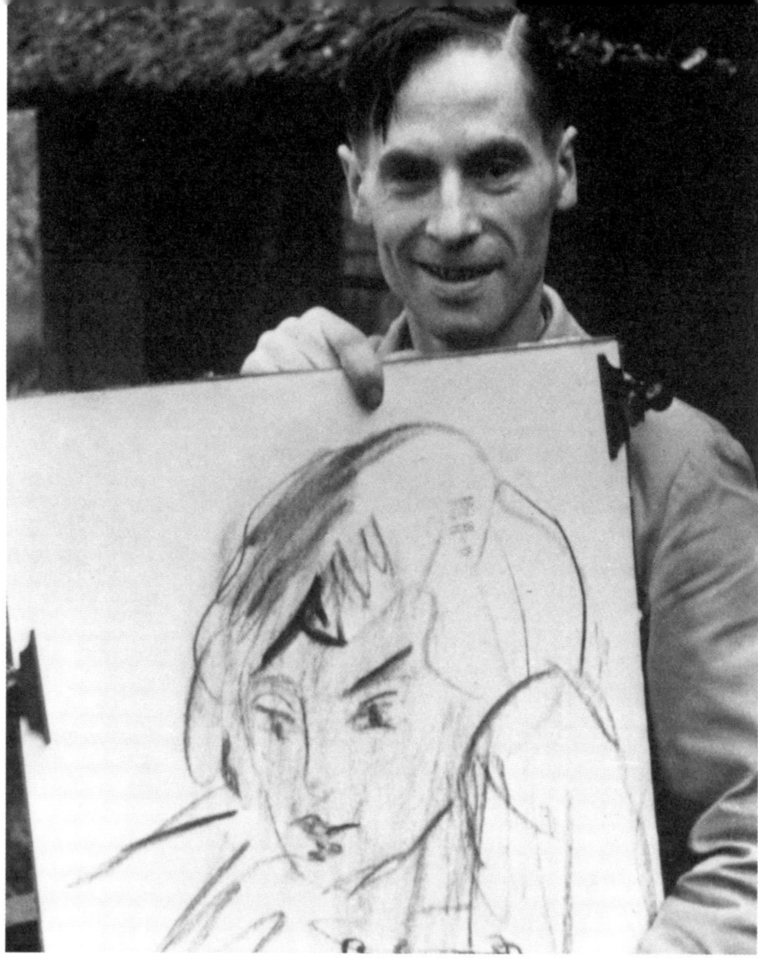

LEFT: Lothar Malskat in 1954, holding a drawing in the style of Henri Matisse, which he drew in 80 seconds.

14th-century painting. At the same time, he criticized the experts who had praised his forgeries. 'One art critic raved about the "prophet with the magic eyes",' he laughed. 'It was modelled on my father.'

The experts were furious that they had been tricked. In January 1955, after more than five months of evidence, the court reached a verdict and the presiding judge announced: 'Although the ascertainable material damage done may not have been excessive, it seriously endangered the restoration of Marienkirche as a whole.' Fey was sentenced to 20 months in prison and Malskat to 18 months for fraud and deception. The frescoes in the Marienkirche were all removed, except for a section above the nave, which was left to serve as a warning to future counterfeiters.

Later reputation

Malskat's reputation as an artist was ruined and he struggled to find work. Fey also never restored his career in conservation. Malskat fled to Sweden and there he began trying to benefit from his infamy and

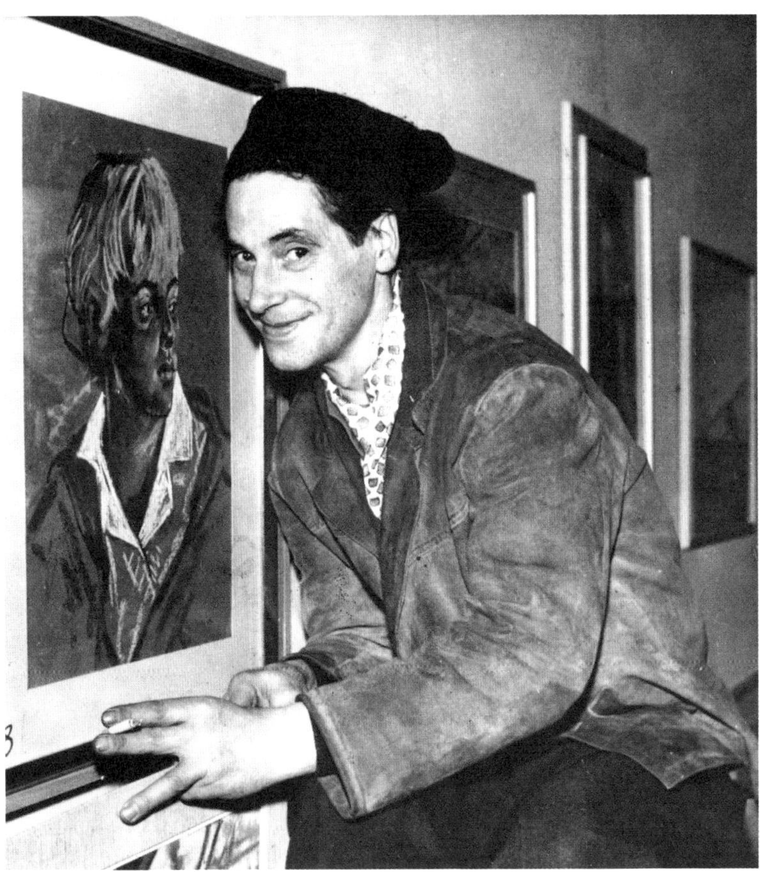

LEFT: Malskat stands next to one of his works in a 1959 exhibition in the Patriotic Building at the Trostbrücke in Hamburg.

prove his creative ability by soliciting commissions. He received some jobs to decorate the walls of restaurants and inns, including Stockholm's Tre Kroner Restaurant in the medieval Gothic style, and he repainted his Schleswig turkeys in murals for the Royal Tennis Court, but ultimately he faded into obscurity.

A fictionalized version of his painting of the Marienkirche frescoes appeared in the 1986 novel *The Rat* by German novelist, poet, playwright, illustrator, graphic artist, sculptor and winner of the Nobel Prize in Literature, Günter Grass. Malskat's forgeries are a major theme of the novel as a symbol of the alleged corruption of post-war Germany.

CHAPTER 11

The Perfect Forger

Ageing his paintings by colouring them with a mixture of coffee and cigarette butts, or baking them in a pizza oven, Tony Tetro (b. 1950) created many paintings, drawings and prints that mimicked original art by famous artists.

However, he maintained that rather than an art forger, he was an 'emulator' who copied artworks, not a forger, as he did not intend to sell them as originals. Nonetheless, in a career that spanned over 40 years, he copied artworks by artists in every genre that were regularly passed off as authentic in museums, galleries and auction houses worldwide.

BELOW: Tony Tetro stands next to one of his paintings for a newspaper interview.

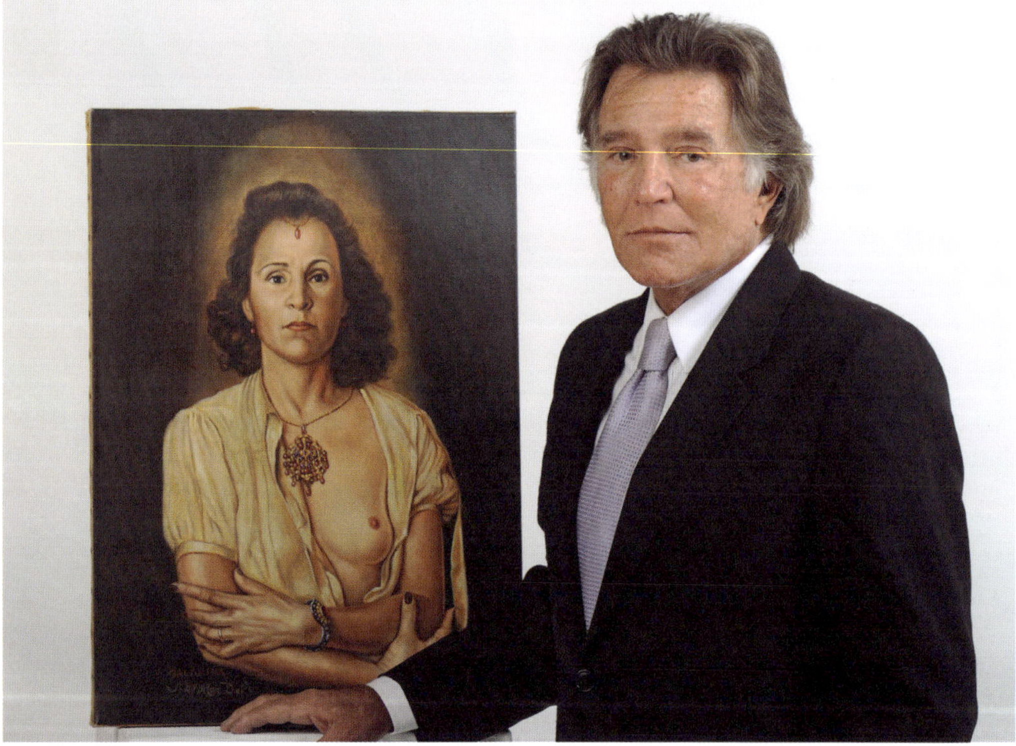

Self-taught

Born in Fulton, Oswego County, New York, Tetro was one of four children. At the age of 16, he married his high school girlfriend. Three years later, he moved to southern California and worked as a furniture salesman. A few years after that, he and his wife divorced. By 1972, he had read the 1969 book *Fake!* by Clifford Irving (1930–2017) about the forger Elmyr de Hory (see Chapter 12), and he decided he could do that. He made a drawing based on a 1920s oil painting of a nude by Amedeo Modigliani and sold it to a relatively small art dealer, and the success of that spurred him on. From then on, he studied art earnestly, reading books, visiting museums, and experimenting with paint, canvas and paper. Using the age-old learning process of copying the masters, he also painted and experimented with methods to produce the craquelure that often occurs in old paintings. He travelled to Florence, Italy, and visited the Uffizi Gallery where, he recalled, he met a man called Carlo who taught him to paint flesh like the old masters.

From 1972 to 1989, he produced many paintings, lithographs and portraits, copying the styles of great artists from the 17th to the 20th centuries, including Rembrandt, Caravaggio (1571–1610), Giambattista Tiepolo (1696–1770), Matisse, Miró, Chagall, Salvador

BELOW: The Uffizi Gallery, Florence, at night, where in the early 1970s Tetro met a man named Carlo who taught him to paint flesh like the old masters.

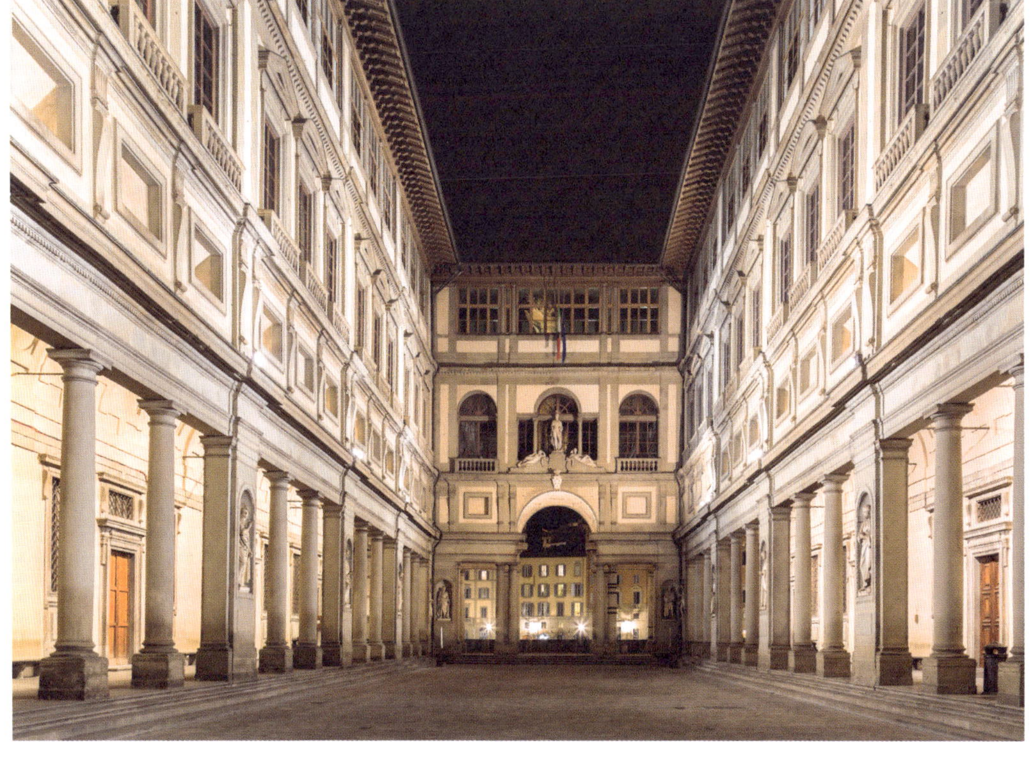

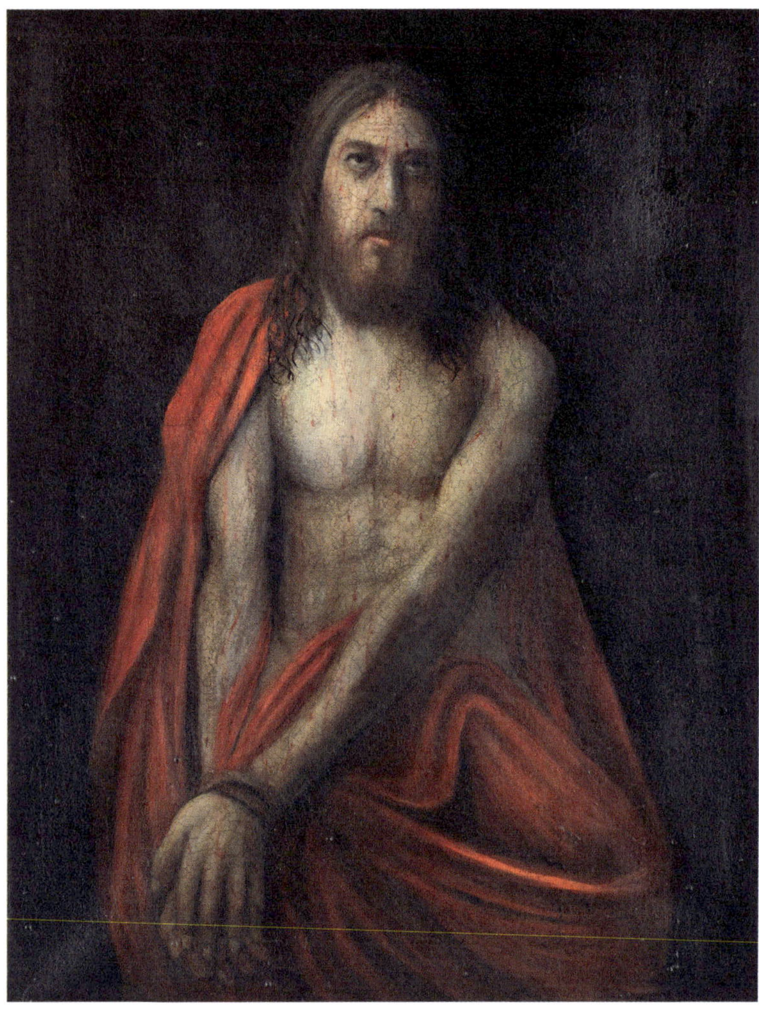

LEFT: *Christ Sweating Blood,* Tetro, in the style of Caravaggio.

Dalí (1904–89), Norman Rockwell (1894–1978) and others. He worked painstakingly. He searched through antique books from the appropriate eras to find blank pages so that he could draw on the right type of paper and always worked with canvases and pigments from the same era as each artist he copied. He developed a technique to create watermarks on papier d'Arches, a handmade French paper that many famous artists use for their lithographs. He found a system of embossing paper to leave a mark that looked similar to those on many original prints.

Initially, he sold directly to dealers, inventing vague provenances that lacked detail about the works having belonged to his dead grandfather. Still, eventually some of the dealers started asking him to create works specifically for them to sell. His accomplished works were convincing, complete with accurate-looking signatures, gallery

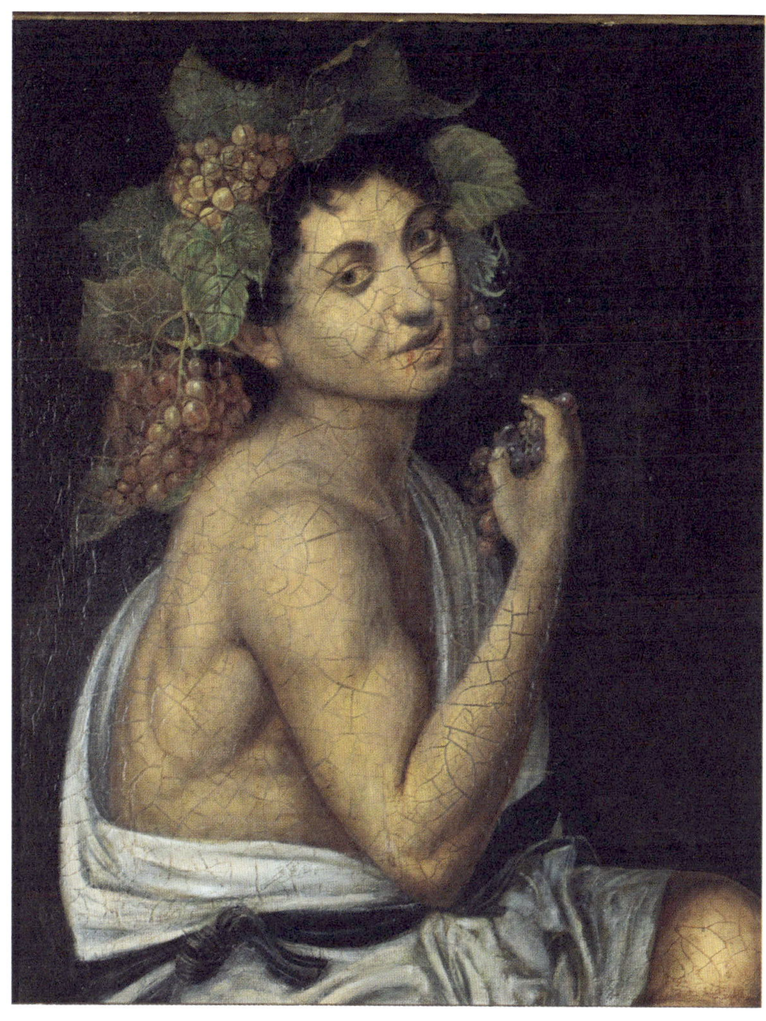

LEFT: *Bacchus,* Tetro, in the style of Caravaggio.

stamps and discolourations of age. Profiting from the craze for a 1977 limited edition lithograph, *Lincoln in Dalivision* by Salvador Dalí, Tetro printed dozens of counterfeit versions. To create these, he used an old printer and worked out a way to remove the half-tone dots that usually reveal a fake print to a knowledgeable dealer. During the 1980s, the art market expanded, and he became incredibly prolific. Reproductions of famous works were in demand, and by then he was known by some dealers for his expertise. He focused so closely on accuracy that he even travelled to Europe to buy wooden stretchers and canvases from where a particular artist had lived and worked. He later maintained that he never marketed his paintings and lithographs as originals, and his business card read, 'Tony Tetro. Art reproductions'. He said dealers told him his work would be sold to people who could not afford originals.

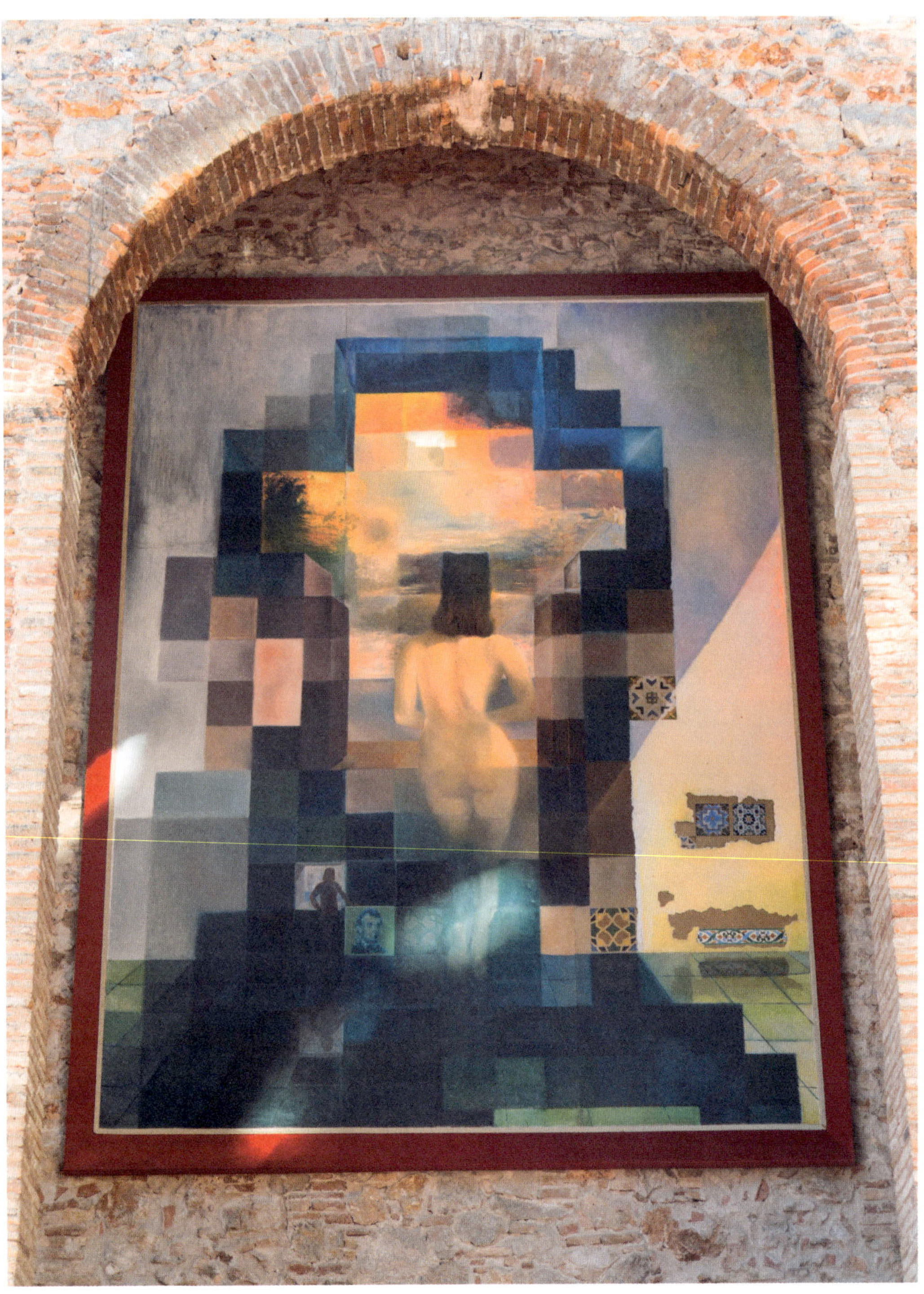

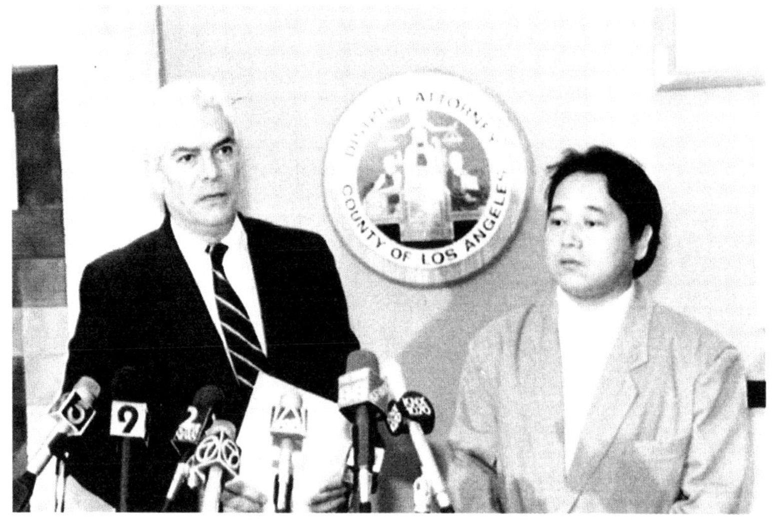

LEFT: In August 1989, Los Angeles County District Attorney Ira Reiner and artist Hiro Yamagata addressed the media during a press briefing. Reiner cautioned that the discovery of over 250 counterfeit artworks attributed to artists like Yamagata and Picasso might only scratch the surface of a burgeoning realm of art counterfeit.

Over a short time, he became successful and wealthy, owning a luxury home, a Rolls-Royce, two Ferraris and a Lamborghini. He gambled in Monte Carlo and regularly travelled to Paris and Rome. With no visible source of income, local police and residents thought he must be a drug dealer, and his car was frequently searched. However, the more he denied being a drug dealer, the more suspicious others became.

Arrest

In 1989, Tetro was discovered. The Japanese, California-based artist Hiro Yamagata (b. 1948) came across an artwork falsely claiming to be one of his own for sale in a Beverly Hills art gallery and called the police. The dealer who had sold the painting to the gallery told them that Tetro had painted it, and in April 1989, police found 250 forgeries in Tetro's home. He was accused of conspiring with art dealer Mark Henry Sawicki to deceive four other art dealers by selling them fake artworks. He was arrested and tried in court in Los Angeles, charged with 44 counts of forgery and one count of conspiracy. The costs of his defence forced him to liquidate his assets and ruined him financially.

In court, Tetro insisted that he was not a forger but rather an 'emulator' who copied artworks but did not intend to sell them as originals. He blamed art dealers for the fraud and said they merely commissioned him to create copies of paintings. Jurors were deadlocked for 17 hours; some argued that he was guilty, others insisted that he was innocent. To convict, they had to be convinced of Tetro's intent to commit fraud, and as they could not come to that conclusion, the district attorney retried the case. By then, Tetro had no more money to pay for his defence, so in February 1993, he

OPPOSITE: Tetro printed many counterfeit versions of a 1977 lithograph by Salvador Dalí, *Lincoln in Dalivision* and profited hugely from its popularity. He used an old printer to create the prints and worked out a way to remove the half-tone dots that usually reveal a fake print to an experienced dealer.

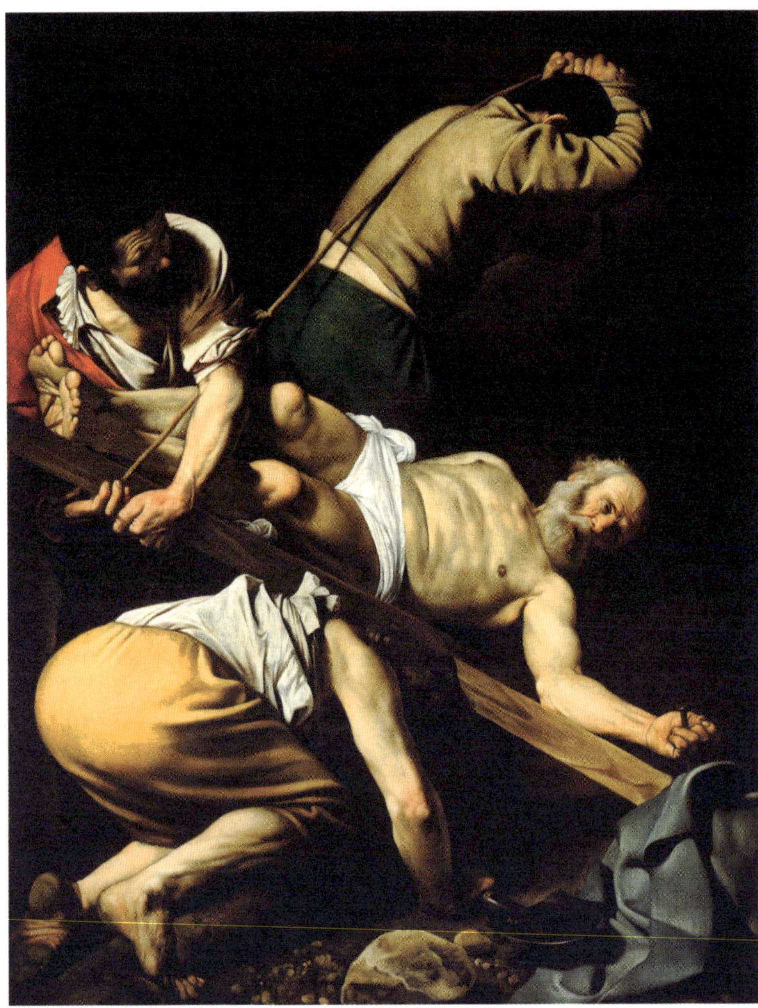

LEFT: One of Caravaggio's most celebrated works, *Crucifixion of Saint Peter*, was created in 1601 for the Cerasi Chapel of Santa Maria del Popolo in Rome. Caravaggio is one of the most influential and popular artists of all time.

pleaded 'nolo contendere' to six counts of forgery, one count of conspiracy and one count of attempted theft. In American law, 'nolo contendere' is when a defendant agrees to be convicted and punished for a crime while not actually admitting that he is guilty. He was sentenced to 200 hours of community service and was ordered to paint a mural on a public building. He was also sentenced to six months in a work release programme in prison, where he painted prototypes for traffic safety murals, and to five years' probation. He was released from prison in 1994.

'All of my paintings are out there'

Tony Tetro has been featured in TV documentaries and magazine articles. In 2022, he published his book, *Con/Artist: The Life and Crimes of the World's Greatest Art Forger*, which he wrote in collaboration with

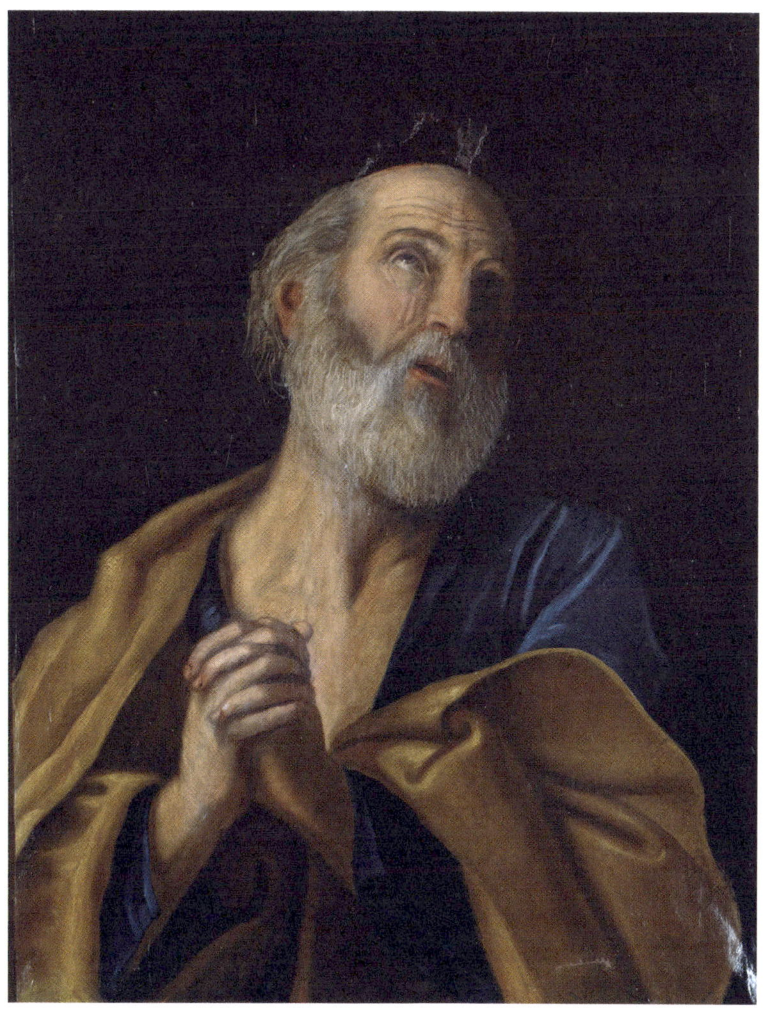

LEFT: *Saint Peter,* Tetro, in the style of Caravaggio.

writer, reporter and documentary-maker Giampiero Ambrosi. His artworks have been featured in exhibitions and auction houses around the world. Nowadays, he creates copies and other paintings for private clients, but signs them all with his own name. In 2011, the Australian Art Series Hotel Group launched a competition. Guests could select an original work by Warhol from a display of fakes created by the 'world's greatest living art forger', Tony Tetro. By using a forgery for marketing purposes, the competition caused huge controversy. In November 2019, it was reported that 4 of the 17 paintings that had been loaned by their owner to Dumfries House, a historic estate and house in Ayrshire, Scotland, were not by Picasso, Dalí, Monet and Chagall, but were fakes painted by Tetro. Tetro would not be surprised at this discovery. He has reflected, 'All of my paintings are out there, and people still think they're real.'

CHAPTER 12

F is for Fake

Hungarian-born painter and art forger Elmyr de Hory (1906–1976) was an inveterate liar.

He claimed that he came from an aristocratic family, that his father was an Austro-Hungarian ambassador and his mother came from a family of bankers. They divorced when he was 16. However, subsequent investigation suggested that he probably had a middle-class childhood, his father's occupation was listed as 'wholesaler of handcrafted goods', and his parents did not divorce when he was 16.

Classical art training

What did happen when de Hory was 16 was that he began formal art training in the Nagybánya artists' colony (now in Romania). He claimed to have studied art in various other places, but the accuracy of these statements is questionable. In 1926, he possibly moved to Paris and attended the Académie de la Grande Chaumière, where he was taught by Fernand Léger. By the time he finished training in 1928, his classical style had been overshadowed by more modern approaches such as Fauvism, Expressionism and Cubism, and his work appeared dated. The ensuing Great Depression that swept across the Atlantic to Europe reduced his prospects of making a living from his art still further. Evidence shows that between 1927 and 1931 he was convicted ten times in five European cities for various minor crimes, including counterfeiting documents and falsely claiming an aristocratic title.

By 1939, as war broke out, he returned to Hungary. He became involved with a British journalist and suspected spy, and ended up imprisoned in a Transylvanian jail for political insurgents. He befriended the prison camp officer by painting his portrait and was released, but within a few months he was imprisoned again, in a German concentration camp for being Jewish and homosexual. He was severely beaten and transferred to a Berlin prison hospital, from which he escaped. He returned to Hungary, and later related that on arrival he learned that his parents had been killed. However, at least one source claims that both his mother and brother survived the war.

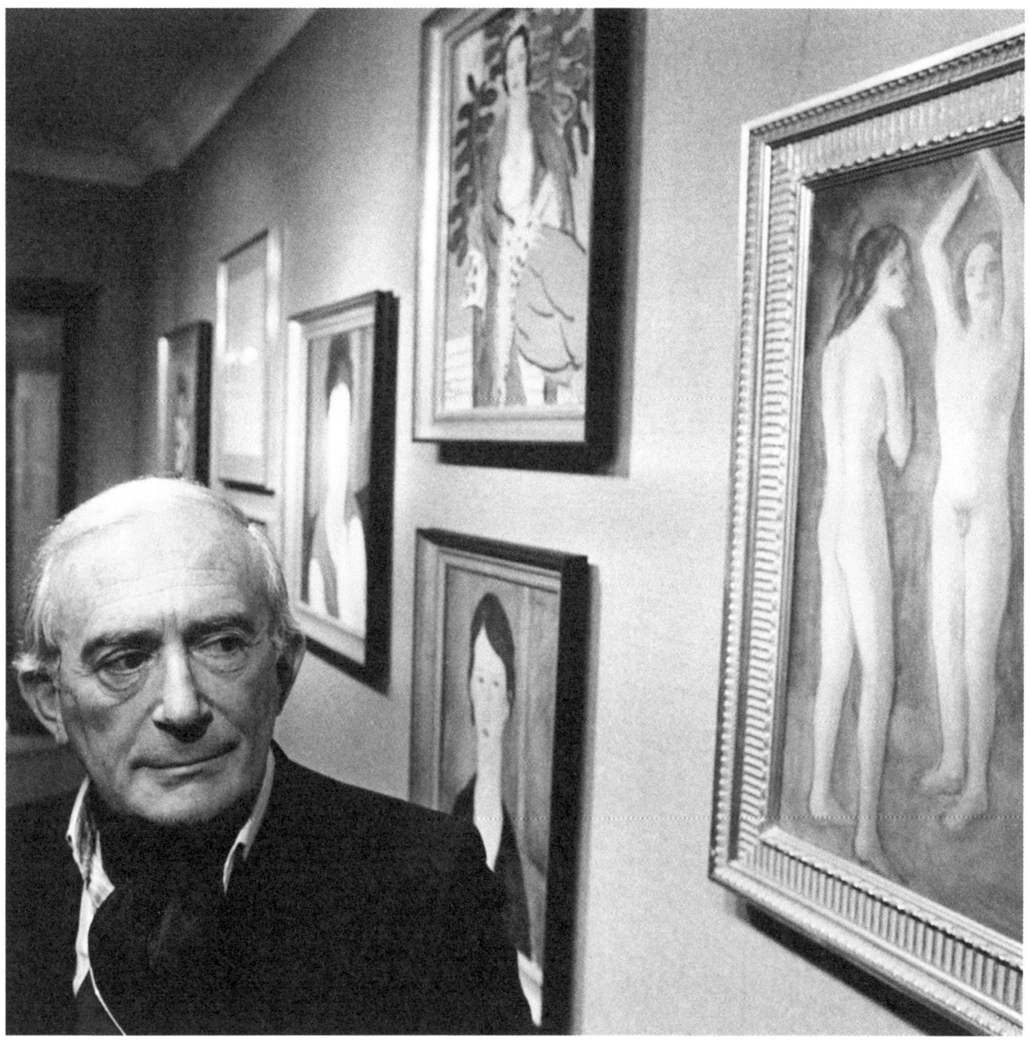

Making money

After the war, de Hory moved to Paris and once more tried to make a living as an artist. He soon discovered that he could copy the styles of various renowned painters and could make far more money doing this than he would be able to make selling his own work. In 1946, he sold a pen-and-ink drawing to Lady Malcolm Campbell, a wealthy British woman who misidentified it as an original work by Picasso. Gaining increasing confidence, he began to sell his Picasso imitations to art galleries around Paris, claiming that he was a displaced Hungarian aristocrat and the paintings he had to sell were the remains of his family's private art collection, or that the artworks had been gifts from individual artists he had befriended during his years in Paris.

ABOVE: De Hory at one of his art exhibitions. During his life, he organized and held several exhibitions where he presented his forged artworks as original creations.

That same year, he formed an association with Parisian gallery owner Jacques Chamberlain; together they travelled in Europe and South America, with de Hory producing fake Picasso drawings and Chamberlain then selling them. However, when de Hory discovered that Chamberlain was keeping most of the profits, he terminated the partnership and began working by himself. After selling several drawings in Sweden in 1947, he made enough money to buy a one-way ticket to Rio de Janeiro. There, he returned to painting his own works: portraits, landscapes and still lifes in his own style. Although they did not earn the kind of money he wanted, he still had money from his fake artworks to live on. Then he visited America, and stayed there for 12 years, moving between New York City, Los Angeles, Miami and Chicago. He tried to make his living once more as a fine artist in his own right, but ultimately failed. So he continued to sell fakes to anyone interested in buying them. He also began to develop more lies about his life. In order to sell his works, he built on the fake identity he had started creating: a Hungarian aristocrat with no Jewish ties who had fallen on hard times after the war and who owned a collection of artworks by important artists that he needed to sell to live on.

He began producing more forgeries, including paintings and drawings in the styles of Matisse, Modigliani, Renoir and others. However, galleries began to become suspicious when he returned with more artworks, so he started to sell his work by mail order, using multiple pseudonyms, including E. Raynal, Louis Cassou, Elmyr Herzog, Edgar Raynal, André Kay, Elmyr Hoffman, Count Joseph Dory, Michel K, Michel C, Count von Szigethy, Frederic Pierre, Louis Martin, Michel Verte, Peter G. Alston and Viktor Olson.

Most of the artists whose work de Hory forged had worked within the previous 50 years or so, which meant that he did not need to use any particular aged materials. Furthermore, the war had created chaos in the art world. So many private and public collections had been seized by the Nazis that many unprovenanced works were exchanging hands without too many questions being asked. In 1955, the Fogg Art Museum at Harvard University in Massachusetts bought a 'Matisse' drawing by de Hory. Soon after its sale, he also offered them drawings by 'Modigliani' and 'Renoir'. A curator noticed a stylistic similarity among the three drawings and refused to buy any more. She then began contacting other institutions and galleries, asking if they knew or had purchased artworks from the same source. That same year, an art broker based in Chicago, Joseph W. Faulkner, filed a complaint against de Hory for forgery of a painting and several drawings. Faulkner sued de Hory for 'intentional deception made for personal gain or to damage

OPPOSITE, ABOVE: Elmyr de Hory holds up a work of art in the style of Fauvist painter Raoul Dufy. It was 1973, the same year he appeared in the Orson Welles documentary *F for Fake*.

OPPOSITE, BELOW: Maria Rogers holds a lithograph by de Hory that imitates various 20th-century avant-garde artists.

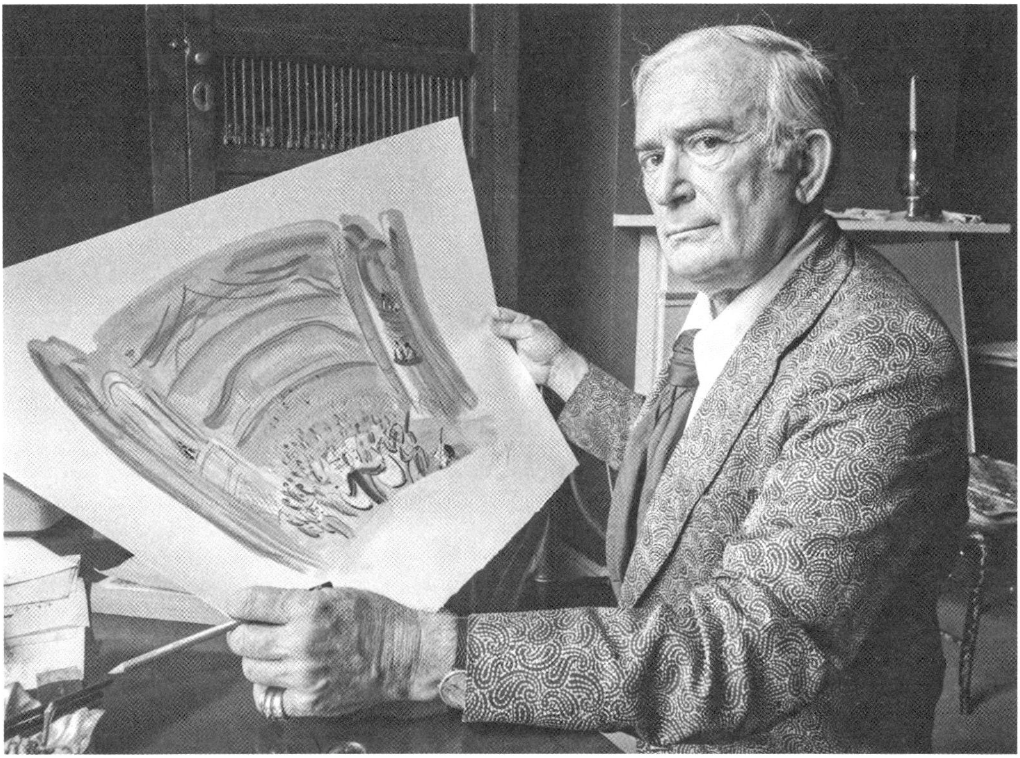

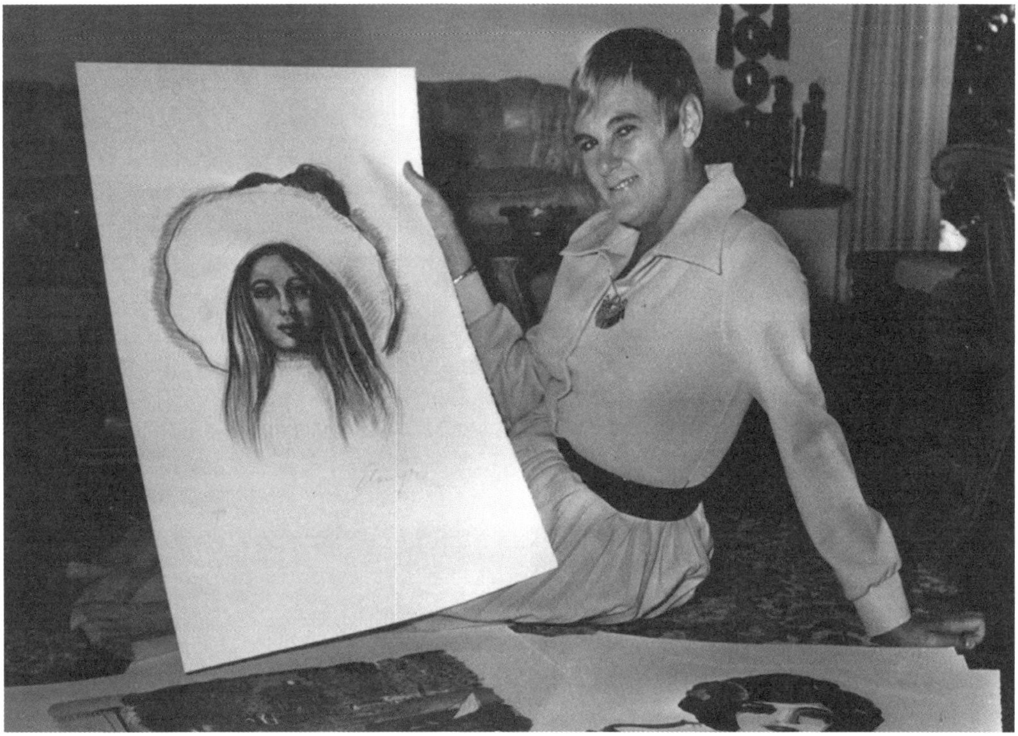

another individual'. To avoid trial, de Hory fled to Mexico City, where he became embroiled in a police investigation and paid a large sum of money to a lawyer to escape more serious consequences. He returned to the United States, where he continued to evade trial by exploiting legal loopholes and inconsistencies in the charges against him.

Complications

By then, de Hory could not resume his large-scale forgery of paintings and drawings, so he began selling forged lithographs by knocking on strangers' doors. It was difficult and he tried to end his life. However, while he was rehabilitating in a New York hospital, he met French art dealer Fernand Legros and the two men developed a relationship. They became lovers and, after Legros convinced de Hory to resume making forgeries, business partners. Throughout the 1960s and 1970s, they flooded the European art market with counterfeit paintings. Meanwhile, from 1958, de Hory also became involved with another art dealer and artist, Canadian Réal Lessard. Both Legros and Lessard convinced de Hory to accept a straight fee of $400 a month for any works they sold. From 1962, he moved to Ibiza, where he lived in a luxurious villa and hosted lavish parties. As a consequence, he became a bit sloppy, his forgeries less professional. Meanwhile, the American investigation was progressing and Interpol was contacted by more of the galleries that had acquired his counterfeits. It was

OPPOSITE: A visitor studies a painting by de Hory in the style of French artist Henri Matisse (1869–1954) during the opening of the exhibition 'Elmyr de Hory – Fake Project' at the Círculo de Bellas Artes in Madrid, in the spring of 2013.

BELOW: Art dealer Fernand Legros holds up a painting at his home in June 1979. Legros sold works by de Hory as authentic paintings by famed artists for years.

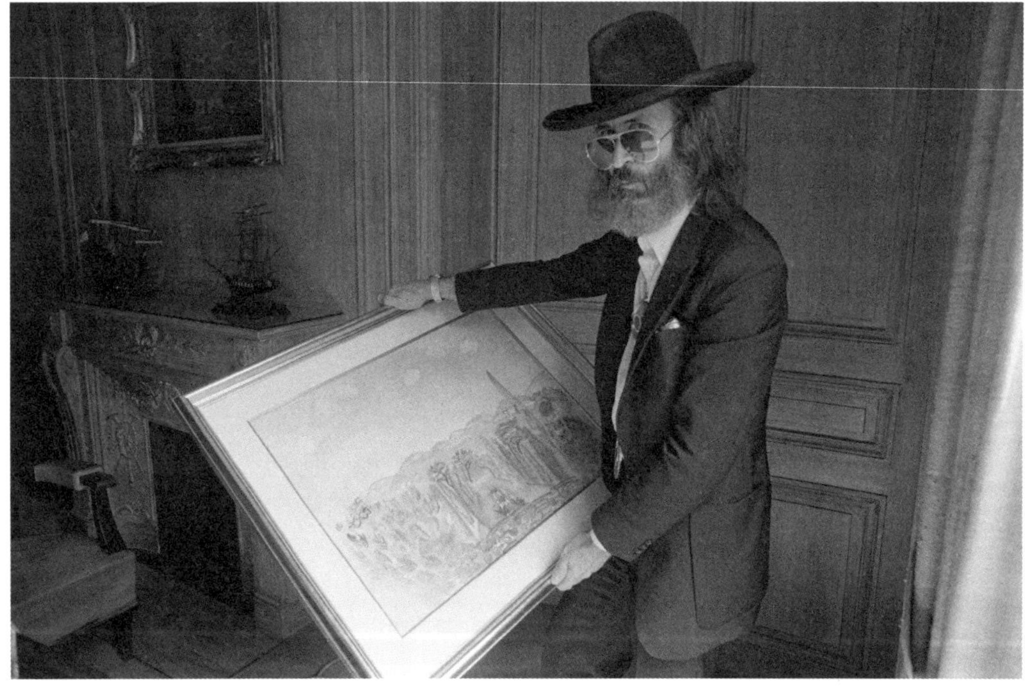

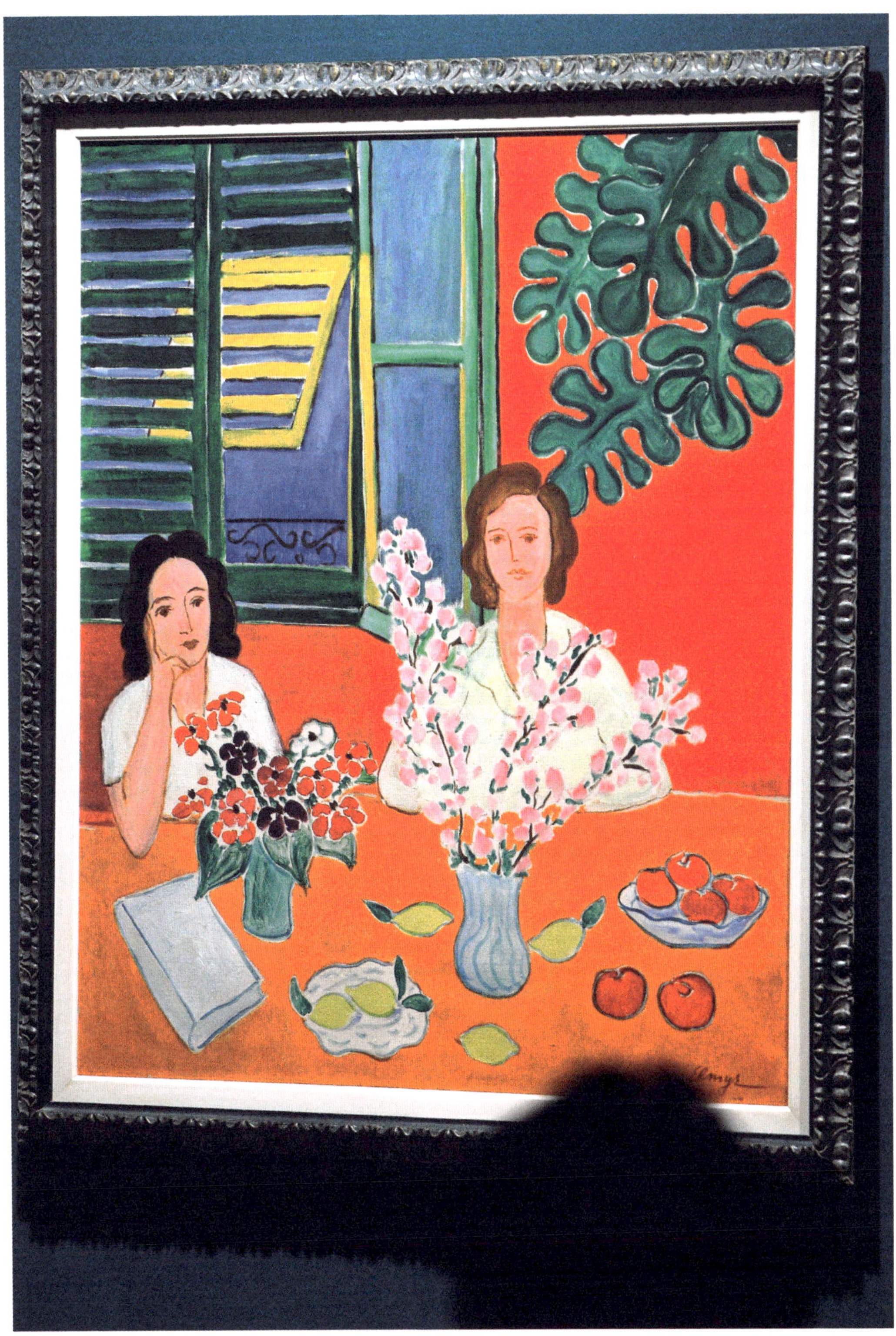

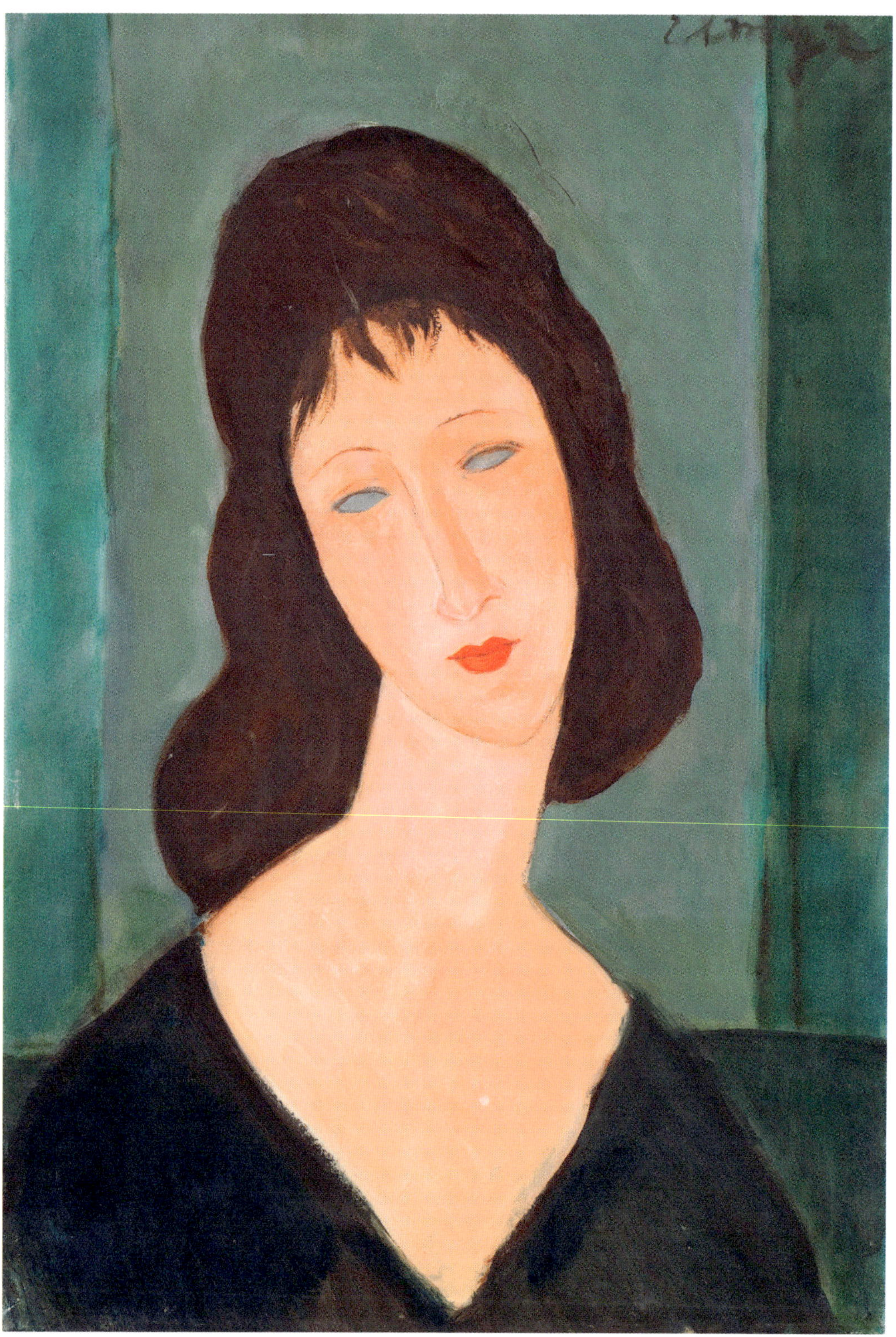

generally known that all the canvases sold through Legros were fakes. The oil tycoon, art collector and benefactor Algur Hurtle Meadows was seething. He had bought 56 works from Legros that turned out to be forgeries and he was determined to prosecute him. Legros escaped to de Hory's villa on Ibiza, but when the relationship became violent, de Hory fled.

Legros and Lessard were soon caught and charged by the Spanish police; tired and depressed, de Hory surrendered to the Spanish authorities. Convicted of homosexuality and consorting with criminals, he was sentenced to two months in prison. However, he was never charged with forgery because the court could not prove that he had ever created any fake artworks while he was in Spain. He was released in October 1968 and expelled from Ibiza for one year, though he continued to live in Spain, this time in Torremolinos.

After a year he returned to Ibiza and became a celebrity. His biography *Fake!* – written by Clifford Irving – was published in 1969, and he was filmed in a 1973 documentary called *Truths and Lies* (also *F for Fake)*, in which he described how his paintings deceived several experts. He began producing his own paintings again and was about to exhibit them when he learned that French authorities were trying

OPPOSITE: De Hory painted a portrait of this young woman, closely resembling the style of Amedeo Modigliani in 1975.

BELOW: De Hory with Clifford Irving, who wrote his biography.

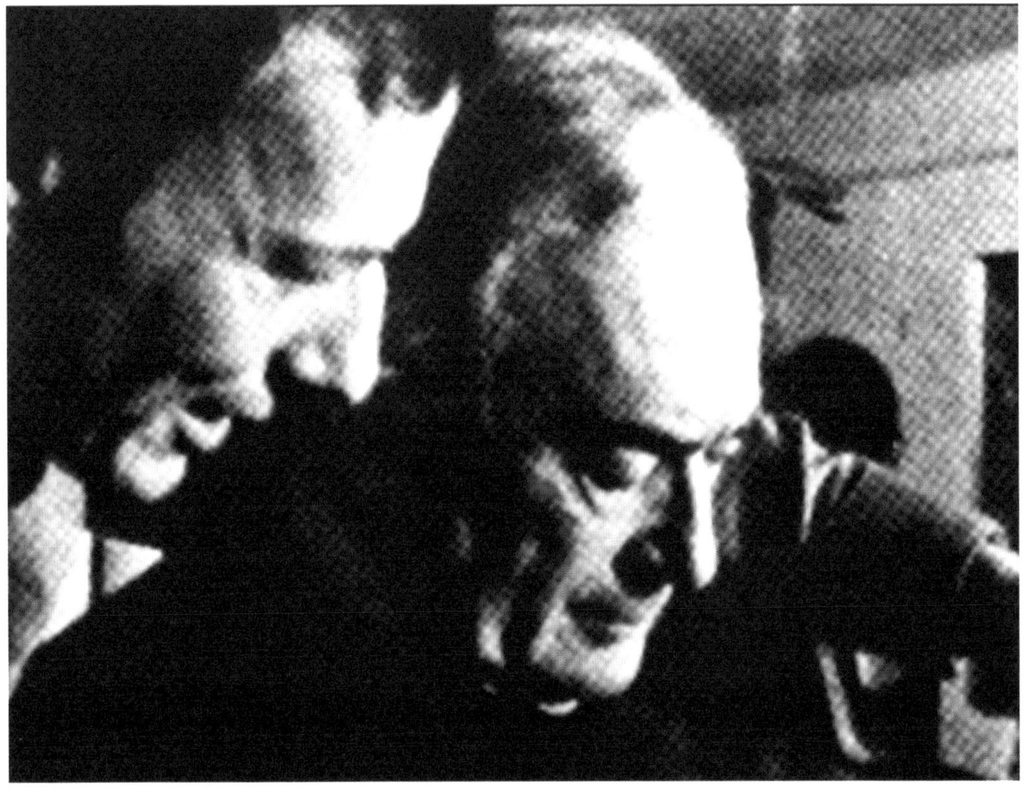

to have him extradited to face trial on fraud charges. In 1976, Spain accepted the French extradition request. When de Hory heard of this, he swallowed a lethal dose of sleeping pills and died in the arms of his partner and bodyguard Mark Forgy.

On reflection

Today, de Hory's forgeries are much easier to identify due to new forensic techniques like X-ray fluorescence and raman spectrometry. However, many of his claims remain unverifiable, leaving him a truly enigmatic and elusive persona. Despite many newly uncovered facts, a legend continues to surround him; some of his stories have stuck.

Initially, when he began his fraudulent career, he mainly faked works on paper – including drawings, paintings and lithographs – simply by staining the paper with tea; it is impossible to know how many forgeries by him there are and where they are. Then he began to work with old canvases, often from the 19th century, that he bought from flea markets and carefully scraped off the paint of previous works. After he had

BELOW: Elmyr de Hory being interviewed in May 1972.

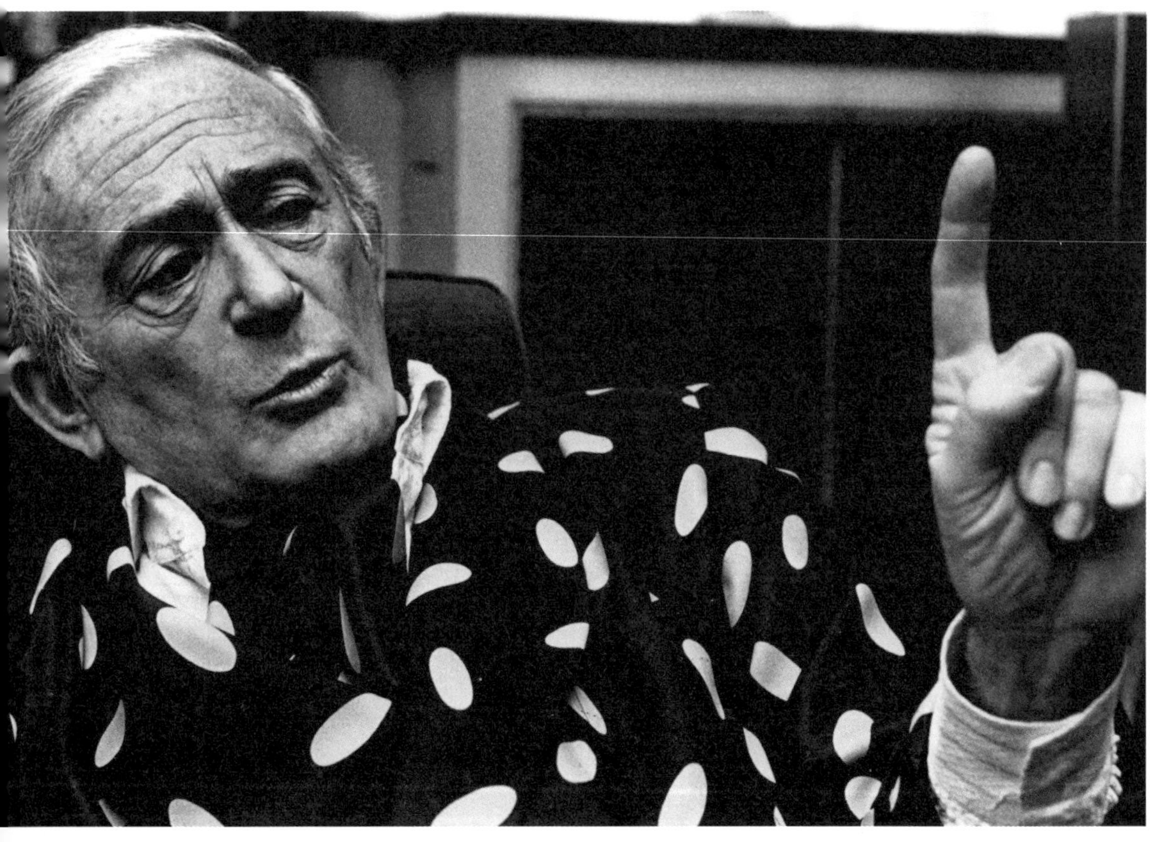

finished these paintings, he applied specialist materials such as *vernis à craquelure*, a varnish that creates craquelure, and *vernis à vieillir*, which creates a rich golden hue that gives the impression of age; then he baked them to dry the oil paint.

The director of the Modigliani Project, Kenneth Wayne, has remarked that because de Hory produced so many Modigliani forgeries, it is almost impossible to create a definitive catalogue of Modigliani's actual work. The forged works were bought by highly respected art galleries such as the Nelson-Atkins Museum of Art, Kansas City, the Niveau Gallery, New York, the now defunct M. Knoedler & Co., New York, and others.

After his death, de Hory left all his money and works of art to Forgy, who later returned to America with hundreds of counterfeit artworks. In 2007, Forgy began writing a memoir about de Hory, which he self-published in 2012. He also created a website devoted to the life and work of de Hory. It will probably never be known how many forgeries de Hory made, nor how many are still being displayed as genuine works of art. It is estimated that he was probably the author of over a thousand forged artworks that sold for more than $50 million.

BELOW, LEFT: Hungarian-born Elmyr de Hory was photographed here in July 1973 in advance of the Orson Welles documentary *F for Fake* that aired that year.

BELOW, RIGHT: Elmyr de Hory photographed in his studio in Madrid, Spain, in 1970.

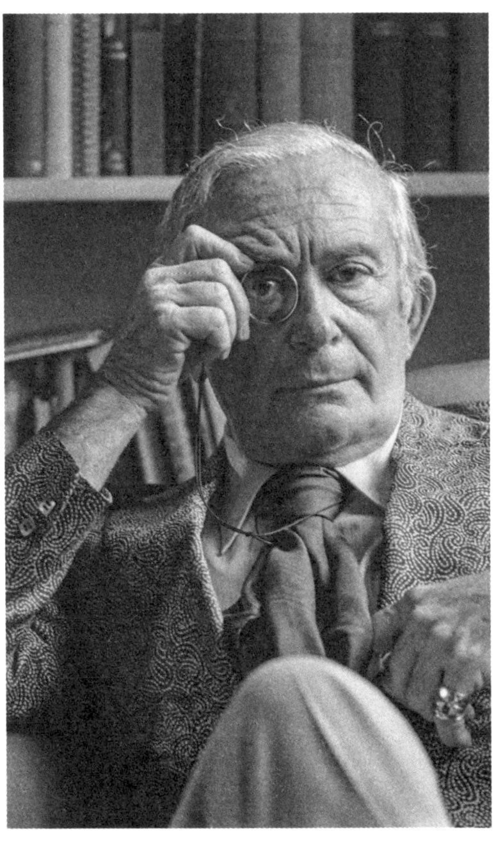

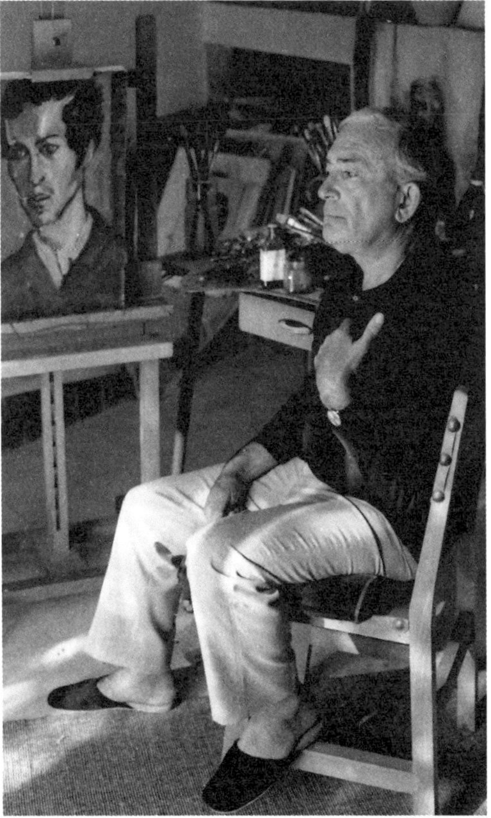

CHAPTER 13

From Garage to Gallery

Pei-Shen Qian (b. 1940), an immigrant based in Queens in New York City, was the artist behind a huge forgery scandal that resulted in a prestigious art gallery closing its doors after nearly two centuries.

Over 14 years, Qian produced artworks for Long Island art dealer Glafira Rosales and her partner and his brother, Spanish art dealers José Carlos Bergantiños Díaz and Jesús Ángel Bergantiños Díaz, respectively. They sold Qian's paintings under famous 20th-century artists' names, including Jackson Pollock and Mark Rothko.

The scandal of the counterfeit paintings became known as 'the Knoedler Affair' because many of the works were sold through New York's prestigious Knoedler Gallery, which had first opened (under the name Goupil & Cie) in 1846. In 2009, it was discovered that a painting sold by the Knoedler Gallery to a well-known couple in the

BELOW: Entrepreneur, marketer and gallerist, José Carlos Bergantiños Díaz (left) became infamous for his involvement in the Knoedler Affair in New York. Ann Freedman (right), art dealer, gallery owner and former director for 31 years of the now-defunct Knoedler Gallery in New York City.

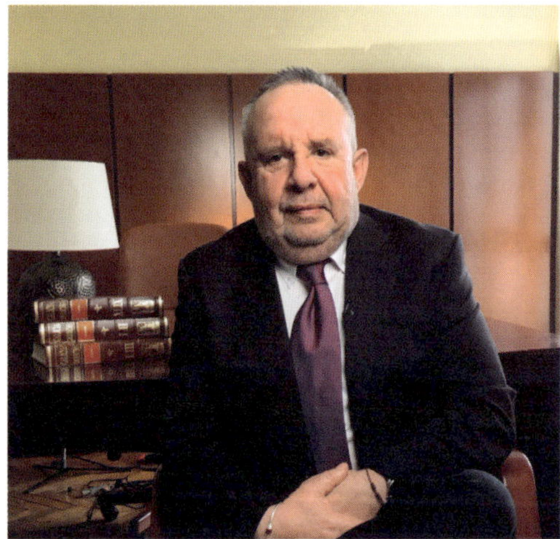

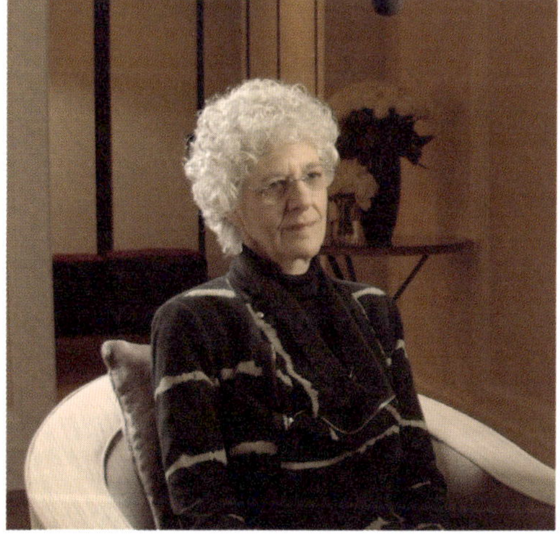

fashion industry had been a fake, and the gallery, under the director Ann Freedman, was brought to court. In 2011, 165 years after it opened, the Knoedler Gallery closed its doors for a final time. Two years later, Rosales appeared in court and admitted that the painting was a fake by Qian. By then Qian had left the United States, maintaining he had been unaware that his paintings were being sold under the names of famous artists.

Mr X Junior

It was later discovered that between 1994 and 2011, under Ann Freedman's direction, the gallery had sold almost 40 counterfeit Abstract Expressionist paintings purportedly by famous artists. Freedman had bought the paintings for the Knoedler Gallery from Rosales. It seems incomprehensible now that Freedman never tried to find out more about Rosales, the polite woman who brought her so many recently discovered artworks. Nor about the Bergantiños Díaz brothers. Rosales built up her relationship with Freedman and the Knoedler Gallery by bringing in the paintings one by one. She told Freedman that her seller was called 'Mr X Junior' and that his parents had been based in the Philippines, but little else. She later said that he had been based not in the Philippines, but in Switzerland. Even this dramatic change in story was not picked up on. Privacy and anonymity are common in the art world among sellers and buyers, so the lack of and changes in detail did not raise undue suspicions. Rosales was not known to Freedman, nor to the Knoedler Gallery, but she was quiet and well dressed, and seemed knowledgeable about the art. She explained that the parents of Mr X Junior had been friends with the Abstract Expressionist painter Alfonso Ossorio and

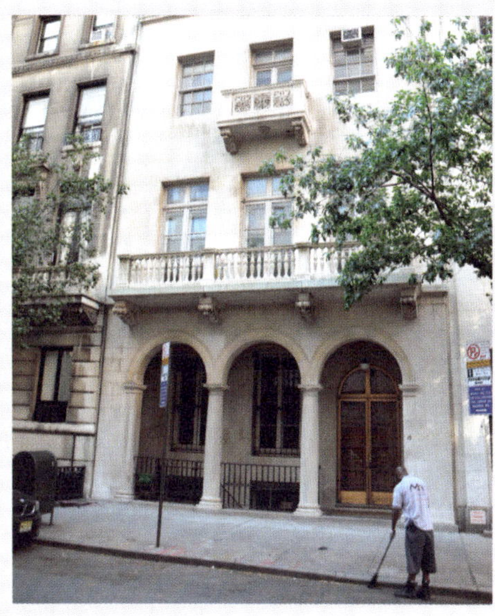

KNOEDLER

Founded in the mid-19th century, M. Knoedler & Co. (also often known as the Knoedler Gallery) became a highly respected art dealership in New York City. It remained one of the oldest commercial art galleries in the USA until it closed in 2011, damaged irreparably by lawsuits for fraud. Michel (later Michael) Knoedler, who was born in 1823 in the German state of Baden-Württemberg, had started to work for the art dealership Goupil & Cie in Paris in 1844, then moved to New York in 1852 to run the New York branch. In 1857, he bought the New York gallery, changing its name from Goupil & Cie to Knoedler. Later, he was joined by his sons Roland, Edmond and Charles; Roland took charge of the gallery after his father's death in 1878. Over its history, some of the most famous art collectors bought works through Knoedler, including Cornelius Vanderbilt, William Rockefeller, John Jacob Astor, J. P. Morgan and Henry Clay Frick, as well as some of the world's most prestigious art institutions, including The Metropolitan Museum of Art, the Louvre and the Tate. In 2012, months after it had closed its doors for the final time, the Knoedler's archives from 1846 to 1971 were bought by the Getty Research Institute to keep them for posterity.

that Ossorio took the couple to individual studios, where they purchased paintings from the artists directly. She said that the paintings remained in storage while the parents were alive until a while after Mr X Junior inherited them, so none appear in the catalogues raisonnés of the now dead artists.

To transport the paintings, Rosales merely put them in the back of her car. She maintained that they were all masterpieces that had been kept for decades in one family's private collection, and once the Knoedler and a few other galleries bought them, dozens were sold to buyers and collectors, having been convinced by the experts.

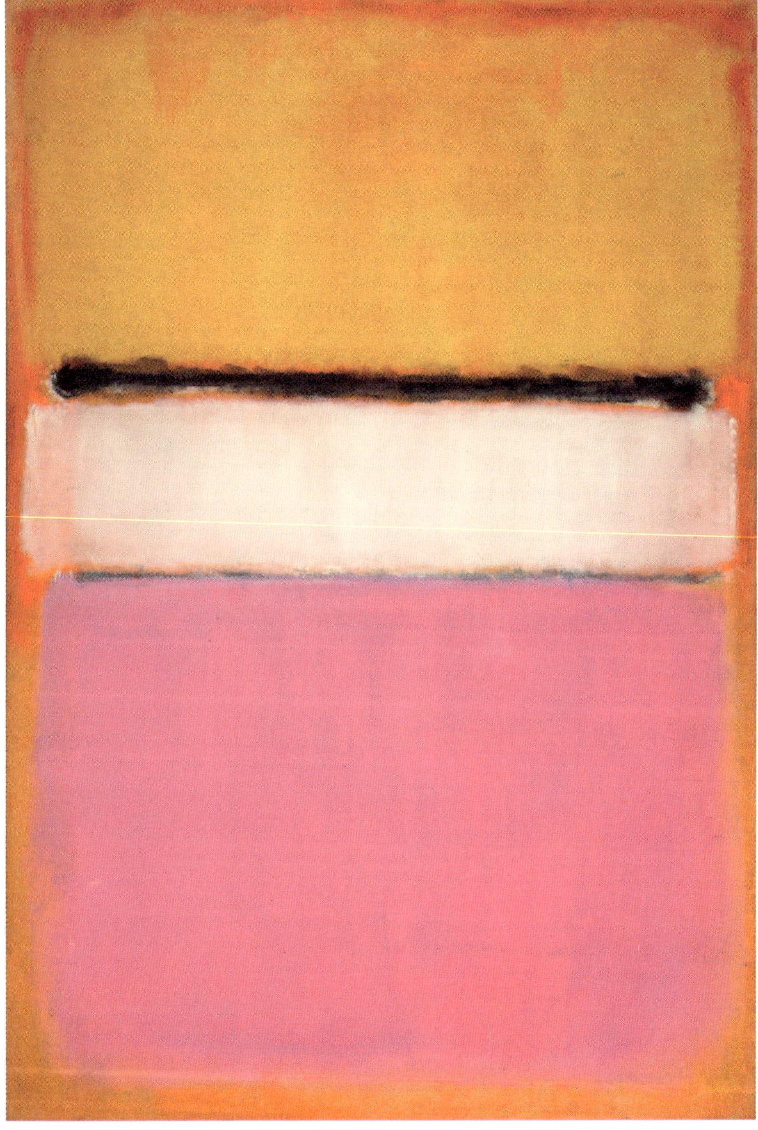

LEFT: *White Center (Yellow, Pink and Lavender on Rose)*, painted by Mark Rothko in oil paints on canvas, 1950.

Overall, tens of millions of dollars exchanged hands between art dealers, galleries and art collectors from 1994 and 2011.

The first artwork that Rosales showed to Freedman was a Rothko on paper, which appeared to be genuine. Freedman later said that she consulted Rothko experts who confirmed the work's authenticity, although it is not known exactly who these were. Rosales agreed a price for each painting that she would accept on behalf of Mr X Junior. Knoedler kept any profit on the eventual sale. For each painting, Freedman recalled, Rosales would go to Mexico or Switzerland, the two locations where she said Mr X Junior lived.

LEFT: Closely resembling the style and techniques of Mark Rothko, this painting was later proven to be a fake.

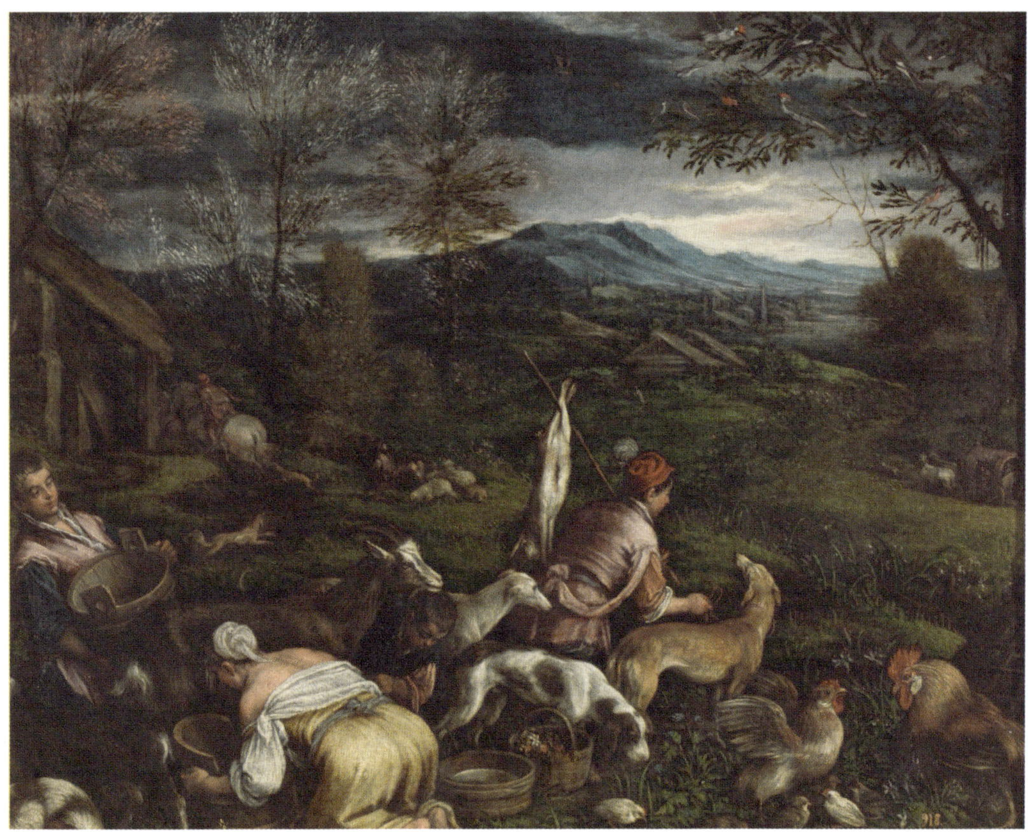

ABOVE: *Spring*, painted in the second half of the 16th century by the workshop of Jacopo da Ponte (Il Bassano). It is relatively similar to the painting, *Spring Sowing* by Bassano (1510–1592), which was returned to Italy after it was discovered that the painting had been war loot.

When she returned with another work, she and Freedman would celebrate over lunch at a nearby restaurant. One summer, Rosales's daughter was accepted into Knoedler's famous art library as an intern and Rosales was invited to gallery openings. 'There was nothing covert about it,' Freedman says. Although Mr X Junior remained a mystery, Freedman says that he conveyed his approval about how the works were selling, as Rosales would tell her, 'He's happy with you, Ann, with what you're doing.'

The downfall

Late in 2001, an executive of the financial institution Goldman Sachs, Jack Levy, bought a Jackson Pollock painting, *Untitled 1949*, for $2 million. As the work was not in Pollock's catalogue raisonné, Levy asked for it to be checked by the International Foundation for Art Research (IFAR). When IFAR checked it, they could not definitively verify the work, so declined to authenticate it. The link with Ossorio was also looked into as part of the verification process. As Pollock was no longer alive, his partner, Ted Dragon, was asked about the parents of Mr X Junior. Dragon said that Ossorio had never mentioned them or Mr X Junior, and that if it had happened, he, Dragon, would have known about it.

In 2003, Jack Levy asked for and received his money back for the painting. The whole matter was kept quiet and nothing made public. However, at the same time in an unrelated incident, the Springfield Library and Museum Association in Massachusetts sued Knoedler for the loss of a $3 million painting, *Spring Sowing* by Jacopo da Ponte (Il Bassano) (1510–1592), which Springfield had to return to Italy after it was discovered that the painting had been war loot. Although this intensified the pressure on the gallery, nothing else of major significance happened until the end of November 2011. Then the Belgian economist, hedge fund manager and financier Pierre Lagrange decided to sell *Untitled 1950*, a work by Jackson Pollock that he had bought from Knoedler in 2007 for $17 million. Lagrange sent the

BELOW: One of Jackson Pollock's artworks, *Untitled*, painted in 1950.

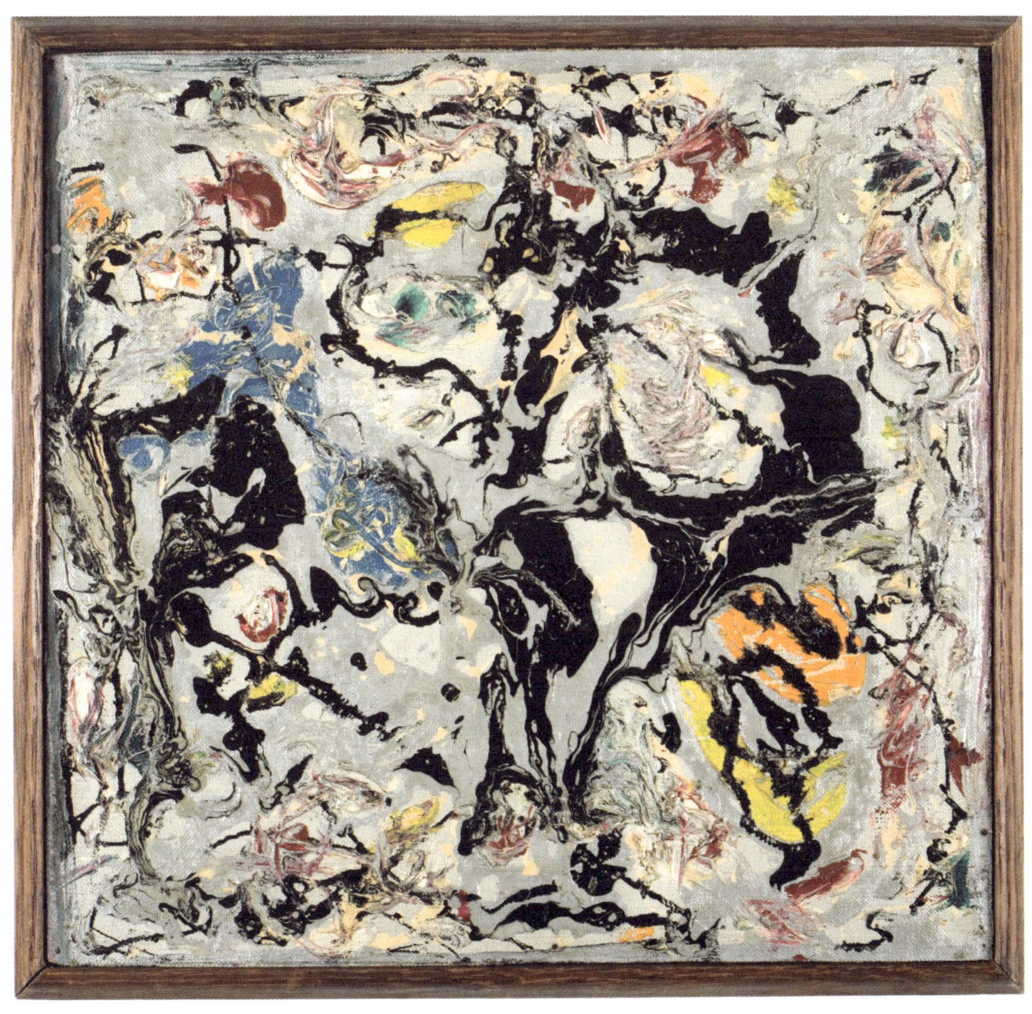

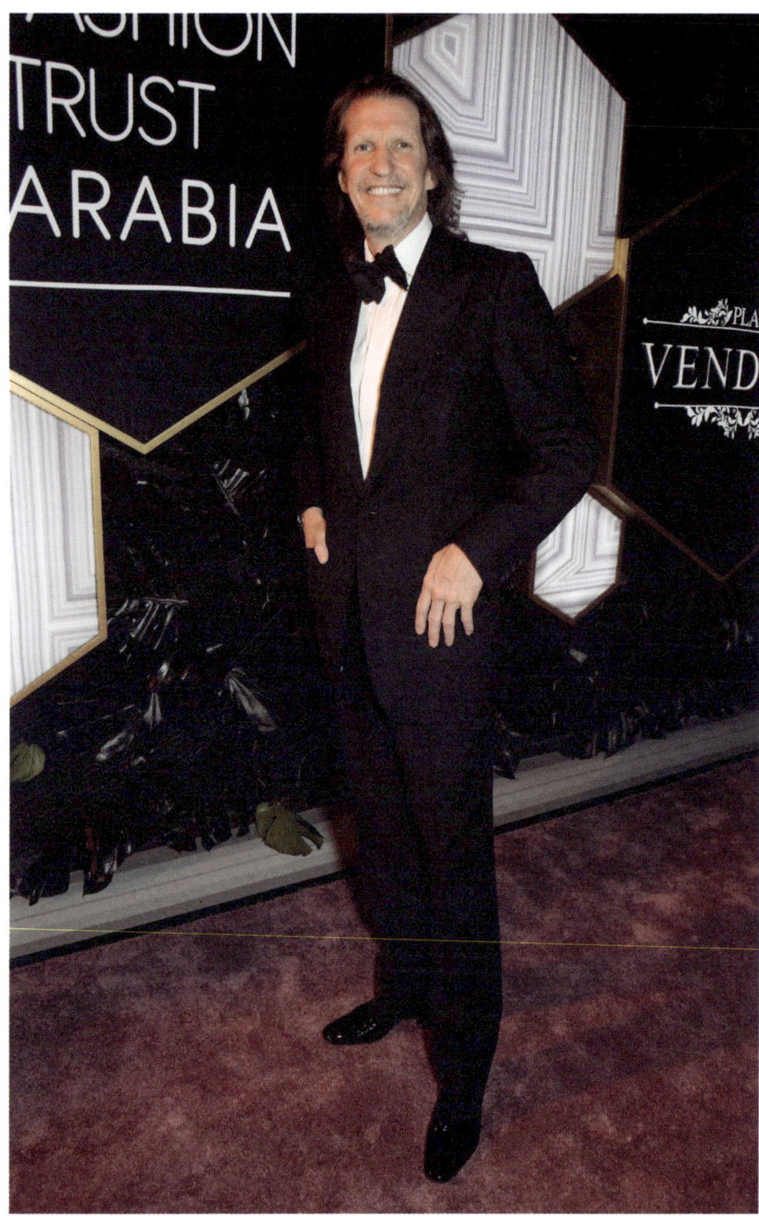

LEFT: Pierre Lagrange bought a Jackson Pollock painting from Knoedler in 2007 but, on having it forensically tested, discovered it to be a fake.

work for forensic testing, and it was discovered it contained a yellow paint that was not available before the 1970s. Pollock had died in 1956.

Following the discovery, Lagrange told the Knoedler Gallery to reimburse him all the money he had paid for the painting within two days or he would sue. In response, to the shock of the international art world, Knoedler closed its doors for good. It had no more money to reimburse claimants or to survive a lengthy legal battle. A statement issued on 28 November 2011 by Knoedler stated simply that it was closing permanently for business reasons unrelated to the lawsuits it faced over the sale of forged paintings.

The case between Lagrange and Knoedler was settled out of court in 2012. Also during that year, business couple Domenico and Eleanore De Sole claimed that the gallery had sold them a fake Mark Rothko, *Untitled 1956*, for $8.3 million in 2004. They sued Knoedler and Freedman and then settled out of court with Freedman in 2015 but continued their suit against Knoedler. Also in 2012, Wall Street executive John D. Howard sued Knoedler and Freedman, claiming that a Willem de Kooning painting he bought for $4 million in 2007 was a fake. The suit was settled out of court in December 2015.

The David Herbert Collection

By 2012, the FBI was investigating 'at least two dozen paintings' that were supplied to the Knoedler Gallery by Rosales. The trial that ensued revealed that at least 20 of these fake Abstract Expressionist paintings had been part of the 'David Herbert Collection', and each had sold for at least eight-figure sums. The David Herbert Collection included works allegedly by some of the greatest 20th-century Abstract Expressionist artists, including Pollock, Motherwell, Rothko, Willem de Kooning, Barnett Newman, Clyfford Still, Richard Diebenkorn and Franz Kline.

Freedman later explained that she understood Ossorio and Ted Dragon had been part of a gay art world circle in the 1950s that had included a gallery assistant named David Herbert. Herbert worked for several important galleries in New York, had his own art gallery from 1959 to 1962, operated as a private dealer, and also had a partnership with another dealer for a few years. Rosales had explained that Mr X Senior was married but also wealthy and gay, and after the two men met, they embarked on a romantic relationship. Herbert took Mr X Senior to various Abstract Expressionist artists' studios, where he bought numerous paintings for cash. Then the romance ended. Mr X Senior returned to his wife and two children in Switzerland, keeping his gay life secret. Because of the clandestine nature of his gay life, he did not want to sell any of the paintings in case Herbert heard of the sales and revealed secrets about both their relationship and the unlawfulness of the transactions. Freedman explained, 'There's no question that the paintings would have been paid for with cash, taxes not paid, assets not declared, and you can go to jail for that.'

Freedman said she was told that even after Mr X Senior died, the paintings were kept by his son, Mr X Junior, until David Herbert died in 1995. Only then could they be sold, in turn, to hide the weak provenance. However, it seems to have been ignored or dismissed as unimportant that not one of the paintings from the so-called David Herbert Collection was catalogued as being a genuine part of any of the artists' collections.

Defence

When Freedman was asked in court why she would take on paintings with no provenance, she replied, 'Because we haven't yet sorted out the provenance doesn't mean there's no provenance.' When questioned further, she continued her defence: 'Every time we got a painting from Glafira, we'd hang it in the [Knoedler's] booth at the [Park Avenue] Armory.' The Armory is an annual show hosted in New York by the Art Dealers Association of America (ADAA), which nearly all top dealers attend. Throughout each day of the show, professional dealers would stop to look closely at the paintings. 'Had anyone found anything wrong, meaning they weren't "right", believe me, I would have been told: "Take that down off the wall." No one ever did that.'

Richard Diebenkorn was one of the artists whose work was bought by Freedman. However, the late artist's son-in-law, Richard Grant, head of the Diebenkorn Foundation, said that in 1995 he learned of paintings by Diebenkorn being bought by the Knoedler Gallery which he had not been aware of. Both Diebenkorn's widow and daughter said that they met with Freedman at Knoedler and advised her that they had no records of any of the paintings she had bought that she thought were by Diebenkorn. Next, the same paintings began appearing elsewhere, suggesting that Freedman had sold them anyway, despite what the artist's family had told her.

In 2006, when Grant learned that Knoedler had sold one of these questionable paintings to the Kemper Museum of Contemporary Art in Kansas City, Missouri, out of courtesy he went first to Freedman to explain that it was not by Diebenkorn. He recalled that she was uncooperative. In her defence, Freedman said that Knoedler's legal counsel had advised her not to respond to Grant directly. So Grant contacted the Kemper Museum and, soon after, the painting was removed from view. In its place, another *Ocean Park* by Diebenkorn was displayed. This had a clear provenance. It had been a gift to the Kemper Museum from Ann Freedman and her husband.

However, still in her own defence, Freedman said that the forensic tests on the artworks were meaningless. For example, artists of the 1950s were often given experimental paints long before those paints hit the market, so the yellow paint discovered in Lagrange's Pollock could feasibly have been used by him. While waiting for further results of the forensic tests on other artworks, she continued to maintain that they were all authentic. It was never clear whether

OPPOSITE, ABOVE: In 2016, Domenico and Eleanor De Sole sued the Knoedler & Co gallery and Ann Freedman for $25 million, for the sale of a fake Mark Rothko painting.

OPPOSITE, BELOW: A drawing by Victor Juhasz of the defence team for the Knoedler Gallery forgery trial, with the president Ann Freedman.

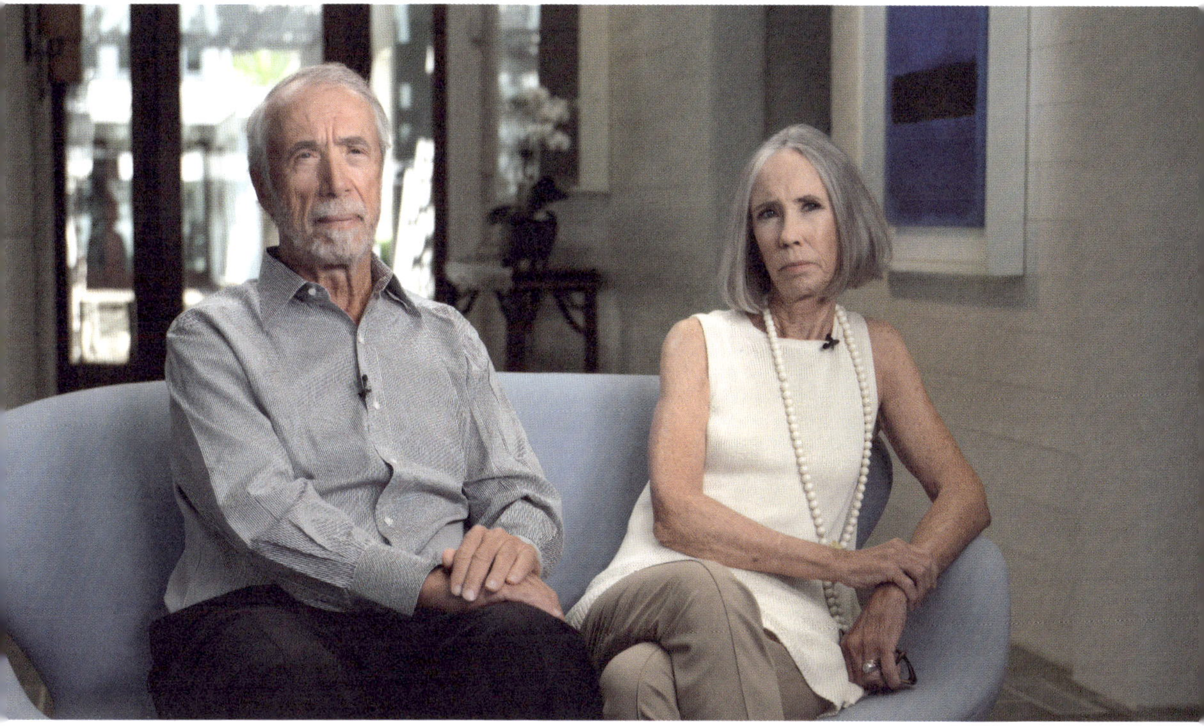

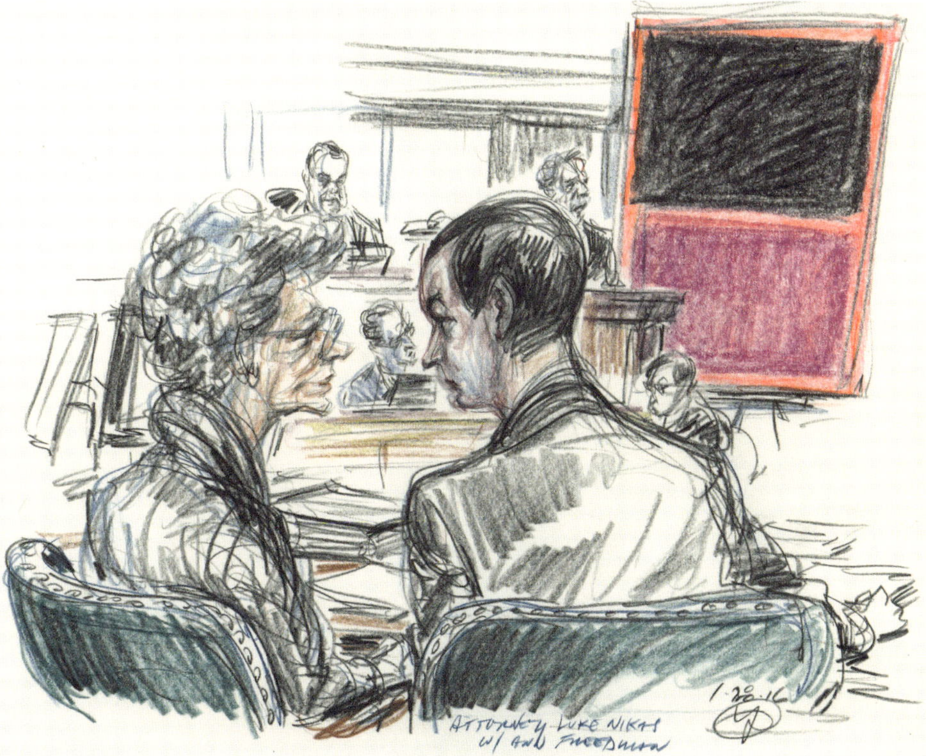
ATTORNEY LUKE NIKAS
W/ ANN FREEDMAN

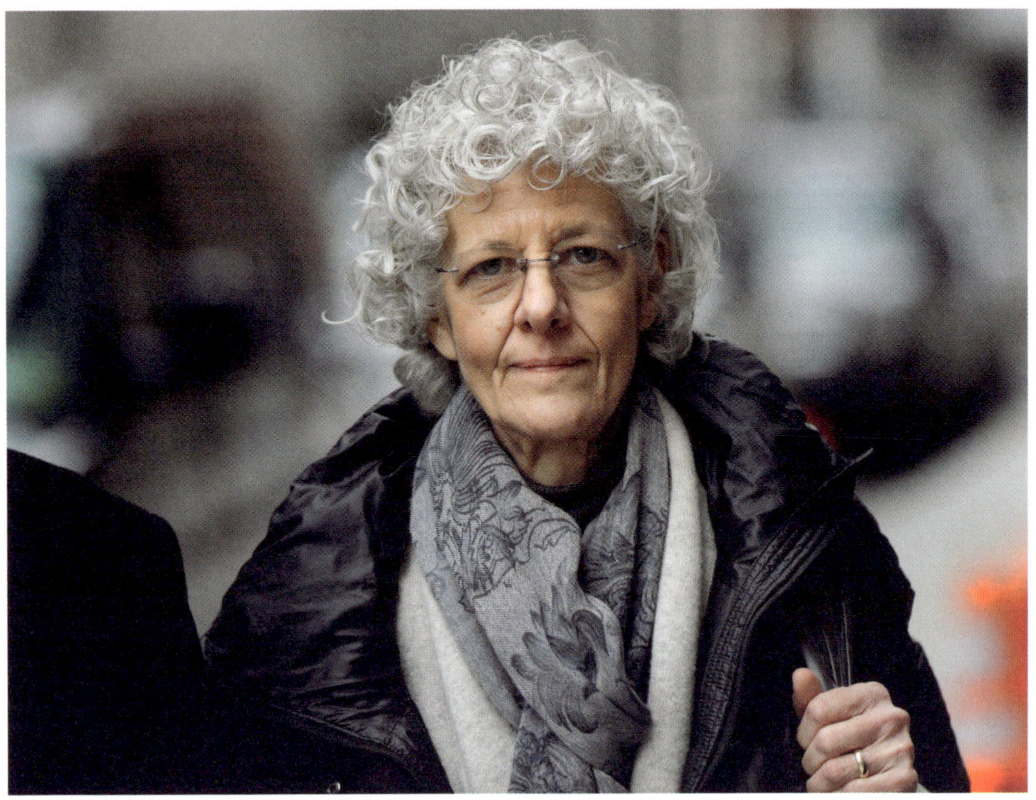

ABOVE: Ann Freedman during her trial in 2016.

she was actually aware they were counterfeits or she was duped. Either way, her reputation was ruined.

Aftermath

Although at first Rosales pleaded not guilty, in 2013 she confessed to selling more than 60 fake artworks to two New York art galleries, Knoedler and Julian Weissman Fine Art, conspiracy to commit money laundering, money laundering, tax evasion and wire fraud (a criminal offence that involves using electronic communications, such as the internet, to intentionally deceive and defraud). She admitted to having promoted artworks by Robert Motherwell, Jackson Pollock, Mark Rothko and others that she knew were actually 'fakes made by an individual in Queens'.

It seems that sometime before 1994, Rosales and José Carlos Bergantiños Díaz discovered the artist Pei-Shen Qian and commissioned him to paint forgeries for them. Little is known about him apart from the fact that he moved to the United States from Asia and lived in Queens, New York. Working from a garage there, he was able to mimic the styles of various artists, replicating their techniques and using similar materials and palettes, and even

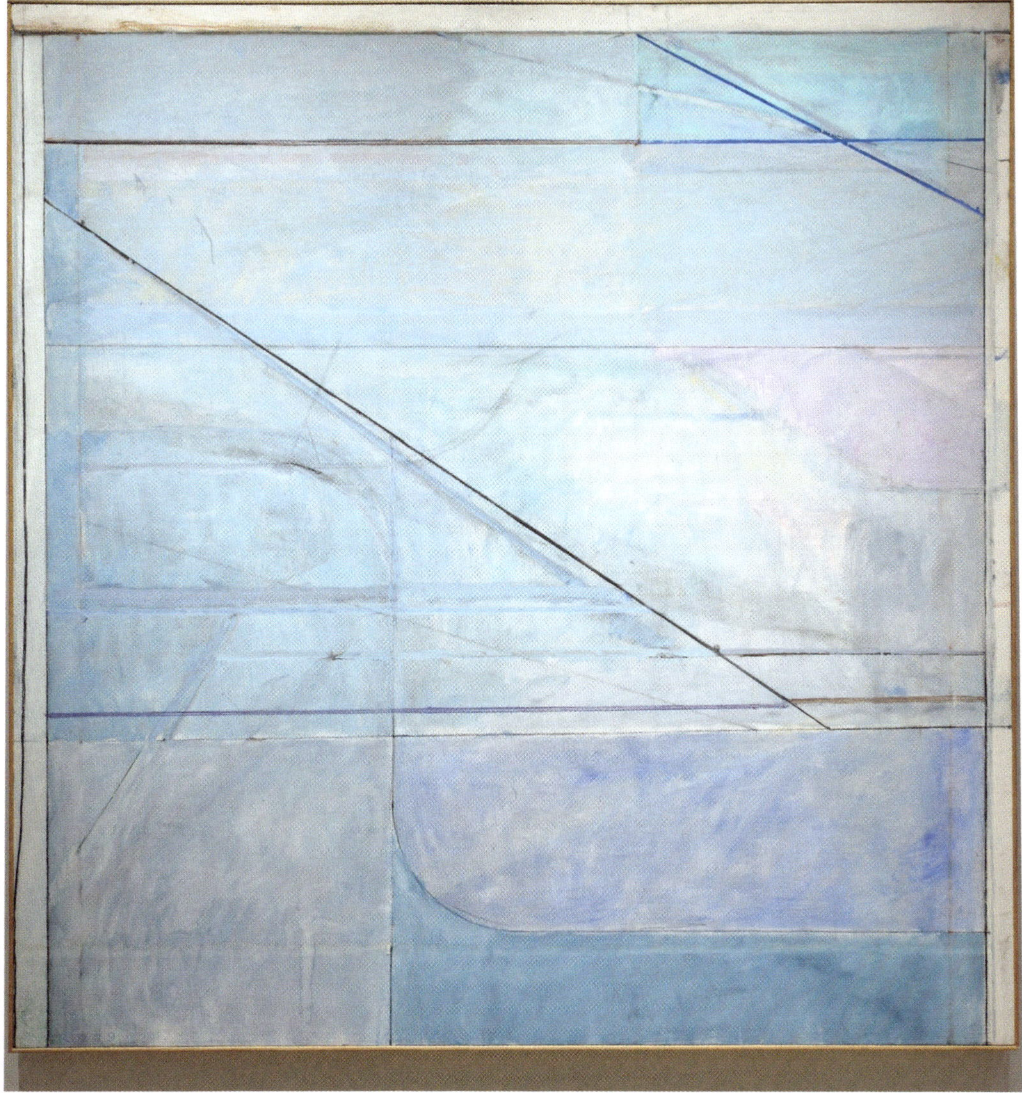

making them look suitably aged using tea or dirt from a vacuum cleaner. Allegedly, he received less than $9,000 for each painting from Rosales, while she sold them for millions of dollars to Knoedler. When the forgery scandal was exposed, Qian fled.

It was estimated that Rosales and the Bergantiños Díaz brothers earned $33.2 million and the two New York galleries, Knoedler and Julian Weissman Fine Art, made $47 million between them. In 2017, Rosales was ordered to pay $81 million to the victims of the Knoedler art fraud scheme, but she received leniency in sentencing as she cooperated with the government. Shortly before sentencing, her lawyer released a long statement outlining years of abuse that she

ABOVE: Richard Diebenkorn painted a series of artworks called *Ocean Park* that were designed to reflect the landscape around his California studio. This artwork (*No.114*) is part of the series, but not the painting donated by Ann Freedman.

had allegedly suffered at the hands of her partner Bergantiños Díaz. The statement claimed that she was in constant fear he would take their daughter to Spain where Rosales would not be able to find her and these threats and others forced her into continuing the fraud. She served three months in prison, nine months of house arrest and three years' probation. The Bergantiños Díaz brothers were also prosecuted for the fraud, but by then they were living in Spain and avoided extradition. Pei-Shen Qian was summonsed to court but avoided prosecution, as he was out of the country.

With three of the perpetrators never brought to justice, the truth about Freedman's knowledge of the crimes never made clear and many prominent people losing big money over this affair, the case continues to fascinate. In 2019, director Daria Price created the documentary *Driven to Abstraction*, which explored what it described as 'the $80 million forgery scandal that rocked the art world and brought down Knoedler, New York City's oldest and most venerable gallery'. The following year, filmmaker Barry Avrich directed and produced a Netflix film, *Made You Look: A True Story About Fake Art*, another documentary on the scandal.

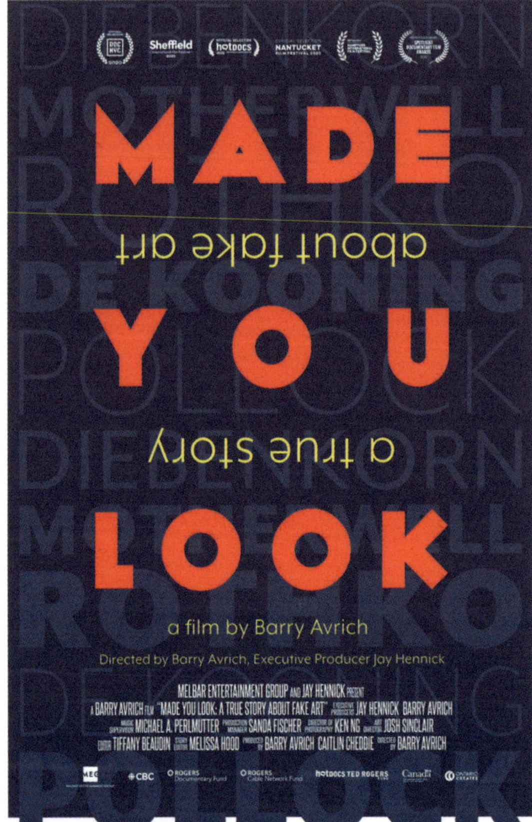

LEFT: A poster advertising the 2020 Netflix film *Made You Look: A True Story About Fake Art* that explores the Knoedler Gallery story.

Along with the lawsuits, settlements and criminal charges against individuals, the scandal provoked increased scrutiny and stricter authentication processes within the art world to prevent similar incidents from occurring in the future. Repercussions continue to be felt in the art market. The case raised serious questions about the responsibility of galleries, dealers and collectors in ensuring the authenticity of artworks.

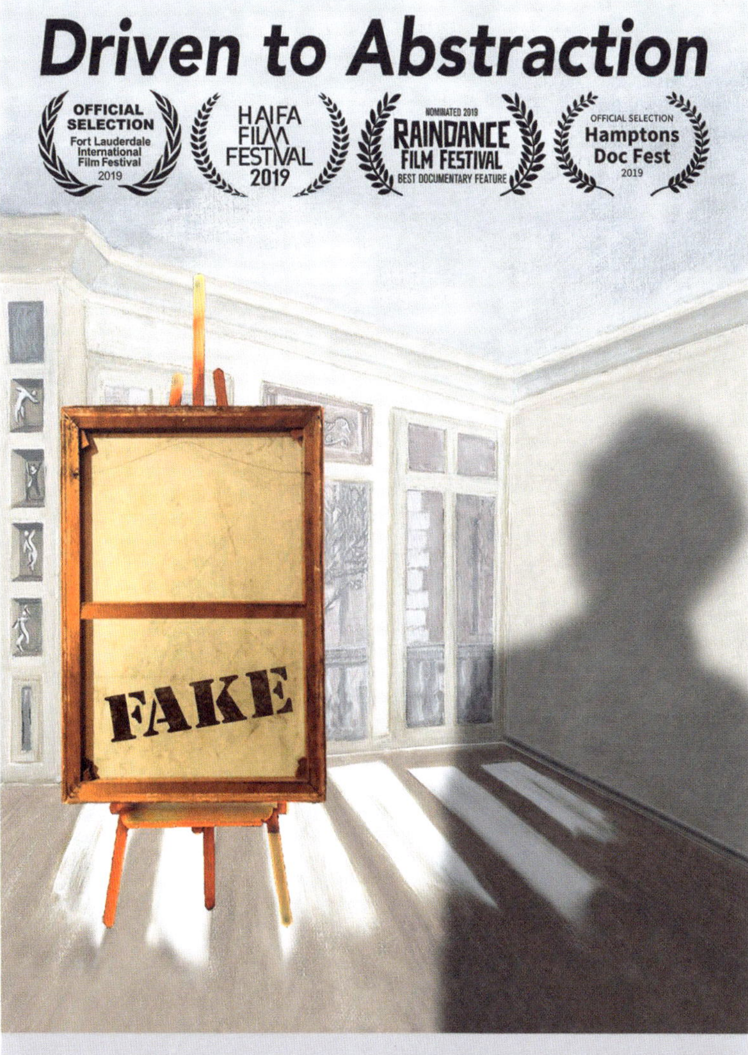

LEFT: A 2020 poster about the film *Driven to Abstraction* that explored the forgery scandal that shocked the art world and brought down Knoedler, New York City's oldest and most venerable gallery.

CHAPTER 14

Revenge on the Art World

During the 1990s, William 'Billy' Mumford (b. 1949) from West Sussex created up to a thousand fake paintings which he sold to oblivious buyers.

Mumford copied the styles and images of many artists from different periods and backgrounds, including van Gogh, Picasso and L. S. Lowry, along with some lesser known 20th-century figures such as Welsh landscape painter Kyffin Williams, English painter and designer John Tunnard and Indian artist Sayed Haider Raza, and he sold them as originals.

From a young age, Mumford wanted to be a painter, but this eluded him and he ended up as a chef in a local pub. He reflected, 'For forty years, I had painted the same picture, then I put a different name on it and they queued up . . . I know it sounds a bit stupid, but maybe it was my revenge on the art world. But I would have rather remained a failed artist than a successful forger.'

Some of Mumford's paintings that were sold as genuine were paid for by collectors for up to £30,000 each. He had a group of accomplices including several friends who sold his paintings on eBay and at auction houses throughout the UK. As incentive, these sellers each received 20 per cent on every artwork sold. Then, in 2009, a major London auction house identified an unusually high number of paintings being offered for sale by Indian artist Maqbool Fida Husain (1915–2011), who was known for his bold, vibrantly coloured narrative works. The auction house notified the Metropolitan Police Art and Antiques Unit. The subsequent police investigation was called 'Operation Sketch'; police found hundreds of paintings in the back bedroom and garage of Mumford's home, plus gallery stamps, ink pads and Victorian paper that he used to create false provenances. They tracked down 40 paintings sold by the group. Many of the paintings were sold abroad, and some were sold on several times.

OPPOSITE: One of Billy Mumford's forgeries in the style of a Renaissance drawing using red chalk on tinted paper.

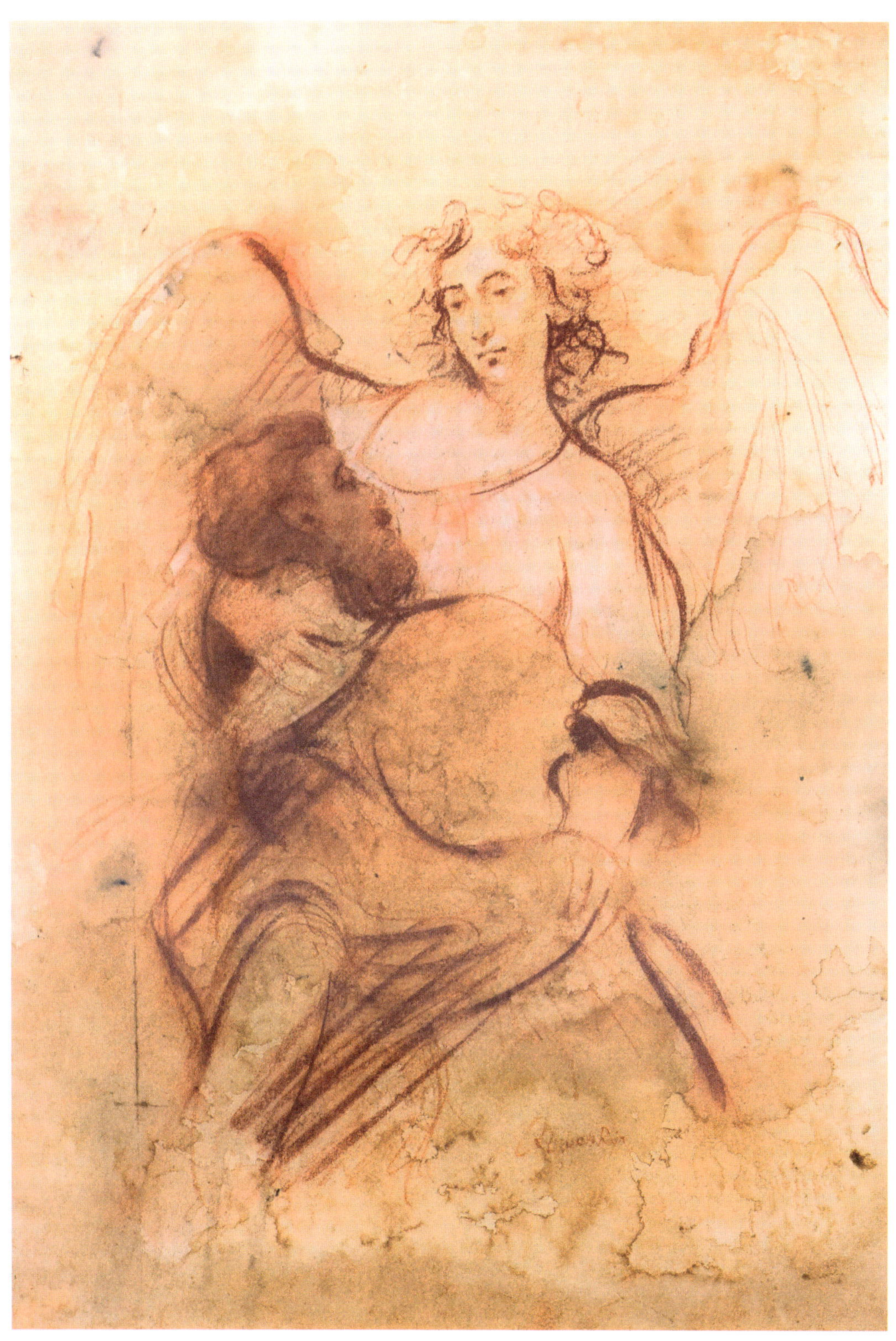

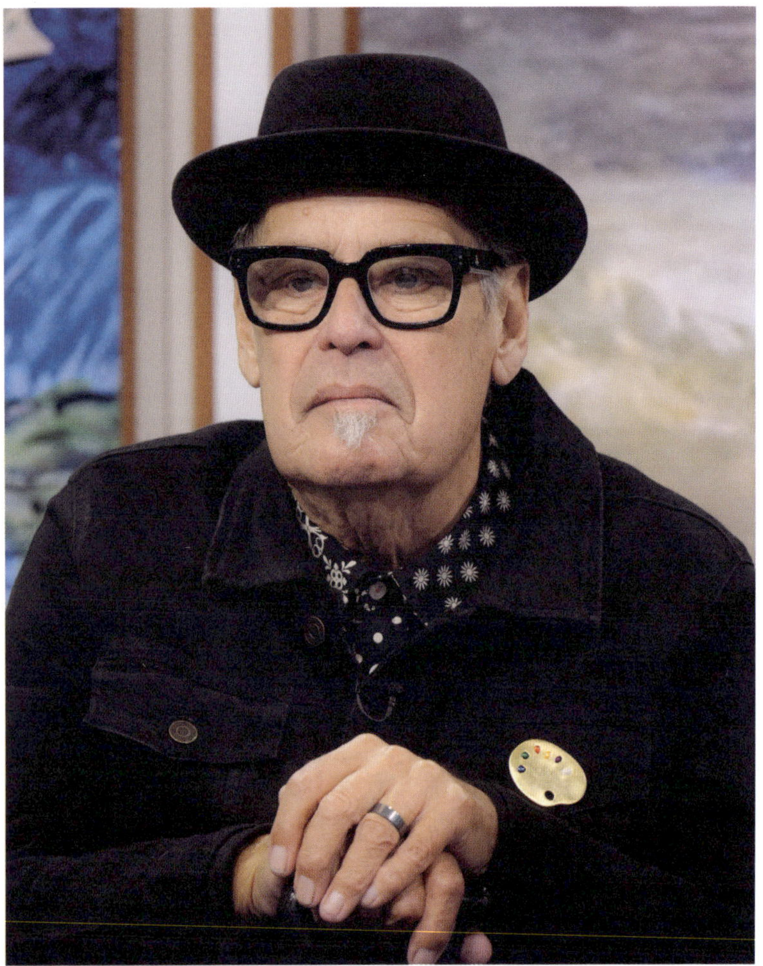

ABOVE: Mumford appearing on a morning news programme in the UK, explaining how he forged images for Jeffrey Archer's novel *An Eye For An Eye*. Archer wanted two strategic artworks for his book: an imagined Rembrandt drawing of *Jacob Wrestling with the Angel*, and Thomas Jefferson's *Fair Copy of the Declaration of Independence*.

It is conjectured that hundreds of Mumford's forgeries probably remain in circulation.

Sentencing

In 2009, Mumford and his accomplices were sentenced at Southwark Crown Court in London. Having already admitted to creating the forgeries, Mumford pleaded guilty to conspiracy to deceive potential buyers and launder the proceeds of the crimes. He was jailed for two years. His co-conspirators were also convicted. Martin Petrskovsky admitted conspiracy to defraud and was imprisoned for 21 months. Karen Petrskovsky, Martin's wife, also admitted conspiracy to defraud, and was given a one year jail term, suspended for two years. Anthony Resse admitted conspiracy to defraud and was sentenced to a year's imprisonment that was suspended for two years, plus he was ordered to do 200 hours of unpaid work. Paul Shepherd admitted

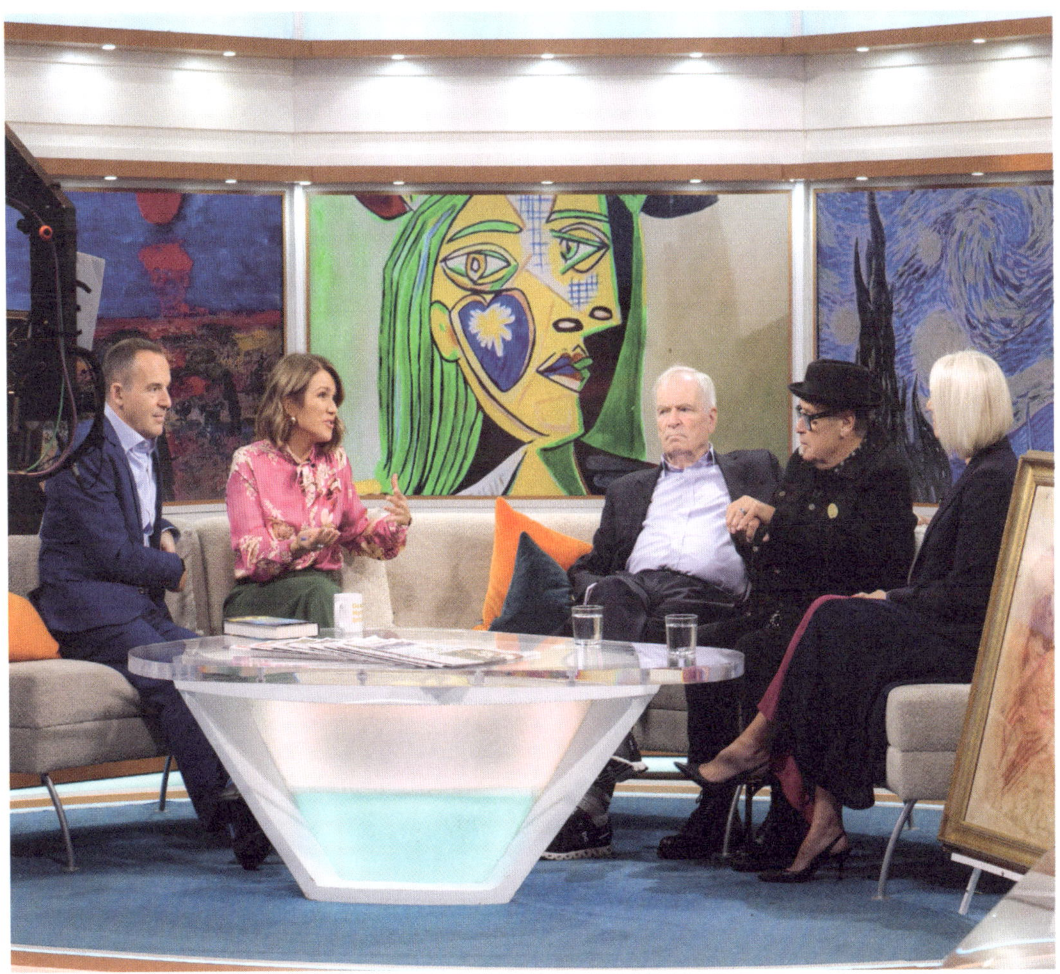

fraud by false representation and was also sentenced to a year's imprisonment suspended for two years with the order to do 100 hours of unpaid work.

Afterwards, Mumford continued to paint and in 2021, the Billy Mumford Gallery opened in Bridport, Dorset, where his works are available to buy.

ABOVE: Billy Mumford in 2024. He sits next to the novelist Jeffrey Archer, and explains how he went about copying the artworks that Archer commissioned him to do.

Conclusion

As we have seen, forgery continues to pose significant challenges to the art world. In general, most forgers are artists who fail to attain recognition and status under their own names. They want success and resent the art world when that seems unobtainable. Art made by forgers is often created purely to make money or to exact revenge on an uncaring world. However, forged art can have serious consequences. In addition to making money out of their deception, forgers often damage the reputations of established artists, art dealers and auction houses, and erode trust in the art market as a whole. Forgery can falsify historical records by introducing fake artworks into an artist's catalogue, leading to confusion about their true body of work and so distorting history. The repercussions can be huge.

BELOW: Detective Sergeant Vernon Rapley poses with forgery tools in a preview of an exhibition on the 'Art of Crime', which included famous forgeries at the Victoria and Albert Museum, London, England.

OPPOSITE, ABOVE: Detective Constables Ian Lawson and Halina Racki from the Metropolitan Police Art and Antiques Unit stand outside Bolton Crown Court.

OPPOSITE, BELOW: The Carabinieri Protection of Cultural Heritage present some of their finds to the press, in 2021 in Rome, Italy.

The future

To try to prevent art forgery, institutions, experts and collectors employ ever more rigorous authentication processes, including scientific analyses, provenance research and stylistic examination.

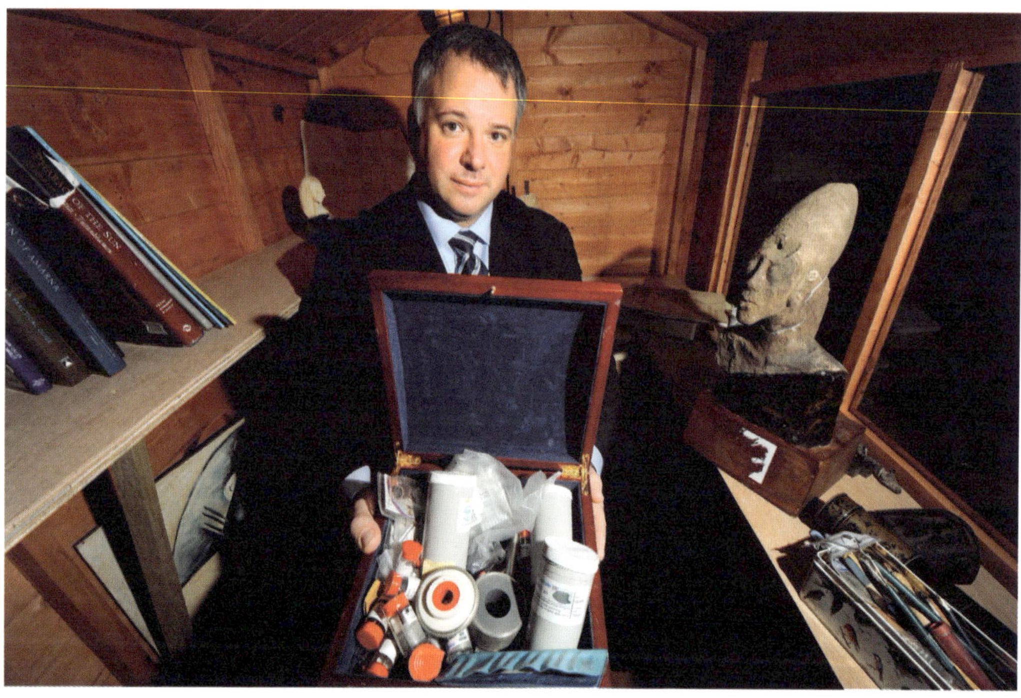

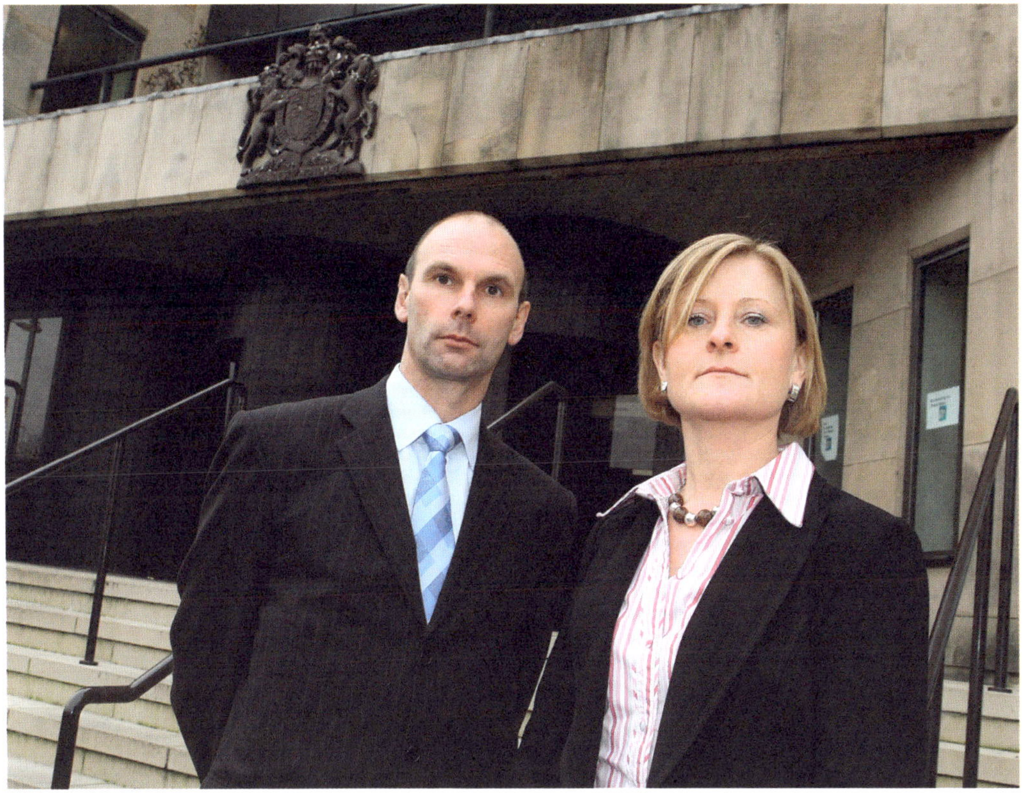

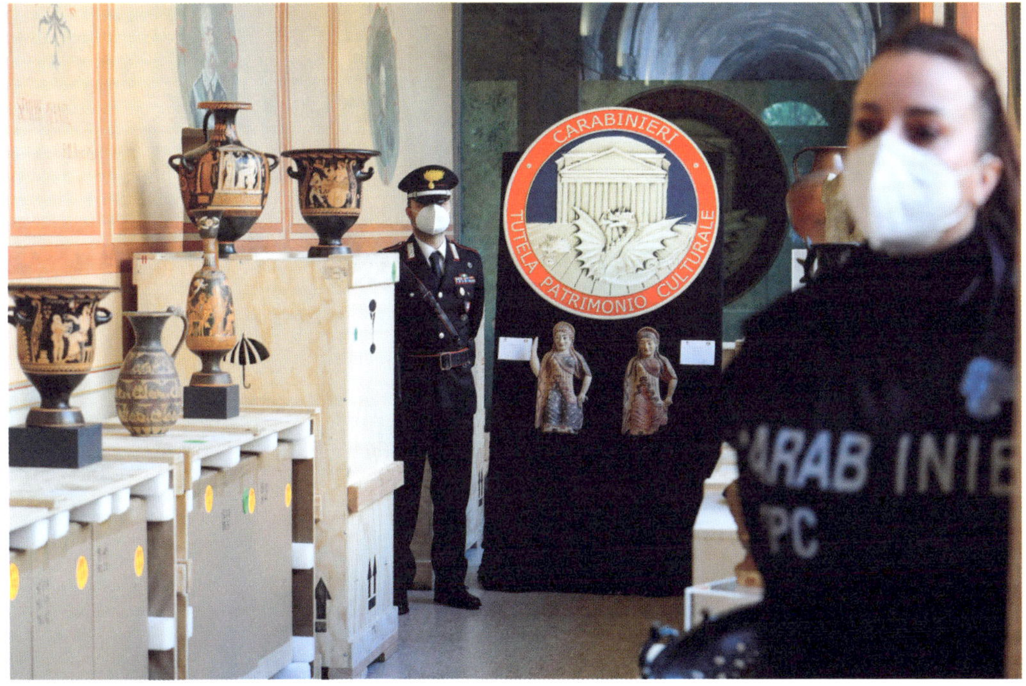
CARABINIERI
TUTELA PATRIMONIO CULTURALE

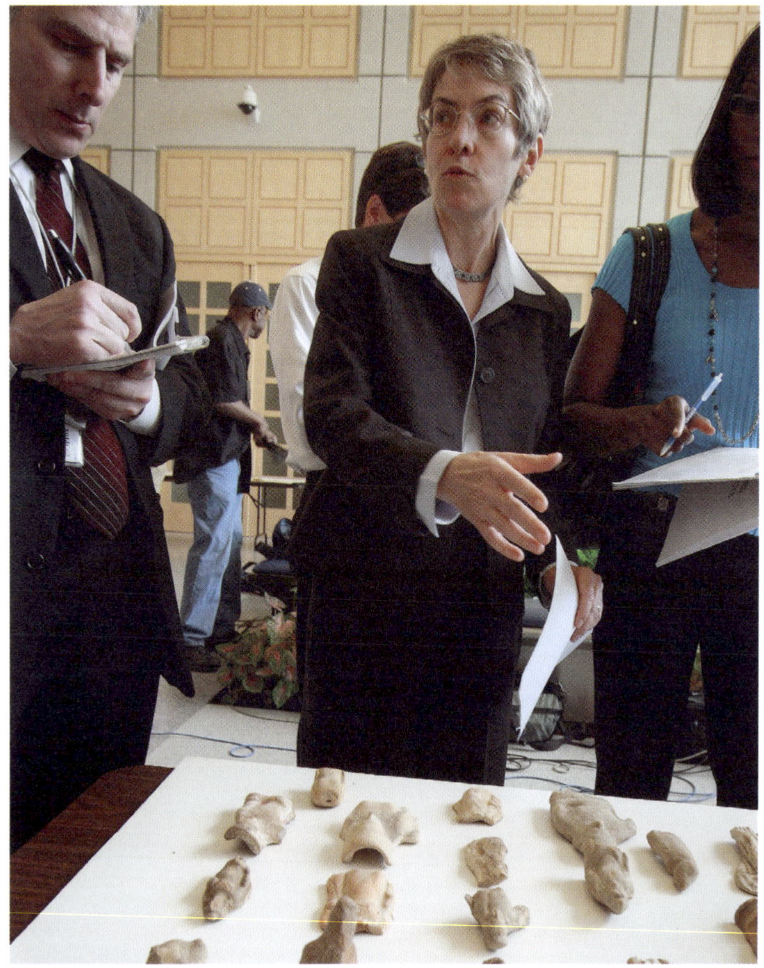

LEFT: The FBI has an active Art Theft Program and Art Crime Team (former manager Bonnie Magness-Gardiner is pictured here) which was formed in 2005 to investigate thefts of art and cultural artefacts, and to combat art forgery.

Many countries have established laws and regulations to prosecute individuals involved in fraudulent practices. Advances in technology, such as forensic analysis, imaging techniques and blockchain (a tool that keeps digital records safe and accurate that stores data simultaneously across many computers), are now being utilized by some to enhance the verification and provenance tracking of works of art. Promoting education and awareness about forgeries is also helping both collectors and professionals to recognize the signs and make more informed decisions. Collaboration between international organizations, law enforcement agencies and art institutions is also critical in combating forgery on a global scale, but as the case studies in this book highlight, none of this is infallible.

Art forgery remains a multifaceted and persistent issue requiring constant vigilance, expertise and collaboration to overcome, but in many ways this is becoming more difficult, for technological advancements can assist as well as combat forgers.

How technological developments are affecting forgery

By making use of technological innovations, some modern forgers have entered new territory, presenting a formidable challenge to the art world. Here are some of the ways in which new technology is helping forgers:

- Criminals can use high-resolution scanning and printing technologies to imitate artworks with greater accuracy.
- Digital tools such as Photoshop allow forgers to manipulate images, alter details and create fake documentation or provenance records to reinforce the faked authenticity of forged artworks.
- Nowadays even more advanced pigments, materials and techniques are known and available that can imitate the ageing and patina of authentic artworks, making it more difficult to detect forgeries based on visual inspection alone.
- Blockchain can be used to create secure digital records of an artwork's provenance, making it harder to trace the origins of counterfeit artworks and potentially abetting the sale of forgeries with fabricated histories.
- Counterfeiters can exploit scientific developments in techniques such as carbon dating, pigment analysis and X-ray imaging to create forgeries that are more difficult to detect through traditional methods of verification.

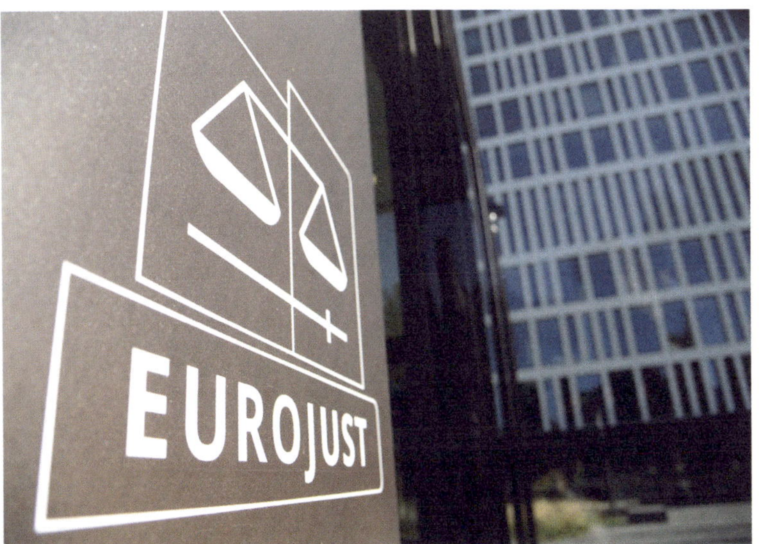

LEFT: The Eurojust building in The Hague, the Netherlands, is where, in November 2024, 38 people were indicted following an unprecedented operation against a criminal network for forging over 2,000 works of contemporary art. It followed an 18-month-long investigation by Italian authorities, in cooperation with Belgian, French and Spanish counterparts.

- The rise of online marketplaces has created new opportunities for forgers to sell counterfeit artworks to a global audience, often avoiding traditional inspection processes and making it easier to deceive unsuspecting buyers.
- AI and machine learning algorithms can be used to analyse and replicate artistic styles, helping forgers to create artworks that copy the techniques and characteristics of renowned artists even more closely.

Overall, the increasing sophistication of forgeries creates continued and often even more difficult challenges for experts and institutions tasked with authenticating artworks. To combat the changing and advancing threat, investors in the industry have to constantly remain vigilant and to continue to adapt their authentication methods, regulations and practices. Although art forgery might appear to be unthreatening or victimless, something that affects only anonymous institutions and the wealthy, it can have huge repercussions on us all: on our culture, our history and the fabric of our society.

Weakening the art market

Art fraud is complex and it frequently ruins lives. The allure of high profits, coupled with a lack of regulation and human error, have created an environment where fraudulent activities flourish, and far beyond the financial loss, artists' legacies can be tarnished, collectors' investments devalued and public trust in the art market eroded. For those affected directly by art fraud, their mental health is usually harmed.

Forgery usually has significant economic impact on the art market, affecting collectors, dealers and the broader economic landscape. The introduction of forged artworks into the market can result in a depreciation in the value of authentic works by undermining trust. When collectors are aware of the prevalence of forgeries, they can become hesitant to buy art for fear of acquiring a counterfeit, which reduces overall market activity and fluidity. This can lead to reduced sales and potentially impact the livelihoods of genuine artists and dealers. Moreover, many of the resources that need to be used in the authentication of artworks, including experts' fees and technological methods, often increase transaction costs and slow market dynamics.

These economic consequences extend beyond the market to affect cultural institutions and investment sectors. Museums and galleries, strategic players in the cultural economy, may suffer reputational damage if found to have inadvertently displayed

OPPOSITE, ABOVE: The increasing sophistication of forgeries is creating continued and even more difficult challenges for experts and institutions trying to stop the criminality. To fight these threats, authentication methods, regulations and practices are constantly being improved. Here, Valeria Ciocan, scientist and imaging specialist, analyses an infrared image of a painting, searching for signs of forgery at the Fine Arts Expert Institute (FAEI), in Geneva.

OPPOSITE, BELOW: Sandra Mottaz, a specialist in conservation and analytic restoration, analyses a painting with ultraviolet light at the Fine Arts Expert Institute (FAEI) in Geneva, searching for signs of forgery.

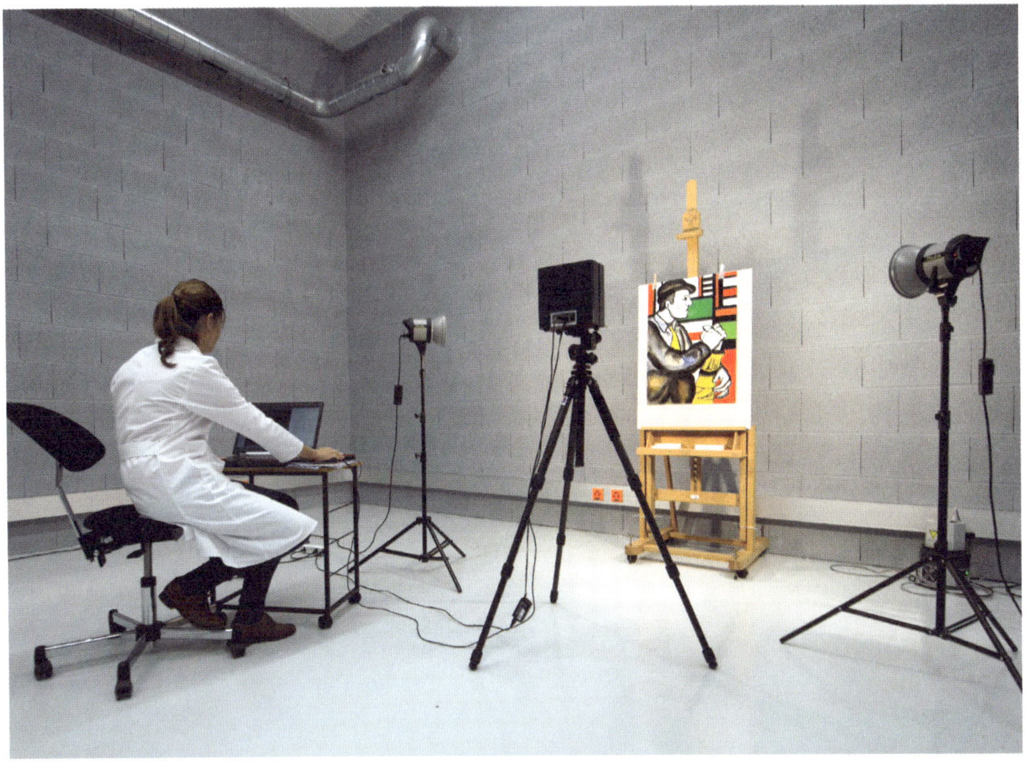

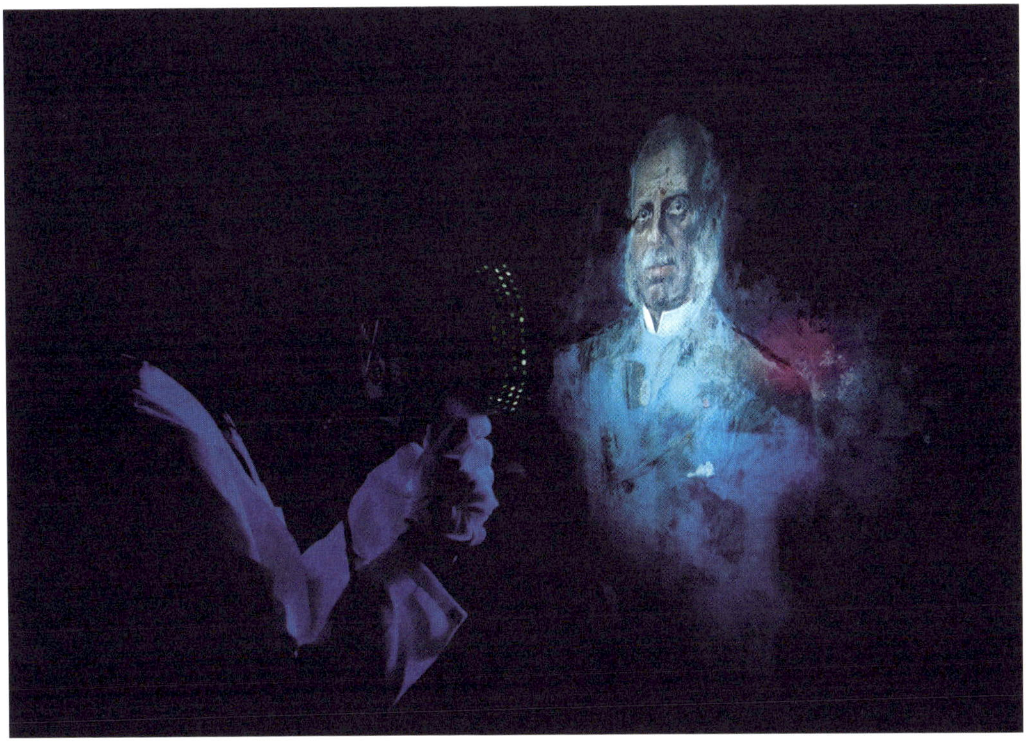

forgeries, potentially affecting visitor numbers and sponsorship deals. For investors the presence of forgeries – whether they are actual or suspected – can make the market particularly volatile. The uncertainty introduced by forgeries can lead to increased risk premiums and deter new investments, affecting the overall stability and growth of art as an investment. Most collectors state that the worry of mistakenly buying a fake artwork outweighs any other concerns they might have in their buying and ownership of art. So the impact of art forgeries is deeply interwoven with economic confidence in the art market, affecting both the cultural and investment dimensions of the industry.

The cultural and scholarly impacts of art forgeries are similarly profound, affecting the integrity of our artistic heritage and the accuracy of historical knowledge. Forgeries can distort the understanding of an artist's legacy, leading to misinterpretations of style, technique and evolution. When forgeries are mistakenly accepted into an artist's recognized body of work, they can mislead researchers, art historians and educators, perpetuating inaccuracies in academic publications, exhibitions and lectures. This not only misinforms the public and specialists but also distorts the historical record, complicating efforts to understand the cultural context and artistic developments of certain periods.

Art is central to cultural heritage institutions such as museums. When forgeries infiltrate museum collections, they undermine trust in their roles as custodians of human history. The presence of forged works of art in exhibitions can initiate public scepticism regarding the authenticity of other artworks, diminishing the cultural value and educational potential of collections. In response, significant resources are diverted to the verification and re-verification of artworks, straining budgets and shifting the focus away from educational and preservation activities. Overall, art forgeries erode the cultural authority of heritage institutions and complicate the scholarly pursuit of art historical knowledge and legacies.

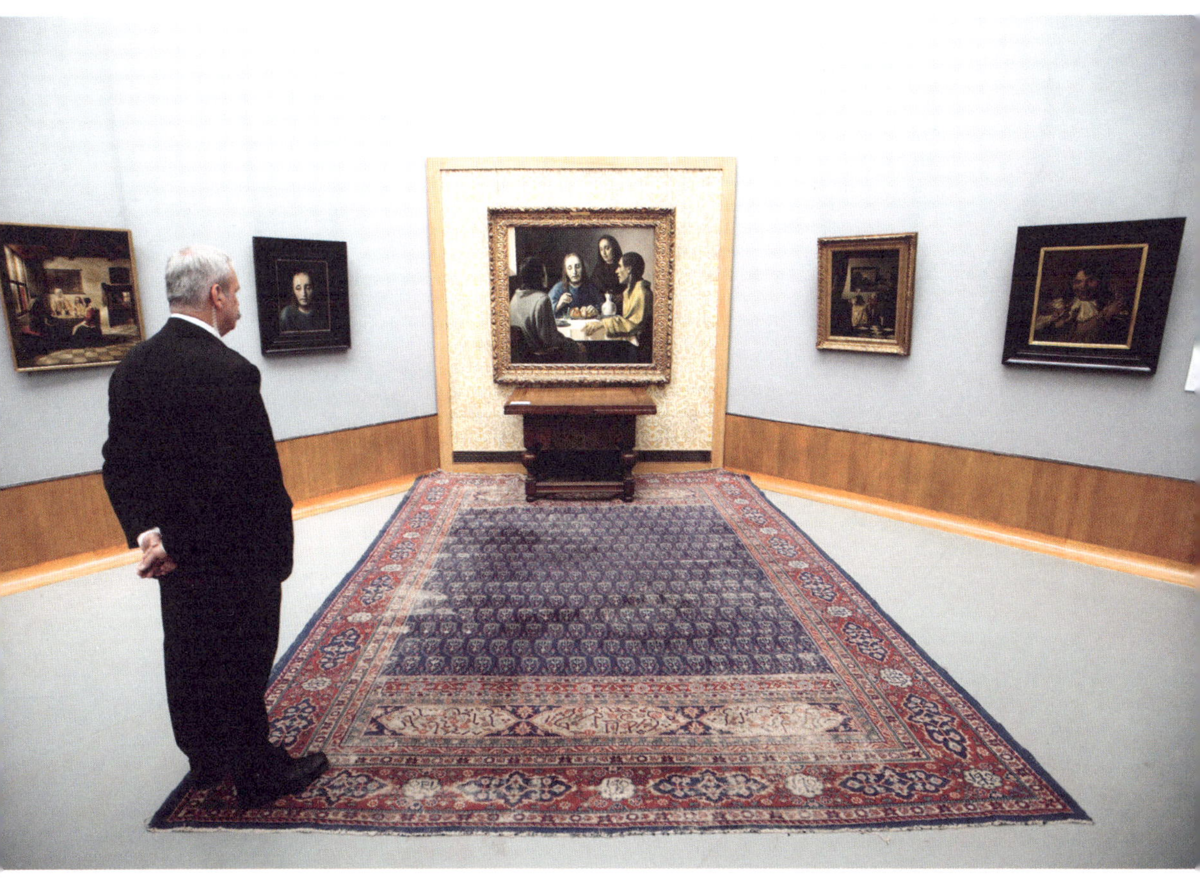

ABOVE: When forgeries infiltrate art collections, they undermine trust, diminish cultural value and educational potential, and complicate art historical knowledge and legacies. Here *The Supper at Emmaus* and other paintings by Han van Meegeren are displayed in the Boijmans Van Beuningen Museum, Rotterdam.

Acknowledgements

This was such a fascinating book to research and write; I hope it's as fascinating to read!

Art is such an incredible subject and so much of it is rather like alchemy. What makes a talented artist turn to forgery? What makes the art world accept it as genuine? What crucial aspects do the experts miss and why? And who are these artists and experts? How many forgeries are still hanging on walls in our galleries and museums, in plain sight, and how much damage does this do to the art world?

In my experience, the men who forge artworks (and they are all men) are not vindictive or vengeful; they are not focused on damaging the wider art world, but they have their reasons for doing what they do.

My thanks to everyone involved in this book at Quarto; Richard Green, Jenny Barr, Kat Menhennet, Nancy Marten, Stephan Behan, Ginny Zeal, Ramona Lamport and Richard Rosenfeld – what a team!

Thank you, too, to Robert Driessen, Mark Landis and Tony Tetro for being so gracious and fascinating. And thanks to everyone else who has helped me with the research aspects of this book.

About the Author

Susie Hodge, MA, FRSA, is an art historian, author, artist and journalist with more than 150 books in print on art history, practical art and history, including several best-selling and award-winning titles, such as *Why Your Five Year Old Could Not Have Done That*, *How to Survive Modern Art*, *50 Art Ideas You Really Need to Know*, *Art: Everything You Need To Know About The Greatest Artists and Their Works* and *My Big Art Show*. She also writes magazine articles, web resources and booklets for museums and galleries, runs workshops and gives talks and lectures for groups, galleries, businesses, schools, universities, museums, festivals and societies around the world. She is a regular contributor to radio and TV news programmes and documentaries.

Further Reading

Thomas McShane with Dary Matera, *Loot: Inside the World of Stolen Art*, 2007, Maverick House

Noah Charney, *The Art of Forgery: The Minds, Motives and Methods of Master Forgers*, 2015, Phaidon Press

Jonathon Keats, *Forged: Why Fakes are the Great Art of Our Age*, 2013, OUP USA

Aviva Briefel, *The Deceivers: Art Forgery and Identity in the Nineteenth Century*, 2006, Cornell University Press

Shaun Greenhalgh, *A Forger's Tale: Confessions of the Bolton Forger*, 2018, Allen & Unwin

Index

Page numbers in *italics* refer to image captions.

Picture Credits

t=top, b=bottom, r=right, l=left

Fine Art Images/Heritage Images/Getty 6–7, 7; akg-images 8; Photo © Minneapolis Institute of Art/The John R. Van Derlip Fund and Gift of funds from Bruce B. Dayton, an anonymous donor, Mr. and Mrs. Kenneth Dayton, Mr. and Mrs. W. John Driscoll, Mr. and Mrs. Alfred Harrison, Mr. and Mrs. John Andrus, Mr. and Mrs. Judson Dayton, Mr. and Mrs. Stephen Keating, Mr. and Mrs. Pierce McNally, Mr. and Mrs. Donald Dayton, Mr. and Mrs. Wayne MacFarlane, and many other generous friends of the Institute/Bridgeman Images 9(l); Photo Scala, Florence - courtesy of the Ministero Beni e Att. Culturali e del Turismo 9(r); Carlo Bollo/Alamy Stock Photo 10(t); Photo © The Courtauld/Bridgeman Images 10(b); Geoffrey Clements/Corbis/VCG/Getty 11; The Met, Gift of Henry Walters, 1917 12; The Met, Rogers Fund, 1918 13; By Rembrandt - -gHQe8vbiHn2xw at Google Cultural Institute maximum zoom level, Public Domain, https://commons.wikimedia.org/w/index.php?curid=23594212 14; By Rembrandt - -gHQe8vbiHn2xw at Google Cultural Institute maximum zoom level, Public Domain, https://commons.wikimedia.org/w/index.php?curid=23594212 15; By Leandro Neumann Ciuffo - Meta-pintura, CC BY 2.0, https://commons.wikimedia.org/w/index.php?curid=28378602 17; Collection of the University of Pittsburgh Art Gallery. Courtesy of University of Pittsburgh, Pennsylvania 19(ALL); Dennis Hallinan/Alamy Stock Photo 20; GRANGER - Historical Picture Archive/Alamy Stock Photo 21; RealyEasyStar/Claudio Pagliarani/Alamy Stock Photo 23; BG/OLOU/Alamy Stock Photo 24(l); Album/Alamy Stock Photo 24(rt), 61, 140; DEA PICTURE LIBRARY/Contributor/Getty 24(rb); Peter Horree/Alamy Stock Photo 25(lt); By Wmpearl - Own work, CC0, https://commons.wikimedia.org/w/index.php?curid=19611629 25(lb); David Lees/Contributor/Getty 25(r); The History Collection/Alamy Stock Photo 25, 39(t); ullstein bild Dtl./Contributor/Getty 29; Tallandier/Bridgeman Images 31; IanDagnall Computing/Alamy Stock Photo 32; By Pieter de Hooch - Royal Collection, Public Domain, https://commons.wikimedia.org/w/index.php?curid=57996619 33; Sepia Times/Contributor/Getty 34, 85(b), 89; Heritage Image Partnership Ltd/Alamy Stock Photo (Collection Cultural Heritage Agency of the Netherlands. The NK collection includes objects that were returned from Germany to the Netherlands after the Second World War and were taken into the custody of the Dutch State with the express instruction to return them – if possible – to the original owners or their heirs.) 35; Heritage Images/Contributor/Getty 36(ALL), 38, 59, 101(b), 103; Smith Archive/Alamy Stock Photo 37; HENRY NICHOLLS/Contributor/Getty 39(b); Geoff Wilkinson/Shutterstock 41, 45, 48(b); Keith Waldegrave/Mail On Sunday/Shutterstock 42(t); Newscom/Alamy Stock Photo 42(b), 44; Shutterstock 46; Fabio De Paola/Shutterstock 47, 114; Ak Suggi, Castle Fine Art 48(t), 49(ALL); Evening Standard/Stringer/Getty 51, 137(t), 143(l); Historic Images/Alamy Stock Photo 53; Clive Limpkin/ANL/Shutterstock 54; PA Images/Alamy Stock Photo 55, 109, 110, 111, 162, 163(t); © Tom Keaton/Bridgeman Images 56(t), 58, 60; Fine Art/Contributor/Getty 56(b), 115(r); Bill Cross/ANL/Shutterstock 62; Neville Marriner/ANL/Shutterstock 63; Licensed through DACS, 2025 © Pechstein - Hamburg/Tökendorf/akg-images 64; Associated Press/Alamy Stock Photo 66, 131, 154; © DACS 2025/Christie's Images/Bridgeman Images 67; dpa picture alliance/Alamy Stock Photo 68, 70, 71, 72, 93, 145; Harold Cunningham/Stringer/Getty 69; dpa picture alliance archive/Alamy Stock Photo 74(ALL); Everett/Shutterstock 75; ©Royal Academy of Arts, London; photographer: John Hammond 76; The Met, Robert Lehman Collection, 1975 77; Courtesy National Gallery of Art 78, 80, 81; Mauro Toccaceli/Alamy Stock Photo 82; Brendan Beirne/Shutterstock 83; Universal History Archive/Contributor/Getty 85(t); Mr John Moss UK 86(ALL), 87, 88, 91, 92; © The Estate of Alberto Giacometti (ADAGP, Paris), licensed in the UK by DACS, London 2025/Bridgeman Images 90; Bridgeman Images 95; The Oklahoma City Museum of Art 96(t), 99(bl), 101(t), 102; The Picture Art Collection/Alamy Stock Photo 96(b); Image courtesy of Hilliard Art Museum, University of Louisiana at Lafayette 97(t); Zip Lexing/Alamy Stock Photo 97(b); Charles O. Cecil/Alamy Stock Photo 99(t); Larry Busacca/Staff/Getty 99(br); By Cerdsp at English Wikipedia, CC BY 3.0, https://commons.wikimedia.org/w/index.php?curid=9431645 106; David Crump/Daily Mail/Shutterstock 107, 112, 113(ALL); Courtesy of Allen and Unwin_9116Ni5ZT2L._SL1500_ 115(l); ullstein bild Dtl./Contributor/Getty 117, 121 (ALL), 122, 123(ALL), 124, 125; Bettmann/Contributor/Getty 119; By Bjoertvedt - Own work, CC BY-SA 4.0, https://commons.wikimedia.org/w/index.php?curid=37579420 120; Craig Hibbert 126; imageBROKER.com/Alamy Stock Photo 127; Photography by Peter Calvin 128, 129, 133; © DACS 2025, photo: Toniflap/Alamy Stock Photo 130; By Caravaggio - Self-scanned, Public Domain, https://commons.wikimedia.org/w/index.php?curid=15219514 132; William Lovelace/Stringer/Getty 135; Houston Chronicle/Hearst Newspapers/Contributor 137(b); jean-Louis Atlan/Contributor/Getty 138; Kote Rodrigo/EPA/Shutterstock 139; Everett Collection Inc/Alamy Stock Photo 141; Fairfax Media Archives/Contributor/Getty 142; Gianni Ferrari/Contributor/Getty 143(r); Courtesy, "Made You Look", Melbar Entertainment Group 144(ALL), 153(t), 156; © 1998 Kate Rothko Prizel & Christopher Rothko ARS, NY and DACS, London, Photo Bridgeman Images 146; Pei-Shen Qian, Painting in the style of Mark Rothko. Courtesy Winterthur Museum, Garden & Library 147; By workshop of Jacopo Bassano - https://www.museodelprado.es/coleccion/obra-de-arte/wd/ed1bb91e-51ff-4894-8536-2f5f299c9df0, Public Domain, https://commons.wikimedia.org/w/index.php?curid=114809676 148; Pollock - © The Pollock-Krasner Foundation ARS, NY and DACS, London 2025, Photo © Davis Museum at Wellesley College/Bequest of Merrill Millar Lake (Class of 1936)/Bridgeman Images 149; Dave Benett/Contributor/Getty 150; VICTOR JUHASZ FOR ARTNEWS 153(b); © DACS 2025, photo: Stephen Smith/SIPA US/Alamy Stock Photo 155; Grasshopper Film/Everett Collection Inc/Alamy Stock Photo 157; Ken McKay/ITV/Shutterstock 159, 160, 161; AGENZIA SINTESI/Alamy Stock Photo 163(b); Scott Olson/Staff/Getty 164; copyright Eurojust 165; RICHARD JUILLIART/Stringer/Getty 167(ALL); ROBIN UTRECHT/Stringer/Getty 169